THE PANTHER IN
MY KITCHEN

BRIAN BLESSED

THE PANTHER IN MY KITCHEN

SIDGWICK & JACKSON

First published 2017 by Sidgwick & Jackson
an imprint of Pan Macmillan
20 New Wharf Road, London N1 9RR
Associated companies throughout the world
www.panmacmillan.com

ISBN 978-1-5098-4158-5

1 3 5 7 9 8 6 4 2

A CIP catalogue record for this book is available from the British Library.

Typeset by Palimpsest Book Production Ltd, Falkirk, Stirlingshire
Printed and bound by CPI Group (UK) Ltd, Croydon, CR0 4YY

Visit **www.panmacmillan.com** to read more about all our books
and to buy them. You will also find features, author interviews and
news of any author events, and you can sign up for e-newsletters
so that you're always first to hear about our new releases.

Contents

'If having a soul means being able to feel love and loyalty and gratitude, then animals are better off than a lot of humans.'

– James Herriot,
All Creatures Great and Small

PROLOGUE

One evening, in the spring of 1988, I was visited at our home in Windlesham by two local police officers. As I saw their car pull into the drive two possibilities entered my mind: either they'd seen my performance on *The Basil Brush Show* and wanted some answers, or they were bored and wanted a laugh. Either way, I thought it best to go outside and bid them welcome.

'Good evening, fellow coppers,' I quipped, subtly reminding them that I was PC Fancy Smith in *Z-Cars*. 'I suppose you've come for an autograph? Go on then. Who's it to? Or do you want me to say GORDON'S ALIIIIIIVE?'

I thought it best to break the ice just in case I was about to be transported to a faraway penal colony.

'If your wife's in I'd love an autograph, Mr Blessed,' parried PC Prendergast, who was driving.

Before I could remonstrate with the varmint he continued.

'Actually, we need your help with something. Do you mind if we come in?'

'Not at all. I'll put the kettle on.'

My wife Hildegard, who, as well as being an actress is also the world's most patient woman, was away on tour at the time and so there was just me, our daughter Rosalind and our merry little menagerie in residence. This happy band was comprised of about ten dogs, nine cats, four ponies and three ducks and seemed to grow almost by the day. Many of these animals had been rescued and, bar the ponies and the ducks, they all had a free run of the house. Saying that, I did catch one of the ponies in the kitchen polishing off some dog food one day. The entire place was absolutely animal crackers and what's more, we loved it!

But I digress. I'm rather good at that.

I led the way into the kitchen, and so didn't immediately realize that the policemen, who we knew quite well, were entering the house carrying a very large dog cage. When I caught sight of it I drew a sharp breath.

'I'm under strict instructions not to take in any more waifs or strays,' I said to them quickly. 'Hildegard will murder me!'

The menagerie to which I just referred was more of an animal sanctuary really and the local police and RSPCA used to bring animals to us all the time in the hope that we might be able to offer them either a temporary or a permanent home.

Obviously undeterred by the prospect of me being bludgeoned by my spouse, PC Barr opened the cage and very carefully began removing its contents.

'We found him abandoned on the M3,' he began. 'Worst case of animal abuse I've ever seen. I mean look at him. He's barely alive. The RSPCA are closed and if we took him anywhere else they'd probably have him put down. You're his last hope, Mr Blessed.'

No pressure then.

The reason the officer had taken such care in removing the animal, which we later deduced was probably a cross-breed with some Bull Terrier in him, was because as well as having hardly any fur there were open wounds all over his body and he had skin so thin it was almost transparent.

'Not pretty, is he?' said PC Prendergast.

'Well he was once,' I replied. 'What on earth do you think happened to him?'

Both officers had undoubtedly dealt with dozens, if not hundreds of abused animals over the years and there was a weariness on their faces as they surveyed the poor creature with sympathetic eyes.

'If I didn't know better I'd say somebody's been pouring boiling water over him,' said Prendergast grimly. 'Or maybe even acid.'

'Almost definitely,' confirmed PC Barr.

'My God!' I cried. 'But why?'

The officers shrugged.

'We ask ourselves that all the time, Mr Blessed,' said PC Barr.

After imagining what I would do to the perpetrators, were we ever to meet – which, while we're here, involved some electrodes, some testicles and a jack hammer – I informed the policemen that they would be leaving the house alone and with an empty cage.

'Don't you worry. We'll take care of him,' I said. 'I'll give our vet a call and ask what to do with him tonight and then first thing tomorrow we'll get him seen to. In the meantime, let's give the poor little bugger some grub. I've seen more bloody fat on a gnat's knackers!'

Just then, my daughter Rosalind entered the room and on seeing the dog almost fainted in shock.

'But Dad, you can't possibly look after him,' she protested. 'He needs specialist treatment.'

She was right, of course, but then so were the officers. If that dog had been taken anywhere else he'd have been put to sleep and I simply could not allow it.

The thought of that poor soul being tortured and then abandoned sparked a rage in my belly that words alone cannot do justice to. Until now, your common or garden bully had always been my quarry of choice and since childhood I'd leathered dozens of them. Apart from boxing, judo and Cumberland wrestling, bully bashing was the only sport I've ever been good at.

Torturers though, and abusers of innocent animals? They deserved justice of a different kind.

As I again began mentally rehearsing the retribution I'd administer to these arseholes I made eye contact with our new guest. Suddenly, all the thoughts of violence and electrocuted testicles dissipated and I was left with an overwhelming compulsion to make him well again.

'Right then you!' I whispered. 'Let's get you some food while I call the vet. And don't you dare even think of dying!'

As soon as I'd finished giving out my orders, the haggard hound, who had listened intently to my instructions, began wagging his tail. It was as if he'd forgotten his pain in the joy of recognizing he was finally at home. This didn't just play on my heart strings, ladies and gentlemen, it belted out an entire symphony! I knew now that whatever happened my new chum was up for the fight and after dishing out the dog food I got straight on to the vet.

'Give him a warm bath and put plenty of salt in it,' was the vet's immediate instruction. 'That'll help clean the wounds. Then, after that, put plenty of antiseptic cream on them and try and make him as comfortable as possible.'

We called our new friend Bodger, on account of him looking like a bit of a botched job, and after introducing him to the rest of the family I set about running the bath. I knew it was going to be agony for the boy, but it had to be done.

Sure enough, poor old Bodger found this experience hellish and if it hadn't been for about fifty dog biscuits, a few kisses, endless words of comfort and a couple of saucy jokes I think he might have given up the ghost.

After drying him off I then covered his wounds in about half an inch of Savlon cream. He must have had at least forty wounds in total and we went through tubes of the stuff. My God, how that dog must have suffered.

After seeing the vet the following morning we were told we had to repeat this rigmarole twice a day for at least the next two weeks. Neither of us got much sleep, but as Bodger's wounds began to heal his fur started to grow back and before you could say 'sausages', he was starting to look like a dog again!

Watching young Bodger gradually recover and then eventually start enjoying his life must be one of the most life-affirming processes I have ever had the pleasure of witnessing, and this was enhanced further when his personality began coming to the fore. For a start, Bodger was obviously a lover, not a fighter, and in the ten years we had him he never once so much as growled at another animal. Then there was his curiosity. I shudder to think what Bodger's life was like prior to coming to us but every minute of every day seemed to be precious to him; his life now set on a permanent cycle of explore, enjoy, repeat. Just like yours truly, I suppose.

One of funniest things about old Bodger was his inability to tolerate farting, either from human beings or any of the other dogs. In fact, if any one of us ever dared let one go in his presence Bodger would stand up like a king, put his nose in the air and then march out of the room in disgust. Occasionally I'd wind him up by blowing raspberries out of my mouth and he would glare at me, as if to say 'Don't you dare'. When he broke wind he would look incredulously at his rear end then turn his head away in total disdain.

As well as being adept at expressing shock and outrage, Bodger was also rather proficient at articulating boredom, and nothing bored Bodger more than somebody talking about Mount Everest. At the time, I was, for want of a better phrase, a bit of an Everest obsessive and whenever

I set off on one of my mountainous mouth-athons Bodger would sigh and then fall asleep instantly. Hildegard, who always bore the brunt of my ramblings, would look at Bodger enviously. 'If only we could swap places,' she once said out loud. Bloody cheek!

Anyway, the reason I have decided to open my tome with Bodger is simple.

You see, without wanting to sound like a conceited old bar-steward, I have genuinely lost count of the number of mountains I have climbed over the years and the same applies to the films, plays and television programmes I've appeared in, not to mention the voice-overs. There must be thousands. Yet despite having recalled many of these experiences in a number of what are now considered to be literary masterpieces, not one of the occurrences therein has been anywhere near as worthwhile as bringing Bodger back to life and giving him a second crack of the whip. I wouldn't say it makes me proud exactly. It just makes me feel grateful. Very grateful! Give me a choice between a restaurant full of humans or a shed full of previously unwanted dogs and the shed wins every time. No contest.

The French poet and novelist Anatole France once said, 'Until one has loved an animal, a part of one's soul remains unawakened.' Well, my rampant little reader. The book you have just opened recounts my own awakening and at the same time grants me the inordinate pleasure of being able to celebrate animals. I hope you enjoy it.

WARNING!

Now, if you're reading this book you either have a love of animals or a love of actor/adventurers with beards, stentorian tones and beautifully marked bottoms. Either way, my dear, sweet reader, you are most welcome and I promise you we're going to have a marvellous time together.

Before we start let's go through the house rules, shall we? If you read my previous book, called *Absolute Pandemonium* (available in all good bookshops priced ten trillion groats), you will no doubt be familiar with some of these instructions. However, for those of you who have never sampled the delights of Brian Blessed in book-form, might I suggest you proceed with caution!

First of all, there's the style, which is to say, how I write. Once again, I'm keeping things conversational which means you must imagine that I am sitting in a *huge* armchair opposite you and am reading this book to you, and to you alone. Do you think you can manage that? Try it now, will you? Picture me walking into the room, shaking you warmly by the hand and then sitting down in a big red armchair just a few feet away. Hello! And how are you? Are you well? Are you ready? Of course you are! See, it's not hard, is it. Don't worry. I'll keep on reminding you.

Writing in this conversational style helps to bring out the real me, I feel. It enables yours truly to really open up! That's what you want, isn't it? You want warts-and-all Brian, not guarded, sheepish Brian. If there is such a thing. I've certainly never seen him. My God, I'm waffling already. HEEL, BLESSED! You see, writing off the cuff like this can be rather dangerous. At the end of the day though, forewarned is forearmed. Which brings me nicely to the language herein. Things may get a little bit colourful from time to time – the odd expletive floating about – but there's nothing gratuitous and you must, simply must bear in mind that when I swear, I MEAN TO BLOODY SWEAR! I call a spade a spade.

Finally, I must stress that I am incapable of writing any of that bog-standard chronological formulaic actor autobiography tripe and I do tend to flit around hither and yon. This could be by time or indeed by distance. Bear with me though, dear reader, as together, we shall prevail!

Good! Then off we go.

1

AND TIBBY CAME TOO

Tibby was the first animal I ever befriended. The first of many, I am happy to say. He was not my first pet as I never *owned* Tibby and even suggesting as much would be a gross misrepresentation of our relationship and on the effect he had on my life. Tibby was the first 'best friend' I ever had and we were, for many years, constant companions. As a child I enjoyed numerous human friendships, and yet none of these gifted me anywhere near the amount of joy and fulfilment that my kinship with Tibby did and this is one of the reasons why I just know that I'm going to derive more pleasure from writing this book than any that have come before. Even thinking about Tibby makes me smile almost uncontrollably.

You mark my words boys and girls; the love of an animal is one of the greatest things you can ever attain as a human being. If not *the* greatest. Why? Because their love is unconditional, providing you don't abuse it, and it knows no bounds. Very few human relationships can boast such emotional totality, except perhaps for the love that a parent feels for its newborn child.

Once again you must forgive me if I am about to tread on old ground but for the sake of all the lovely newcomers among you I must first set the scene for Tibby's tale, and the scene is 30 Probert Avenue, Goldthorpe, South Yorkshire, circa 1942. Right in the middle of the Second World War.

My father, Bill, was a coal hewer in nearby Hickleton Main Colliery, and my mother, Hilda, was a housewife. Our home comprised of a sitting room, a large kitchen, a bathroom and three bedrooms with a small garden at the front and a larger one at the back. The avenue itself curved around like a horseshoe embracing, in total, about a hundred brick council houses. I went back there a few years ago to have a few photographs taken and it was exactly the same. Just marvellous!

Back then, most of the people living in Probert Avenue were in the process of having families and so a whole new generation was being born there. From house to house the noise of screaming babies heralded the presence of new life and my father once likened the road to a giant incubator. All the men on the avenue worked, as my father did, in one of the nearby collieries and so were either on a night shift or a day shift. With military punctuality they would don their work clothes, appear at their front doors, plant a kiss on the cheek of their respective wives, and then march in straight lines to their respective pits.

How are you getting on so far? OK? Good stuff. Tibby won't be long.

My recollection of those early days are of complete

calm and happiness. Like one continuous hot dreamy summer. How much of that is actually true I can't honestly say as I think it's very easy to romanticize much of one's early life. One thing I am sure of is that the love my parents had for me was self-evident and our house was simply brimming with it. Love was all around, all of the time. Perfect.

When I was about two years of age my mother used to sit me on a rug in the garden while she hung out the washing. Can you picture a baby Blessed, by the way? Some people find it impossible and seem to assume that I was born with a beard and wings and that my first words were GORDON'S ALIVE! They may well be my last, dear reader, but they weren't my first. No, no! That particular honour goes to one of my all-time favourite naughty words – bugger! I was certainly born with a big gob then, but not a big beard. I'm distracting myself now! Anyway, my one abiding memory from my time on the rug was seeing cats. Lots and lots of cats. At first, being only two, I didn't know what to make of them all and according to my mother I would scream with delight whenever one jumped over the garden fence and clap my hands together with unbridled glee. Heaven only knows what they made of little me but over time some of the braver among them tentatively began to venture over to where I sat and would allow me to stroke them. This, according to dear mother, never tended to happen more than once as a single stroke from baby Brian was akin to being battered half to death with a rubber cosh.

What delighted me most about my feline friends was that they came in all shapes, sizes and colours, which was obviously manna from heaven to an inquisitive two-year-old, whose life was still but a blank canvas. I was fascinated!

Our next-door neighbours at the time were Mr and Mrs Burns and their daughter Betty. They had a beautiful Golden Retriever called Wendy and she had the kindest face I think I have ever seen. Oh, how I loved Wendy. Mrs Burns used to bring her round to our house and she would babysit me while I was in the garden. Isn't that marvellous! My first babysitter was a beautiful Golden Retriever. Perhaps having so much contact with animals early on in my life might explain why nowadays my home is like a menagerie. You're going to read all about this ark of mine later on in the book but for now let's just say that A) it's rather full, and B) that the animals in charge there are of the four-legged variety and not two! Seriously. I'm run bloody well ragged by animals and what's more I wouldn't have it any other way.

By the age of seven I had graduated from our large back garden to the smaller front garden, which had a big ash tree in the corner that the local cats loved to climb. I'd carry out my small blue chair, set it down in the centre of the lawn, and there I would stand guard – or should I say, sit guard – over the small community of frogs and toads that had, for some reason, decided to make this minute patch of earth their home. They came from the nearby fields (in those days there was no such thing as pesticides) and I was determined to prevent them falling prey to any hungry strays. Should any visiting felines dare to reveal themselves as frog fanciers I would explode into a fit of rage and chase them around the avenue; all the time warning them of exactly what would happen should they ever return.

The only thing that would ever lure me away from the royal throne was the appearance of Dr Morris, the man responsible for delivering all the bonnie babies that seemed to appear on an almost daily basis in and around Probert Avenue. Whenever he appeared in his little Austin car I would leap out of my chair, tear off to wherever he was going and ask if I could be of any assistance.

'Morning Brian. How are the frogs today?' he would say. 'Are you taking good care of them?'

'I am that, Dr Morris. Can I help you? Can I help you deliver the baby?'

This used to make Dr Morris howl with laughter. 'What makes you think I'm here to deliver a baby, young Brian?' he'd say.

'That's the only reason you ever come to Probert Avenue! Is it Mrs Brown at number six? Mum says she's been about to pop for weeks.'

Whatever I said always seemed to have Dr Morris in stitches and although it was probably not ethical having a seven-year-old present at a birth, he happily let me tag along. There were one or two occasions where I was asked to make myself scarce, however. My God yes! I remember once following Dr Morris into a house on Probert Avenue and being greeted with a cry of 'I'm not having him here. He's not even one of mine. Get him out!'

'Not this time I'm afraid, Brian,' said Dr Morris. 'You get back to your frogs and I'll see you soon.'

Come to think of it, if I was about to give birth the last thing I'd want to see would be one of the local ragamuffins staring at my whatsit! I was such an inquisitive little mite. Sorry, that should read, nosy little bugger!

I said at the very start of this chapter that I never owned Tibby, and that's perfectly true. In fact, I don't consider myself ever to have owned any animal. I mean, how can you? We can forge a relationship with an animal and we can even give it a home. But *own* it? Don't be daft. Why, oh why do we humans always have to own everything? When we discover new lands what's the first thing we do? Stick a flag in the ground and claim it as our own. It's ridiculous.

So, not only did I not own dear Tibby but I didn't even choose him. He chose me! I was sitting on my blue throne one day on frog-watch when all of a sudden one of the hedges started to move. *Hello, hello*, I thought. *Another whiskered chancer.* That very morning I'd given chase to at least three amphibian assailants and so I stood up from my chair and readied myself for yet another royal rumpus. I'm being serious now, if you want to send Uncle Brian into a tizz, you try getting your hands on his amphibians. Deadly! Anyway, before I could make a move, out from under the hedge strolled the most beautiful animal I had ever clapped eyes on. So stunning was he, in fact, that for a moment I couldn't move a muscle. I was transfixed!

He was a red tabby, quite large, and had the purest, gentlest face; something that I would later find out belied his ability to fight. Tibby was quite obviously a stray; in fact, the vast majority of cats were at that time. Even so, he appeared to be healthy and well fed, but instead of entering the garden and then going straight for one of the frogs, like all the other cats invariably did, he calmly strolled up to where I was standing, bold as brass, and began weaving in and out of my legs and purring loudly.

It was love at first sight, or a *coup de foudre*, as they don't often say in South Yorkshire. Wendy, the Golden Retriever, who I still took for walks and played with occasionally, was no longer the apple of my eye. I loved her dearly, and to this very day she still holds a special place in my heart. This was different though. For some unknown but glorious reason, Tibby, as I immediately christened him (I wasn't good on names back then), had chosen me as his companion and from that moment we were inseparable.

Ever since watching the 1942 film *The Jungle Book*, which had been playing at the cinema just a few months previously, I had fantasized about what it must be like having a feline companion like Bagheera. Those were perfect dreams, the sweetest of all, and with the arrival of Tibby they were brought magnificently to life. OK, so there may have been a slight difference in size between Tibby and Bagheera, and as talented as Tibby undoubtedly was I don't ever remember hearing him talk in

English. That didn't matter one bit. Tibby was *real* and as I eventually sank back into my chair he ceased making figures of eight around my feet and jumped up onto my lap. There, my new friend curled up into a large soft ball and as he purred away I began to familiarize myself with the intricate patterns on his reddish brown fur. Looking back, they actually remind me of the patterns you see on the fur of the clouded leopard, which is a rare wild cat found on the foothills of the Himalayas. As I don't have any photographs of Tibby why don't you do a search on the clouded leopard? That way you'll be able to create a picture of what he was like.

After an hour or so of perfect stillness Tibby leapt from my lap, strolled towards the front door of our house like the cock of the north and looked at me as if to say, *Aren't you going to invite me in then? And if there's a saucer of milk going I wouldn't say no!* Food was obviously scarce in those days, but with my parents both out of the way I managed to snaffle my companion a small saucer of milk as requested and then once he'd lapped it up I showed him around the house.

Looking back this really was very strange indeed as it was almost as if he was giving the place the once-over with a view to putting an offer in. That's crazy, even for me! When I opened each of the doors Tibby would stroll nonchalantly into the room. Then, once he'd had a good nose around he'd trot out again with his tail in the air. His favourite room was my bedroom and once inside he immediately jumped onto the window sill, as if judging ease of access. *Yes, quite simple this one. As long as you keep the window open!*

Tibby never attempted to sleep in the house, by the way, and even if he had there was no way my father would have allowed it. Wendy was the only dog on the whole of Probert Avenue because people couldn't afford the food, and it was pretty much the same with cats. Yes, there were hundreds of them, but as I said the vast majority were strays. They survived and, though the weather was often harsh, there was never any shortage of shelter or juicy rodents. No frogs though! It took me a few months to work out where Tibby laid his paws of an evening, but eventually I realized he was sleeping snugly in our old air-raid shelter.

From the very first day we met he would only ever disappear last thing at night, staying until I fell asleep. Come the morning he was nowhere to be found, yet the moment I set foot out of the house, there he was waiting for me.

Do you know, this is the first time I have ever spoken about Tibby to anyone other than a family member and the only thing I regret is not doing it sooner. It's bringing back the most marvellous memories!

Tibby and I took our first trip into the town together one bright Saturday morning. We'd been friends for about a week I think and in that time had spent almost every waking hour together. It was the summer holidays and so the perfect time to make a new acquaintance and cement a beautiful friendship. I recommend it! Anyway, every

Saturday morning my friends and I would meet at the Empire Picture House in Goldthorpe where we would watch the Gaumont-British News followed by an exciting episode of *Flash Gordon*. I wrote about this in some detail last time around so I won't go on. What I will say though is that once Tibby came along absolutely nothing changed. And why should it? Out I trotted at the usual time, greeted Tibby who was waiting for me on the garden wall, and then off we went to the Empire.

In hindsight perhaps it was a little bit strange seeing a small boy strolling along the pavement with a cat by his side, but only to those with absolutely no imagination. A few members of my gang thought it was absolutely fantastic. During the Gaumont-British News Tibby would crawl from lap to lap and allow each of the gang to stroke him. Come the main event, however, there was only one place Tibby wanted to be and that was with me.

Whenever any adults dared to complain about Tibby they got short shrift from my mother.

'Mind your own business and leave the lad alone,' she would say.

Funnily enough, the majority of the adults of fun-loving Goldthorpe eventually started calling Tibby 'the cat that's a dog', on account of him following me around.

The other excursion which used to cause a certain amount of consternation around the town was my weekly trip down to Booths, which was the local paper shop. It also sold little lead figures, and I loved the marvellous Red Indians on horseback. Once again, Tibby and I would convene in the front garden and then make our way down the road and into town. Mr Booth, who was a very kindly old gentleman, didn't seem to mind Tibby's presence one bit and on the rare occasions I went there without him Mr Booth would look sternly at me.

'Is that cat of yours alright, young Brian? He thinks the world of you. Never takes his eyes off you. You've got a good friend there.'

How right he was.

'No, he's fine, Mr Booth. I'm just running an errand for my mum. Tibby's keeping guard of the frogs!'

This was perfectly true, by the way. On first seeing me chase a cat out of the front garden Tibby took it upon himself to share these duties and between the two of us no frogs ever came to any harm. It was then that my parents started to take notice of Tibby and treat him like one of the family. They could see how devoted we were to each other and I think they were moved by the whole relationship. My mother loved Tibby and my dad eventually also succumbed to his charms and allowed him to live in the house.

'I'm not having him sleep here, Brian,' said my father. 'But he's welcome during the day as long as you're with him and as long as he doesn't cost me any brass. Why don't you ask Mrs Dancy next door if she can spare any bacon rind?'

What a great idea! From then on Tibby became part of our family and during the day he treated our house as his home. Great chubby Mrs Dancy did indeed supply me with some bacon rind – she used to bake pies and bread for the whole street – and when Dad wasn't looking my mother would slip Tibby the odd saucer of milk. He was never ever referred to as a pet, however, and because he always maintained his independence I think my parents had a strange kind of respect for him.

One of the reasons why I think Tibby gravitated towards me (this might be absolute nonsense, by the way) was because he was a tremendous fighter and I too enjoyed a scrap. The first time I ever saw him lose his temper was amazing to behold. We were lounging in the front garden one afternoon when all of a sudden two black cats leapt over the hedge and on to the lawn. Before I could move a muscle Tibby had almost doubled in size (or that's how it seemed) and after bending his head forward he began making the most frightening hissing sound. I'd heard hundreds of cats hiss before but nothing compared to this. One minute he was Tibby, the most laid-back, gentle cat on the entire planet, and the next he was a sabre-toothed tiger. My word. Never in my life have I seen two more terrified felines and within seconds they were back over the hedge and halfway to Barnsley. The moment the intruders had left Tibby turned back into his old self and sat by my side again as if nothing had happened. I looked down at my friend, stroked his head and thought *Bloody hell, if I was a cat I wouldn't want to get on the wrong side of you!* From then on I honestly don't remember seeing another cat in our front garden so word must have got around!

Back then I used to fight all the time – in fact I was

known as the cock of the school – and since getting together, Tibby had witnessed several of these scraps. Now it was his turn to show his mettle and my God did he deliver. Hard as bloody nails with no fear whatsoever. What a team we made. Like He-Man and Battle Cat! They were probably based on Tibby and me.

Apart from a wonderful deep friendship, my relationship with Tibby awakened in me what has become a life-long passion, not only for all animals, but for their welfare, and once this obsession began to manifest itself it's fair to say that it has ruled my life. You see dear reader; I don't do anything by halves. If I say I'm going to climb Mount Everest, I will attempt to climb Everest, and if I say I am going to help charities like Animal Defenders International, Born Free, WAP, World Wildlife and the RSPCA, my God, that's exactly what I will do. There's no middle ground with me. I'm all or nothing, ALL OR NOTHING! Unfortunately, this rather single-minded approach got me into a little bit of trouble early on and I ended up shouldering a not inconsiderate amount of shame.

The leader of our gang, Caldeon Williams, had received for his birthday a kind of bumper book of animals which was the size of several bricks and seemed to have inside it a page or so on just about every species known to man – from lions, tigers and elephants to the giant pangolin. On first observing this voluptuous volume I was set upon by an army of green-eyed monsters and without a thought for my young friend began pestering him to lend me his treasured tome. After a horrific amount of badgering Caldeon eventually relented, although reluctantly, and the moment I got the book in my possession I began soaking up every fact, photo and drawing that was displayed within its illuminating pages. A week or so passed and my friend, quite naturally, began asking if I could return the book as he himself had only just started reading it.

'Don't worry,' I said. 'I'll bring it to the Empire on Saturday morning, OK?'

To my eternal shame I did nothing of the kind and from then on I began avoiding Caldeon as a monkey might avoid a hungry leopard. On the rare occasions my friend did manage to catch up with me I simply trotted out one of my never-ending stream of excuses, all of which, I hasten to add, were complete and utter balderdash.

Then, one evening, my friend arrived at our front door.

'*Please*, Brian, can I have my book back,' he pleaded.

'Yes of course,' I conceded gloomily. 'Wait there and I'll go and get it.'

Feeling mortified because Caldeon was a true trusted friend, I went up to my bedroom where the book lay. As I went to pick it up I realized there and then that it was quite literally falling to pieces. I must have thumbed through its pages a million times since I commandeered it and I'm afraid it was now just a pile of loose and rather tatty-looking pieces of paper. The look on my friend's face as I handed the book over is one that will stay with me for the rest of my days. Neither of us knew what to say and at this point my mother took over.

'You shouldn't lend him books, he doesn't know how to take care of things,' she said, giving me a severe look.

Caldeon was devastated. I keep on referring to him as my friend because, and it brings tears to my eyes telling you this, he actually forgave me. His most prized possession ruined and he actually forgave me. Isn't that one of the sweetest things?

From the very first day he accompanied me there, the teachers at Goldthorpe Primary School treated Tibby like some kind of unofficial school mascot, as did all my friends and fellow pupils. At first I was quite nervous about him coming with me as my parents had warned me that the chances were he wouldn't be allowed in.

'You can't take a cat to school with you Brian,' my mother had remonstrated. 'It's unhygienic.'

'But I don't *take* Tibby anywhere with me, Mum,' I countered. 'He just tags along. I can't stop him, can I?'

I remember my mother staring at me with a look of sweet resignation. 'Let's see what happens shall we Brian? But try not to get too upset if they say he's not allowed. Schools have rules you know.'

That first morning after breakfast I grabbed my school bag, gave Mum a kiss on the cheek, my baby brother Alan a pat on the head (he was about one at the time), opened the door and there, sitting on the wall in front of me looking like a reddish miniature clouded leopard, was Tibby. My first words to him were always, 'Morning Tib. Sleep well?' Tibby was a very vocal cat – another fellow big gob

– and so his reply could last until we'd left Probert Avenue. As he mewed happily away I would nod enthusiastically and pretend he was asking me a very important question. 'What do you think is going to happen in *Flash Gordon* this Saturday, Bless?' (Everybody called me Bless in those days.) Then, once he was done, I'd answer him. 'Mmmmm, not sure Tib. Flash looked like he was done for though, didn't he?'

Actually, my intrepid friend, I have a question for you. You are still with me, aren't you? Not falling asleep? Well done you! Do you remember those charming public information films from the 1960s and 1970s? They were wonderful. Full of God-awful acting. Like *Crossroads*! Actually, my old *Z-Cars* colleague, Stratford Johns, once appeared in one about drink driving, so it wasn't all bad. Well, if you do remember them, there was one in particular that used to remind me of Tibby and me. What was it called now? Hang on. That's it! Charley Says. CHARLEY SAYS! I knew I'd get it eventually. There was a series of them, I think, and this young boy and his cat, Charley, would get into all kinds of scrapes together. Then, just before something horrifying happened, Charley would warn his friend using a series of meows, which, I am reliably informed, were voiced by none other than Kenny Everett! I'm an absolute fountain of knowledge you know. Full of it! If you've never seen the Charley Says films why not hop onto the interwobble and have a quick look. Anyway, once Charley had made plain the danger within, his young friend would translate the cat's counsel to the viewer. For instance: 'Meow meow, meow meow meow,' would be, 'Charley says don't go near that dodgy bloke in the dirty raincoat and for God's sake don't play with matches.' Now, not only did Charley and his friend have conversations with each other, just like Tibby and I did, but Charley was also a reddish brown tabby! How about that then? Art imitating life, you might say.

As Tibby and I arrived at school on that cool Monday morning in September, neither the pupils nor the staff batted an eyelid. I'd been friends with Tibby for many weeks by then and because we'd spent almost every waking hour in each other's company (and because the entire school lived in the town) they were already more used to seeing us together than apart. Tibby and Bless, as we were known, came as a pair, like strawberries and cream or Laurel and Hardy. It was a unique situation as nobody ever referred to Tibby as my pet. It was always 'Where's your friend, Bless?' or 'Where's Tib?' He had human characteristics, did Tibby, and so was always treated accordingly.

The assembly on that first day back after the summer holidays demonstrates this fact perfectly as when we all sat on the hall floor waiting for the headmaster, Tibby, who had walked ahead of me, sat quietly by my side, eyes forward, and never moved a muscle. All the rest of us were chatting away like chimpanzees each trying to relay stories of the summer just gone. Not Tibby though. He was setting an example, or at least that's how it seemed. John Dale, who was sitting on the other side of Tibby, was the first one to spot his demeanour and without saying a word he simply stopped talking and faced forward, just like Tibby. *The headmaster will be here soon so best shut up*, was the advice Tibby seemed to be silently emanating. Slowly but surely the rest of the school followed suit and by the time the headmaster entered, we were all paying attention, something he was definitely not used to, especially after the holidays. This made the headmaster very nervous indeed.

'Is everything alright boys and girls?' he asked cautiously. 'I trust you all had a nice summer?'

After we'd all answered in the affirmative the headmaster, very gingerly, continued with the assembly, but the look on his face throughout was a picture. Whenever there was the slightest noise from the floor he'd look up as if expecting some kind of explosion. The Tibby effect was already bearing fruit.

The classroom produced a slightly different scenario, as it was, after all, a place of learning. But providing Tibby remained beneath my desk throughout the lessons and failed to make his presence felt, he was tolerated. Indeed, Mr Loxsby, who was my form teacher, even had the bright idea of leaving a window open for Tibby just in case he was caught short. He was, of course, quite frequently, and after jumping out and doing his business he would sneak back in, wind a quick figure of eight around my feet and ankles and then would curl up again on my school bag and go back to sleep.

The sound of our chairs being pushed back across the

classroom floor signalled playtime, and as we all stood up to leave, Tibby would bound onto my desk, stretch his front paws forward, and together we would join the happy throng as it made its way noisily out of the classroom and down the corridor towards the playground. Tibby was in his element during playtime as he was always the centre of attention. Pupils and teachers alike would go out of their way to stroke him, like some kind of modern-day tribal ritual. He was our totem, I suppose. Our good luck charm.

There were only two events at school where Tibby wasn't welcome; lunchtime, which was fair enough, and exams. Even the school caretaker was tolerant of Tibby, which, bearing in mind what he must have deposited in his flower beds, was remarkable. You see, in my opinion, every school in the land should have a Tibby. I'm serious! Animals bring out the best in children. They engender compassion, promote responsibility and stimulate the imagination. Do you remember animals being brought in to your school? If you do, do you remember the excitement they caused and how you and your fellow pupils reacted when coming into contact with them? I've taken animals into schools on several occasions and the results are beyond price. Watching a child slowly cup their hands and then take charge of a young bird or mammal is a joy to behold. Life held dear, treasured in the moment. That, my friends, is Horlicks for the heart.

One of the things I'm most proud of is being a life-long bully basher. If somebody was to ask me how I'd like to be remembered it would be up there with anything else I've ever achieved. Can you imagine the epitaph?

HERE LIES BRIAN BLESSED
1936–2099 (AT LEAST)
ACTOR, ADVENTURER, BULLY BASHER
AND ANIMAL LOVER

Anyway, I've given all sorts of examples of this in the past, but all the bully stories I have ever told thus far have been about humans bullying humans, whereas this one, which happened when I was about ten years of age, involves a human bullying not only another human – a friend of mine called Philip Harrison – but also his black and white cat. The bully in question was called Adam Potts and he lived in a nearby village. I'd heard rumours that he could be a bit of a bully but I'd never had reason to actually take him apart.

My friend Philip, although not a coward, did not like confrontation at all and so instead of getting involved in these kinds of situations he would slink off shaking his head and leave us all to it. In other words, dear reader, he was a sensible boy! This kind of common sense used to infuriate Adam Potts but because Philip could handle himself if provoked he decided, like bullies do, to find a weaker prey but something that would still provoke a reaction from poor Philip. The victim, I'm afraid, came in the shape of Philip's cat, Pickles, who was black and white and really quite small. He was a cute little thing and Philip doted on him as I did Tibby.

One day, Adam Potts and his gang turned up at Philip's house and after spotting Pickles playing with Philip in the garden they held Philip down, snatched Pickles from him and then took the terrified cat down to the local pond. Philip, who was naturally distraught, immediately ran to tell me what had occurred. As I said, Philip wasn't soft, but with five or six boys to contend with he was going to need help and as I was a fellow cat lover, he came to me.

'Brian, Brian!' Philip exclaimed. 'Adam Potts and his gang have grabbed Pickles. They've taken him down to Brick Pond. You're the best fighter in school! Come on!'

Within a second or so Philip and I were racing toward Brick Pond with Tibby running behind. Tibby could always tell if things were about to get a bit tasty and whenever I got into a fight he would circle the melee, arch his back and his fur would stand on end.

As we approached our destination all I could make out at first was that Adam and his gang had surrounded the pond and were laughing at something. Then, as we got closer, the full horror of what was occurring began to dawn on us. Poor Pickles was being thrown into the pond like you might throw a stone into the sea – tossed high into the air. Then, when Pickles managed to extricate himself, they would throw him in again.

Poor Philip started to cry the moment he realized what was going on and began pleading with the gang to stop. They didn't, of course, and just laughed at him. This hideous state of affairs presented two firsts for me: It was the first time I ever witnessed any kind of animal cruelty and was the first time I remember really losing my temper. Red mist exploded in my brain and I propelled myself forward like a wild animal.

'Philip!' I shouted. 'You jump in and fetch Pickles and leave the rest to me.'

Once Adam Potts and his gang caught sight of the spitting ball of fury approaching them they scattered in all directions. *Fair enough*, I thought. *If I can't have all of you I'll at least have the leader.* And so, with a determination that would have instantly propelled an entire rugby team to the top of K2, I began the quest of first catching, and then punching the living daylights out of the hideous Potts. I'm not ashamed to say that every punch I threw at Adam felt absolutely wonderful, yet the fear I saw on his eyes as I attacked him was enough to persuade me that actually, I should stop. Why, as supposedly intelligent creatures, do we continually fail to appreciate that animals experience fear, terror and pain just as we do? And what gives us the right to inflict these on creatures who A) mean us no harm and B) haven't the means of defending themselves? Cowardice personified.

Now, despite choosing to spare Potts a proper thrashing, I did feel the need to try to knock this behaviour on the head and so later on that day I walked to Adam's house, which was about three miles away. I no doubt appeared much calmer by this time but the anger within me still burned and by the time I knocked on Adam's door I'd been haunted so much by the image of Pickles being thrown into the pond that I was ready to finish off what I'd started earlier that day.

Adam's mother answered the door.

'Yes, can I help you?' she said. 'Hang on. You're Hilda Blessed's boy aren't you?'

'That's right,' I snapped, now absolutely seething. 'Do you know where your Adam was this morning?'

She surveyed me with mild indignation. After all, she was being questioned by an irate ten-year-old!

'No, I do not, young man. As far as I know he was with his pals.'

'That's right!' I exclaimed, as if in the process of revealing the identity of a mass murderer. 'He was with his pals! And do you know what they were doing?'

This was a step too far for Mrs Potts. 'Now see here, lad,' she barked, firing me a look that would have stopped the *Flying Scotsman*. 'State your business or get off home, and unless you change your tone I'll have something to say to your mother the next time you see her.'

Mrs Potts was absolutely right, of course, and I realized there and then that if I didn't change tack I wasn't going to get very far.

'I'm sorry, Mrs Potts,' I said, 'but it's your Adam. This morning him and his gang kidnapped Philip Harrison's cat, Pickles, and then they threw him in Brick Pond and tried to drown him. Time and time again they threw him in!'

'Alright lad, calm down,' she said, then screamed, 'ADAM! Get your backside down here NOW!'

Mrs Potts, as I was fast finding out, was not a woman to be trifled with. As well as having the build of a Sherman tank she had a voice that could cause an avalanche. Come to think of it my dear reader, she was like a female version of an adult me, really!

For as long as I live I will never forget the look on Adam's face when he descended those last few stairs and then began to comprehend the scene that lay before him. Guilt, guilt, guilt. His face was bright red with it. He was well and truly up the creek without a paddle. In fact, without a boat!

'Is it true what young Blessed says about you and your friends kidnapping a cat and trying to drown it?' growled Mrs Potts, and I *mean* growled.

Adam was lost. The look on his face had now progressed from abject horror to fearful resignation as he bowed his head and nodded towards his broad-shouldered mountain of a mother.

'I'm sorry, Mum,' he whimpered. 'It was just a bit of fun. The cat kept following us.'

'FUN!' Mrs Potts exploded. 'You think kidnapping a cat and trying to drown it is FUN? I've brought you up better than that Adam Potts and by the time I've finished with you you'll wish you'd never seen a bloody cat before, let alone tried to drown one. I dread to think what your father will have to say when he hears.'

Bringing the no doubt equally formidable Mr Potts into the equation obviously reminded Adam that the fallout from his mother's rage was only the tip of the iceberg, and what happened next turned his day from a stinker, albeit self-inflicted, into quite possibly the worst moment of his entire life.

I think somewhere down the line Mrs Potts must have been made aware that Adam could be a bit of a bully and so in what I assume was an attempt to put paid to his wicked ways, or at the very least teach him a lesson he'd hopefully never forget, she gave me leave to chin the little bugger.

'Punch him,' said Mrs Potts. 'Go on lad. Punch him.'

Literally a second after the invitation had left Mrs Pott's lips I had landed on Adam's nose a right hook that would have floored a wild boar – he was two years older than me by the way – and he went down like a sack of spuds.

'There,' said Mrs Potts. 'Serves you bloody well right.'

And with that she walked inside, gave Adam a sharp one around the ear for luck, and then slammed the door. For just a few seconds I honestly think I was in love. What a woman! Judge Dredd looked like Titania, queen of the fairies compared to Mrs Potts. Some may call it rough justice, I suppose, although not I. I mean, do you consider it to be rough justice? Of course you don't! Even at the tender age of ten I felt proud that I might have helped prevent something like this from happening again and so I considered it a resounding victory. My knuckles were a bit sore but as I walked back towards Probert Avenue it would have taken a cloth the size of a beach towel to wipe the grin off my happy little face. God bless you, Mrs Potts!

Not long after the incident involving Adam Potts my parents decided that they wanted to move from Goldthorpe to Bolton-upon-Dearne, which is about a mile and a half away. When they broke the news to me the first thought that entered my head was, *What about Tibby?* He may well have treated our house like a home during the daytime but he was still totally independent and so I feared that I might lose him forever. This wasn't the first time in my life that I'd had to contend with the prospect of suffering loss, as not long after I met Tibby my younger brother Alan had come perilously close to death while suffering from the dreaded pneumonia. Although the two events were not of the same magnitude, I was now far more emotionally mature than I was then, and, like any child on the threshold of puberty, prone not only to ruminating over life's issues but producing not an inconsiderable amount of angst.

Come the morning of the move I was at my wits' end and hadn't slept a wink. I'd tried to explain to Tibby what was happening but neither our bond nor my spirited imagination could bridge the obvious communication gap. Tibby was going to be in for a shock and the aftermath of what was about to occur scared me half to death.

When first I opened the front door after breakfast my miniature clouded leopard was waiting for me as usual.

'Morning Tib,' I said, with as much cheeriness as I could muster. 'Sleep well?'

As always my salutation was met with a figure of eight around the feet and ankles but as the day progressed and as the contents of our home slowly began to be transported in all manner of assorted containers to the waiting removal lorry, Tibby became distant. It was as if he knew that I would be leaving him and instead of making a fuss he had decided to give me some space and make the transition easier for me. But how could it be easier? Tibby & Bless, South Yorkshire's very own Mowgli and Bagheera, would shortly be no more and the desperation I felt at not being able to explain to Tibby what was going on was overwhelming. I felt crushed.

Eventually the time came for me to reluctantly board the removal lorry where the driver, my family and all our worldly possessions were waiting patiently. As the driver cranked up the engine I had one last desperate look to see if Tibby, who had disappeared from view at least two hours earlier, would allow me to say goodbye.

My first glance into what was now our old front garden bore no fruit whatsoever, but when I looked again I suddenly saw Tibby. He'd obviously been hiding in one of the bushes at the side of the garden and was now leaping over the front wall towards the removal lorry.

'Wait!' I screamed to the driver. 'Please! It's Tibby!'

Fortunately, my father nodded to the driver to endorse my panicked request and as I opened the door next to me Tibby bound over, leapt up from the pavement below and landed lightly in my lap. By this time, I was in quite a state. That doom-laden sense of impending loss had been merciless and I felt empty inside. Now the relief I felt was even more extreme and I'm afraid I started crying.

Although Tibby was undoubtedly flattered by the reaction his presence had caused he didn't seem to appreciate being showered in a multitude of salty tears, so while I sat there desperately trying to pull myself together he found temporary shelter on my mother's lap.

My dear friend, I'm afraid I must make a confession. I have claimed that as a child I never cried and until recalling this particular episode with Tibby I still believed that. However, I must hold up my hands and admit that I made a mistake. The thought of losing Tibby was too much, even for an obstinate little hard case like me, and the subsequent – and it has to be said, mercifully quick – reunion produced an emotion in me that would have had Ming the Merciless himself reaching for the loo roll.

The look my parents gave me on seeing me blub was one of complete and utter shock. Not a word was spoken, however, and the moment Tibby rejoined me on the seat by the window my father signalled for the driver to carry on and away we went to sunny Bolton-upon-Dearne.

Unfortunately, about three or four weeks after the move, Tibby must have decided that Bolton-upon-Dearne wasn't for him and as I left the house to go to school one morning he was nowhere to be seen. I knew immediately what had happened, as even though we still went everywhere together Tibby hadn't quite been himself since the move and had become quite unsociable. We may not have been the same species, but I could tell that he was pining for something – home, probably – and as devastated as I was when he left, it was no great surprise that he simply disappeared.

That Friday after school I got on my bike and rode back to Probert Avenue to see if I could find Tibby. Not in an attempt to bring him back, by the way – he was very much his own cat! – but to simply try and find out if he was OK. I really missed him and I'd had all my fellow pupils who still lived in Goldthorpe out looking for Tibby after school. They'd been almost as distressed as I had when I told them what had happened, but come Friday none of them had seen hide nor hair of him. In hindsight I should probably have just respected Tibby's decision to leave and got on with my life but ours had been such a unique and close relationship that I felt compelled to act.

When I arrived at Probert Avenue the first thing I did was call on the Burns family, our old neighbours, and on Wendy, their sweet-natured sympathetic Golden Retriever who is still to this very day my all-time favourite baby-sitter. Alas, Wendy was now about thirteen years of age which is old for a Golden Retriever and when Mrs Burns appeared at the front door she was on the verge of tears.

'Hello, Brian love,' she said. 'I'm afraid I've got some bad news. Come in, would you.'

According to my sorrowful hostess poor Wendy had been ill for some weeks. I followed Mrs Burns into the living room and there fast asleep in front of the fire was dear Wendy.

'She's dying, Brian,' wept Mrs Burns, no longer able to

contain her grief. 'The vet came earlier today and says it's only a matter of time. Hours, probably.'

I looked up at Mrs Burns and asked if I could sit with Wendy. 'She looked after me so many times. I'd like to do the same for her, if it's OK with you.'

Mrs Burns, who was a very handsome woman, managed to force a slight smile. 'Of course, Brian love. Wendy's missed you since you've moved. I'll be in the kitchen if you need me.'

Poor Mrs Burns. She and Mr Burns had found Wendy abandoned when she was only a few days old and they were as proud of her as any parent could be of any child. As I've already told you, Wendy was the only dog on Probert Avenue. Everybody on the street loved Wendy and that love was reciprocated ten-fold. Dogs *are* love. I once read a quote by the popular American author, Dean Koontz, that I think sums this up perfectly. He said, 'Once you have had a wonderful dog, a life without one, is a life diminished.' Perfect words.

When I knelt quietly down by Wendy's side she stirred slightly and as I whispered hello to her one of her eyes opened slowly. On registering me, Wendy attempted to rise from the cushion on which she lay but before she could move very far I opened my knees, shuffled myself closer and pulled her gently towards me, so her head was on my leg. She was an old lady now, at the end of her life, yet her eyes were still beacons of affection.

'Hello, Wendy,' I whispered. 'Do you remember that time I took you for a walk and we got lost on the way to

Doncaster? I got into awful trouble that day, didn't I. And do you remember when our Alan came a purler in our garden? You had our mum outside before I could even get up.'

It's no coincidence, my dear reader, that when the great J. M. Barrie was writing *Peter Pan* he decided that Nana, the Darling children's nurse, should be a dog.

Being able to comfort Wendy and say thank you before she died is a gift that I shall always treasure. These days it puts me in mind of Homer's Odysseus, who, after fighting the Trojan Wars for ten years makes the journey back to Ithaca, where, disguised as a tramp, he comes across his faithful dog Argos who has been abandoned and is close to death. Despite his disguise and the intervening years Argos recognizes Odysseus immediately and is able to die a happy death knowing that his master is alive and well.

Wendy died in my arms about forty-five minutes later. I was stroking her and telling her what I'd been up to in Bolton-upon-Dearne when she went. Her breathing had been quite laboured and so when it suddenly stopped I knew immediately what had happened. After saying good-bye and kissing her on the nose and on the forehead I very gently laid Wendy back on her cushion and went into the kitchen.

'I'm sorry, Mrs Burns,' I said. 'But Wendy's gone.'

Once again her tear ducts sprang into action and after giving her a long, lingering hug I decided to take my leave and allow her and her family, when they arrived home, to mourn.

'Thank you, Brian,' she said as I walked out into the street. 'I can't think of a nicer way for Wendy to have gone. She loved you to pieces you know. Send our best wishes to your mum, dad and Alan, would you?'

And with that Mrs Burns closed the door behind her and I ran off to see if I could find Tibby.

I never did find Tibby that day, and every Friday for about the next six months I cycled back to Goldthorpe after school, just in case he turned up. He didn't though, alas, and as the months and years passed Tibby started to become a memory, although a very precious one.

One of the leisure activities I embraced in order to help me get over Tibby was – and I know exactly what you're going to say – crown green bowls. Yes, crown green bowls! Now before you all imagine me smoking a pipe and slipping into comfy shoes, just you hang on a minute, because back then in post-war Bolton-upon-Dearne crown green bowls was as popular and fashionable as cricket or even football. What's more, I – Brian Blessed, the scourge of the Dearne Valley and former South Yorkshire schoolboy boxing champion – can lay claim to being one of the sport's first ever sex symbols. Yes, you read correctly. Brian Blessed was once the David Beckham of crown green bowls! I don't know why I've decided to tell you this but now we're here, what the hell.

This happened about three years after I first graced the sport with my presence so I'm jumping on a bit. It's a nice little story though and as well as bringing a bit of sexiness to the proceedings, not to mention a not inconsiderable amount of glamour, it leads on nicely to the climax of this first chapter.

Just off the green in Bolton-upon-Dearne there lived a spinster who must have been in her late fifties and, for want of a better phrase, was one wave short of a shipwreck. In fact, I'd go as far as to say she was bloody bonkers. She must have been at least five foot ten tall, had a beard that, thirty years hence, I myself would have been proud of and arms like a navvy on steroids. Her name was Mrs Martin.

In addition to an obvious repugnance for razors, not to mention a rather vigorous pursuit of the pleasures of the table, Mrs Martin was also prone to speaking her mind. Sorry, that should have been *shouting* her mind. Now the only real love in Mrs Martin's life, as far as I was aware, was crown green bowls, and although she didn't play the game herself she was certainly an avid and very vocal spectator. An early form of cheerleader, I suppose, with just a hint of all-in wrestler.

The genesis of Mrs Martin's infatuation can be traced back to the time I entered my first competition. This was a great honour for such a young lad and, as I'd been drawn against the formidable yet cantankerous Neddie White, who was a one-time Yorkshire quarter-finalist, I was nervous to say the least. Neddie, like the vast majority of spectators present, was of the opinion that you should be at least ninety-six years of age before you were allowed to participate in a crown green bowls competition. The only thing that stopped the 'crown green glitterati' from running me off, apart from the fact that they couldn't get up, was the presence of my father, Bill, who was a keen bowler himself.

The moment I went to roll my first bowl Mrs Martin, who appeared to be halfway through a round of sandwiches, got to her size tens and began making her feelings known.

'Ooooh, I could fall in love with him!' she shouted. 'He's got it. I'm telling you, he's got it!'

There must have been at least 400 people watching that afternoon and as Mrs Martin made public her opinions every single one of them shot a look at me that said, 'You poor little bastard.' Unbeknownst to me, Mrs Martin had form in this area and I was just the latest in a long line of love interests. Once she'd found out my name from somebody there was no stopping her and every time I went forward to roll she would stand up and start shouting.

'He bowls with dumplings that Neddie White, Brian. You can have him. Come on Brian! Oooh, I'd like to take him home with me.'

The only person, apart from me, who didn't seem to find this funny was my father and after the game had finished (I won 21–19 and pocketed 2 and 6, by the way) he accosted me.

'Please tell me you're not fooling around with her, Brian. Your mother will go spare!'

Well, you could have knocked me down with a bloody feather. I was fourteen at the time and quite a late starter when it came to women. Even though I hadn't even dipped my toe in the water, so to speak, Mrs Martin's attentions probably put me back at least another five years! I was horrified at what my father was suggesting and fortunately just the look I shot him was enough to persuade him that the Blessed cherry was still very much intact.

To close this chapter, we must jump inside my time machine and whizz forward about a year. Although engrossed in crown green bowls – and by then I was acting in the local drama group too – I still thought about Tibby often and was overjoyed when, after playing a match one summer's evening, I returned home to find him perched nonchalantly on our front wall.

'Tibby!' I shouted. 'You've come back!'

It was very rare that I ever picked Tibby up – he really didn't like it – but on this occasion I made an exception and on scooping him up into my arms I kissed him a thousand times before running with him through our front door and into the living room.

'Mum, Dad, look. Tibby's home!'

Mum seemed thrilled to bits to see Tibby again but Dad not so much. There was no Mrs Dancy now and so instead of a reddish brown miniature clouded leopard in my arms all he saw was another expense. He came around though, once I'd promised I'd pay for his food out of my own money.

Tibby and I had eight more precious months together, in which time I introduced him, not only to everyone at my new school, but to all my friends, and enemies, at the bowling club. Yet again he immediately became the centre of attention and had lost none of that totemic quality he'd exuded previously. We were no longer referred to as Tibby and Bless. That represented our salad days. These were now our autumn years and instead of joining me first thing for school as he used to, Tibby would amble along to my school during lunchtime, parking himself contentedly on a bench to soak up the multitude of strokes, caresses and calls of 'Hi Tibby'. I was always so proud of him. Proud that he was my friend.

Then, one school day, not long after the summer holidays had come to an end, he simply didn't turn up. I knew instantly that something had happened to him. When I arrived home my mother confronted me with the news that Tibby was dead, having been shot several times by a pellet gun. My dad had discovered him by the side of his garden allotment. Many people in the area possessed pellet guns so it was very difficult to pinpoint the person responsible, though I did have a pretty good idea. My friends felt certain that it was a lad who kept racing pigeons near the allotments. Tibby, like many of the local cats, liked to sit and watch the birds but he never attacked them. This lad was my age and shook like a leaf when I confronted him.

I had to let it go as I couldn't prove he was guilty, but even to this day if I see him in the Don and Dearne valley I give him the cold shoulder and he still looks guilty.

I dug Tibby a grave in a lovely corner of our garden and, after gently laying his body down, said a silent prayer. My mother kissed me and my dad put his hand on my shoulder.

'Go upstairs and sit in your room, lad,' he said. 'You're fifteen years of age now and a young man should always sit on his own when he cries.'

When Tibby first extended the paw of friendship to me some seventy-four years ago, little did I know that it would be the start of something so very special. My gratitude to Tibby, as with my love for all the animals I have known, is endless. Thank you Tib x

2

FANCY SMITH BUYS A KING'S HOUSE

Now, as much as I enjoyed that chapter it was a little bit short on species, so in order to open things up a little bit I'm going to tell you about the time I had my very own exotic animal sanctuary. OK, that is probably exaggerating the situation slightly but only by a pinch. You see, I once bought, and then renovated, a king's house that was sold just a few years ago for £20 million pounds – although not by me, more's the pity. This all happened back in the 1960s and I lost a fortune on the place. Not that I could give a fig about that.

This is where I started to find my paws as an animal lover, but because of certain acquaintances of mine, including a snake charmer, a man from the ministry and a television star who kept a hamster on his head, the animals in question were anything but domestic.

Stranger than fiction? Yes, dear reader! Yet anything but.

Shall we trot on?

I served the latter part of my national service at RAF Bicester and the USAF base in Upper Heyford, Oxfordshire. The initial square-bashing had taken place at RAF Bridgnorth in Shropshire in the winter of 1954 but Bicester was where the real work began and after being assigned to the Parachute Regiment I spent the majority of my time either packing parachutes or jumping out of aeroplanes. Nice work, if you can get it. Unless of course you're scared of heights, in which case you'd spend half your life screaming like a big girl's blouse.

Anyway, what made RAF Bicester extra special for me was the fact that there was a big educational centre there, and thanks to my mentor Ruth Wynn Owen, a remarkable woman who taught drama, I was now ingesting knowledge like I ingest sausages. Me and my dogs go through literally thousands every week. Anyway, the men and women who frequented the educational centre at RAF Bicester were obviously scholarly types and so I made a lot of friends very quickly. One of these was a ginger-haired chap by the name of Tony Smith. Tony was bound for university once he'd completed his two years and he taught me all kinds of wonderful things about music. Another lad, called Peter Comerford (who wanted to be a priest), used to help me a lot with my grammar and so in many ways it was like having private tuition but without the bill.

Every so often Tony would use his pass to visit places like Hounslow and Twickenham. He had family there and one day invited me to join him.

'I'm actually going up to Richmond today, if you'd like to come,' he said.

I was confused. The only Richmond I knew of was the picturesque market town in North Yorkshire. Which, incidentally, has the most exquisite Georgian theatre. You must go! Surely he wasn't inviting me there?

'No, Brian!' chuckled Tony. 'There's another Richmond down here but it takes its name from the one in Yorkshire. It's on the Thames. Peter's coming too. You'll love it.'

I won't bore you all by trying to describe Richmond but I fell completely head-over-heels in love with the place. It was a foggy day, I remember, which meant I had to examine what lay before me very carefully indeed. This merely enhanced its allure and the more I walked and squinted the more I wanted to see. Richmond Palace, Richmond Theatre, Richmond Green, Richmond Park. It's quite bucolic down there and you can be right in the heart of the countryside in a few minutes. It was already Shangri-La to me and I could not wait to examine it, and the mystical mist, again.

Tony's parents lived in a nice house just outside Richmond and because I got on so well with them they invited me to stay there whenever I liked. All my seventy-two-hour passes were obviously expended travelling north but whenever I was handed a forty-eight-hour pass instead I'd be up that river faster than a Yorkshireman who's seen a pound coin in a puddle.

Over the coming months I took great delight in familiarizing myself with Richmond and spent many a happy afternoon just rowing up and down the Thames in between Teddington Lock and Richmond Bridge, admiring the surroundings.

As the years passed the London suburb of Richmond remained fixed in my psyche and, despite not being able to visit the place much after completing my national service, I often dreamt that one day I would live there.

We all must have a dream, boys and girls. That's *so* important! It doesn't matter who you are, where you live or what you do. If you are without dreams, you are without life.

No more diversions for a bit now, I promise. *I get so carried away!*

OK. Six years or so after I first invaded Richmond I was appearing in the BBC hit series *Z-Cars* playing PC Fancy Smith. Since starring in the show I'd been leading quite a nomadic life and after a couple of years on the road I decided that it was time to lay down some roots. I'd made a few quid beating up baddies on the TV screen and so why not? The question was, where? North London was the place to be back then – villages like Hampstead, Highgate and Primrose Hill – but to be honest I never liked being north of the river. I always feel very hemmed in there and for an explorer like myself that will never do. No, no. I need to walk freely and BREATHE, for heaven's sake, and let the air get to my bits and pieces. These days, of course, north London is absolutely swollen with thespians, rock stars and what have you and is a delightful area but my heart wanted Kew Gardens in the spring and Richmond Hill.

When I first went public with my intention to move to Richmond upon Thames I was rounded on by friends and colleagues alike. They told me that it was a terribly old-fashioned kind of area and that the only people who lived there were expiring octogenarians with arthritic Labradors. 'Perfect!' I said. And so, the following day, I made my way down there and began studying the windows of the local estate agents, all nestled alongside the river.

Ah, that river. Old Father Thames! I felt a bit like Ratty in *Toad of Toad Hall* when I lived in Richmond. 'There's nothing like the river!' he advised Mr Mole. 'There really is nothing like it!' What a clever little English-speaking bespectacled rodent he was. There are thousands of those coming up, by the way. Both tame ones and some horrible wild ones!

You should have seen the looks on estate agents' faces when Fancy Smith walked through the door. Joy and surprise came first, followed quickly by abject fear! I used to get this all the time when I was in *Z-Cars*. I could always read people's minds when they recognized me. First their brains would tell them to smile. *Ooooh, that's him off the telly*, they'd think to themselves. Then, once they realized that 'him off the telly' played a hardnosed copper who used to beat up crooks and bullies they would immediately turn to jelly! They didn't know me as a person, of course, but my character's persona was so strong that it made them react accordingly. In those days there were only three channels, BBC 1 and 2 and ITV, and a show like *Z-Cars* had viewing figures of about 14 million. Television made us famous, but it can play havoc with the life of a performer.

When I first started thinking about buying my own place I was paid £78 a week and believe you me, that was big money! Then, suddenly, the good people over at Equity decided that we telly actors weren't earning nearly enough. We had our beloved heavies at Equity go over to Wood Lane and fight tooth and nail on our behalf and before you could say Bob's your uncle I was on £220 a week! How about that? I couldn't believe it. I was rich beyond my wildest dreams.

On receiving news of my newfound prosperity my bank manager, who I always got on very well with, got rather carried away. 'Brian!' he exclaimed. 'You've just put over £400 into your account! How wonderful.'

I was living in Golders Green at the time and rather than sitting there and pining away I decided to move down to Richmond immediately and rent somewhere. After all, when destiny calls, you don't sit on your backside and wait for it to come and pick you up in a taxi, do you?

The first property that tickled my fancy was a good-sized cottage about halfway up Ormond Road called Ormond House Cottage. It had beautiful bottle glass windows, a large kitchen, a good-looking sitting room, two big bedrooms, a nice bathroom and a staircase that led up to a studio. There was also a garden at the back, which was nicely walled in.

'Wonderful,' I roared with delight at the purveyor. 'That'll do for me!'

Back then, in the early 1960s, you could buy a bog-standard house in Richmond for between about £1,800 and £6,000. You could! I remember an estate agent calling me up about a house one day. It was a 1930s three-bedroom semi and was on the market for £2,200.

'I'm not paying that kind of money for a three-bedroom semi,' I said. 'You've gotta be mad!'

Do you know, that house is now worth over £1.5 million today? ONE POINT FIVE MILLION! One never envisaged property escalating like that.

The part of my great brain that is responsible for making business decisions must be a little bit underdeveloped and operates in a similar fashion to one of the dogs we have at home. Little Rupert, God bless him, is half dog and half amoeba. He's as slow as an eight-day clock and if he was ever let loose in a bone factory I swear he'd come out chewing his own leg. My wife is potty about him, as you'll see later.

Despite having a touch of the Ruperts, I was only paying £13 a week for Ormond House Cottage and so I couldn't see the point of shelling out that kind of cash. I'm also a Yorkshireman, remember, and would never have got permission from God, who has been the mayor of Yorkshire ever since we lost Brian Close.

After saying no to the house, I simply sat back and enjoyed Richmond. With my outgoings being minimal I managed to save a lot of money in my first two years there. About £14,000, in fact! This was after I'd paid all my tax, by the way. My biggest luxury at the time was having a housekeeper, Mrs Bush, who was a gentle old, petite South African lady. I must admit it was a lovely feeling being so financially secure and with visitors dropping in all the time and my parents and brother Alan coming to stay; it was a very happy time for me. I was in a house I adored, in a town I was smitten by and was surrounded by people I loved. Bingo! Blessed had a full house. Well, nearly. The only thing missing now was an animal or six.

This was another one of those delightful Eureka moments onc has occasionally, because when it eventually occurred to me that I could now throw open my doors and offer some creatures of the non-human variety a permanent home, I was cock-a-bloody-hoop! I had a bit of a thing for short-haired and Siamese cats at the time. First to move in was a gorgeous Abyssinian cat that I named Ramesses, after the Egyptian prince. Abyssinians originate from Egypt, you see. Anyway, in those days Richmond was absolutely teeming with big fat pussies and the walls of my garden were covered in them. In fact, it seemed that every cat in the land would turn up just to take a Neville Crump on my geraniums.

Like me, Ramesses was a magnificent creature and as well as having that distinctive 'ticked' tabby coat he had a long slender body and ears that seemed to be slightly too big for his head. But in a good way! Unlike me he was both intelligent and painfully shy, and seemed to move with the grace of a four-legged Fred Astaire. The name Ramesses certainly suited him, although I'm not sure if the Prince of Egypt would have spent quite so much time spraying as his feline namesake. That cat was an absolute sod for it and if you ever got in the way – which I often did – you would end up smelling like an ammonia factory for weeks on end. With the area being riddled with moggies, the deed was quite understandable. Not in Ormond House Cottage though, Ramesses! For the first three or four weeks he did nothing else and Mrs Bush was all for having his tripes out.

'I cannot and will not work in a house reeking of cat piss,' she said to me. 'You're going to have to do something.'

Mrs Bush wasn't the only one suffering the effects of 'Ramesses' Revenge' and I swear to you that after a week or two I lost almost all of my nasal hair. Have you ever tried getting rid of that smell? I dare say some of you have at some point in your lives and it's no fun, is it? After about a month, which seemed more like a year, Ramesses stopped spraying in the house – oh thank you merciful god Osiris! – and turned his attentions exclusively to the garden.

Like the glutton for punishment that I am, I then went out and found a beautiful Blue Point Siamese I called Helen (after Helen of Troy) and then a Seal Point. The Seal Point, who I named Contessa, was a great conversationalist and whenever she heard my voice she would meow away like a faraway siren on a Greek island. It didn't matter if I was on the phone or chatting to the milkman, the moment Contessa heard my dulcet tones she'd start singing her little heart out like a furry Maria Callas . . . Poor Ramesses favoured a quiet life generally and because of the chatter he took to avoiding Contessa like the plague.

I came across Contessa, who was the junior Siamese champion and the most beautiful creature I'd ever clapped eyes on, at a pet show at Olympia one day. As I walked into the Siamese section people started recognizing me and pretty soon a crowd had gathered. It resembled a valuation from the *Antiques Roadshow* and when I managed to persuade the breeder to let me buy Contessa from him a great cheer went up, after which the breeder, a sophisticated silver-haired lady, announced, 'Ladies and gentlemen, PC Fancy Smith has bought Chocolate Wey Missal Four.'

'Has bought what?' I said.

'Chocolate Wey Missal Four,' said the little breeder. 'That's what she's called.'

Some of the names they give these exotic cats. Honestly! Come to think of it, Contessa's not that much better.

Soon after Contessa arrived at Ormond House Cottage a Lilac Point called Sylvia and a Red Point were introduced to my burgeoning feline family, followed then by a Russian Blue. I didn't know it at the time, but this Red Point was so inbred he made Daddy Flintstone look like Richard Dawkins. I called him Fred.

My favourite of all the Ormond House Cottage cats was the Russian Blue who I named Graymalkin, which is from *Macbeth*. His official name was Alkon Bobbydall, which I thought sounded like a 1960s pop star with a blue rinse. What a beauty he was, though. What a specimen! His eyes were like green emeralds, his fur shimmering silver-blue, and he was obviously a very intelligent creature as from the word go he was all over me like a rash. It's the most devotion I've had from a cat outside of Tibby. The reason I called him Graymalkin is because the only noise he ever made was 'malk', and so it seemed rather appropriate. Like Tibby, he used to stick to me like glue so if I was in the house I couldn't even go to the loo without him tagging along. I didn't mind in the slightest as I adored looking at him.

Frank Windsor, who played Detective Sergeant Watt in *Z-Cars*, used to visit me at Ormond House Cottage regularly and after catching the animal bug he decided that he was going to get himself a dog. He lived in Holland Park.

'Make sure you get a small breed,' I advised him. 'Especially as you haven't much room at home.'

Although I wasn't an expert in dogs I still thought Frank would probably heed my advice and come back with something small and yappy. A Jack Russell, perhaps? Oh, no, no, no, no. He came back with a Rottweiler! At 70 centimetres in height, and about 60 kilogrammes in weight, Phyllis was bigger than most male Rottweilers and had the appetite of a medium-sized dinosaur. Well done Frank!

The arrangement, alas, did not start well.

'I can't take her to any of the shops I usually go to, Brian,' he confessed to me one afternoon. 'Or the pub. She's barred from there. And from the newsagents.'

'But why, Frank?' I enquired, trying desperately not to laugh.

'Well, she took a piss in the newsagents, which Harry the owner didn't like much. Or his other customers, for that matter. Then in the pub she took a dislike to one of the regulars and ended up knocking over four tables and smashing about ten glasses. I'm still allowed in, but she's barred for life, and she costs a fortune to feed.'

After taking a sip of tea he sighed. 'Being famous can open many doors, Brian, but not if you happen to have a large pissing dog with you.'

Poor old Frank.

If you go down the hill from Ormond House Cottage you eventually get to Patten Alley, which runs off to the right, and this leads on to a road called The Vineyard. Patten Alley, by the way, has the most wonderful leaning walls which, after dark, give it a delightful creepy quality, like something out of an old Sherlock Holmes movie. I used to peep over them into people's gardens, but about halfway up the alley there was a thick, very large green door that was too high to see over. Having quite a fertile imagination, this used to evoke all kinds of wonderful stories in my head. *What was behind that old green door?* I used to ask myself. *What strange worlds awaited me?* Fate beckoned and I eventually found out.

One day as I walked out of Patten Alley and then right on to The Vineyard, I stopped suddenly as somebody was opening some dark wooden gates. I'd never noticed them before but because they were now parting, and because I'm a nosey bugger, I felt compelled to wait and see what they had been hiding. With the benefit of hindsight, I should probably have walked straight on, but that's life. Before me though, was a vision: a Georgian house, three storeys high and with the most attractive frontage I had ever seen. There was a nice-looking coach house situated to the front left of the building and, on peering down the side of the main house, I guessed that there must have been at least half an acre of land at the back. Perhaps more. The whole place looked rather faded, I remember, which I found very appealing – a bit like the Brontë sisters' house in Yorkshire – and as the person, or people, who had parted the gates drove past me in an old banger I rather cheekily walked forward so that I could take a closer look.

The wisteria on the front of the house must have been at least two feet across at the base and was so thick going up that you could have scaled it right to the top of the house. It was even bigger than the Mitre, apparently, which is the large wisteria at Hampton Court Palace, and the owners had an arrangement with Kew Gardens who helped look after it. I was told that the body of a dead horse had been put under its roots to feed it.

After admiring the frontage for a while, I then sneaked down the side of the house to get a good look at the garden. I was right, it was at least half an acre in size and had a lawn like a cricket pitch. There was an Anglican church at the bottom of the garden, a Catholic one to the left, and to the right of it was Patten Alley, so as well as being smothered in Godliness it was completely walled in. It was just exquisite! I half expected to see Mr Rochester appear. On closer inspection, it was easy to see that the buildings were not in the same condition as the garden, but I didn't care.

The following day I went into a local estate agents just to see if they knew of the house.

'That's Clarence House you're talking about, Mr Blessed,' the estate agent said. 'It's not on our books I'm afraid but it is for sale. Has been for many years, nobody is interested in it.'

I had only enquired about the house because I found it so fascinating, but when I was told it was for sale my heart leapt and I was rendered quite dizzy. I'd never experienced such emotions over mere bricks and mortar before.

On locating the right estate agents, who were called Penningtons, I literally assailed their gates.

'I want that house,' I proclaimed.

'Which house?' said the startled estate agent.

'Clarence House! You may as well put a sold sign up now, love. For it will be mine!'

The look on the estate agent's face was a picture. He was a delightful character called Mr Hester who was always smiling and laughing.

'Really,' Mr Hester said incredulously. 'You do realize, Mr Blessed, that the property needs some attention?'

'Yes, yes, yes. That's half the fun. I'd love a nice project. Now tell me all about it and I promise I will spare your life!'

If Clarence House *looked* like an interesting place, which it did, that was nothing compared to its history. Built in 1696 for a London haberdashery merchant, it was bought in the 1780s by the Duke of Clarence (hence the name), who eventually became King William IV.

'You mean to say it's a king's house?' I said, thrilled.

'That's right, it was King William IV's summer residence,' he replied. 'But its history becomes even more interesting once we reach the end of that century.'

'Really? Then speak on, man, speak on!'

'Well, from 1792 until 1799 Clarence House was a Catholic school and among its students was Bernardo O'Higgins, the Chilean independence leader who, together with José de San Martín, freed Chile from Spanish rule in the Chilean War of Independence.'

'*Bueno, maldita sea!*' I cooed with enthusiasm. As well as a king of England living there we've had one of Chile's founding fathers. Who'd have thought it?

'Who's next?' I asked him.

'Nobody of any note, I'm afraid. Fortnum and Mason used it as a warehouse in the 1940s and were intending to tear it down and replace it with a bakery before they changed their minds.'

'Tear it down? All that history though?'

'Means nothing to them. Anyway, after that it reverted back to being a private dwelling.'

If I was sold on Clarence House going *in* to Penningtons, I was doubly sold going out. It had my heart.

'Let me speak to my bank manager,' I said to him, 'and I'll come back to you next week with an offer. By the way, how many rooms does it have?'

'Seventy-two. All need repairing.'

'Bloody hell fire!'

With that I ran back to Ormond House Cottage, covered the cats in kisses and then telephoned my bank manager.

'I'd like to see you as soon as I possibly can. I've found the perfect house!'

After giving him the details he said he'd make some enquiries and then get back to me.

'Yes, yes, yes, as quick as you can please. I've fallen madly in love with it and I'd like to move in there right away.'

I hadn't even set foot in the place, by the way. Typical me!

When the bank manager eventually telephoned me back he sounded rather flat.

'What's wrong with you, man?' I probed.

'I think you'd better come and see me, Brian. I'll meet you here at the bank, OK?'

On entering his musty lair I was instructed to park my posterior and prepare for a shock.

'I'm afraid Clarence House isn't what you thought it was, Brian,' he began. 'I've been making some enquiries and it is what is known in the property trade as a *sour* property.'

'What on earth's a sour property?'

'Somewhere that is in a state of limbo, basically. You occasionally get these kinds of houses. Nobody can ever decide what to do with them and so after time they fall into a state of disrepair. I'm afraid Clarence House has been falling since the 1940s and I've been advised by those who have already surveyed the house to keep well away.'

I was crestfallen, slightly, but far from beaten. 'I knew it looked a *bit* tatty,' I said to him. 'At least let's go and have a look at the place.'

'You mean you haven't?' he shrilled, looking like a man who'd just been goosed by a nun.

'Nope.'

'Well I have, Brian. And the sooner you do, the better. The entire place is falling to bits!'

Alright, alright, so perhaps I should have taken a butcher's at the inside of Clarence House before contacting the bank. But on doing so I discovered that although the Deity of Dosh had been earnest in his assessment, he had, without doubt, over-dramatized the house's condition more than somewhat.

I thought *Falling to bits my Aunt Fanny*. After all there were people actually living there.

After taking a look and getting some advice it seemed that the plaster, the ceilings, the wiring, the woodwork, the plumbing and the panelling would all need replacing. OK – so most of the interior would need ripping out. That still doesn't constitute falling to bits. What happened to having a little bit of positivity? I was bordering on being a master plasterer for heaven's sake, having spent two years working under one as a teenager, and in addition to my dad and my brother Alan, who both knew their way around a tool box, I was acquainted with dozens of builders, electricians and plumbers. It'd be fine. Damn these merchants of doom and to hell with the lot of 'em. That's what I say! It was a magical place and I had fallen under its spell.

To cut a biblically long story short, ladies and gentlemen, I ended up buying Clarence House in 1965 for £20,000 – complete with three families' worth of sitting tenants. The previous owners, a lovely family named the Ommaneys, were living on the middle floor; a Mr and Mrs Shelford were residing on the ground floor, and an old Colonel and his wife and two children were on the top floor. Naturally I didn't sign for the place until they were all happy with everything and had agreed to vacate the house when they could. They were under no pressure, by the way.

The Ommaneys, who I found out had lived in Kenya for many years, used to have tea delivered from Nairobi and so every few weeks a huge box would arrive that was about four foot by three. Being a tea fanatic I'd be knocking on their door the moment the van arrived and they were always very generous with it. Mrs Ommaney, who was basically bedridden, reminded me a bit of Miss Faversham from *Great Expectations*. The fact that she lived in a bit of a hole merely reinforced the impression, but she was in fact a dear, sweet lady.

When the gentlemen and ladies of the popular press found out that I'd bought Clarence House they had a field day. 'FANCY SMITH BUYS A KING'S HOUSE' was the headline I remember, and it was plastered everywhere. I was maligned at first because of its condition, but once I got in there and began ripping out the innards the press started popping in to see me and their opinions changed almost overnight when they saw me plastering. One day I was a wealthy bohemian chucking all his money away on a dilapidated mansion and the next I was a champion trying to preserve a piece of history. Not only were they all amazed by the amount of money I was spending on the place but they couldn't believe that I'd be doing most of the work myself. Suddenly I was a knight in shining armour!

This became the *new* headline then, after which a steady stream of well-known and very welcome well-wishers wended their way to where I worked. All my old mates from *Z-Cars* popped in, as well as Keith Barron and John Thaw. Then there were a few locals; people like David Attenborough and John Mills. They used to live just up the road at the time, as did Huw Weldon who was in charge at the BBC. Huw pretended to be rather cross with me as at the time I'd started working for ITV – the other side! I used to go running three or four times a week and whenever I passed Huw's house on Richmond Hill he'd open his front door and shout, 'JUDAS! YOU TRAITOR-OUS SWINE!' Huw had the most wicked sense of humour and after berating me in front of passers-by and calling me all the names under the sun he'd drag me in for a cup of coffee and a catch-up.

My endeavours at Clarence House became so well known that numerous comedians mentioned me on ITV's *The London Palladium Show* and even Morecambe and Wise came on stage carrying pick axes and spades, and at the end of their skit they said, 'Right then. We're off to help Brian Blessed. If anyone else wants to lend a hand there'll be a workman's bus leaving in five minutes.'

It really seemed to capture people's imagination and I had no end of letters wishing me luck. People even used to send me ten-bob notes in cards saying 'This is to go towards the wallpaper' or something.

One visitor who was not welcome at Clarence House, but came nonetheless, was a local councillor who I came to loathe. I won't name the gentleman as if he's still alive he might try and sue me, but just prior to me buying the house he'd talked about trying to have it knocked down so that some developer – who he no doubt had connections with – could build some modern houses. Fortunately for me, and for Clarence House, he had only started making enquiries by the time I signed the papers and when he received news that I had purchased the dwelling and saved it from the bulldozers he began kicking up a bit of fuss. Letters were written and meetings held but none of it came to anything. Then, in what I assume was an attempt to try and pour scorn upon my endeavours, he made the almost fatal error of coming to the house uninvited and attempting to communicate his sentiments to me in person.

In two minutes flat I threw him out of the front door (literally). He was shaking like a heavily constipated gorilla with no means of escape. My God, it felt good! He was a bully, dear reader, and I eat them for breakfast. His mere presence ignited a flame in me that could have burned through steel!

I continued to rent Ormond House Cottage because I

couldn't move in to Clarence House until I'd at least finished ripping out the interior. The idea was that the cats and I would move in there the moment I could finish the kitchen, a couple of bedrooms and the sitting room.

I had an additional cleaning lady at the time, called Mrs Cobus, who used to fill in for Mrs Bush. Mrs Cobus was a large Spanish lady in her forties, with a warm and passionate nature. When I'd thrown the disgusting little gentleman out of the front door she looked at me and said, 'You know, Mr Blessed, I can tell you now, you are not English. I don't know where you are from but you are not English!'

She was another sweetie and used to make me the odd evening meal. At the time, I was living mainly on porridge oats because I needed so much energy and Mrs Cobus would supplement the oats with something a bit different, like a home-made meat and potato pie. She was quite a size, was Mrs Cobus, and in addition to having a rear end with its own postcode she had breasts the size of moons and legs that, when they used to rub together, would squeak like a bucket full of randy mice and generate enough power to move planet earth a centimetre closer to the sun. Rubens would have loved her – she was beautiful.

I'll never forget the day that Spain first won the Eurovision song contest. It was 6 April 1968, a date etched on my busy brain. The song what won it, which was imaginatively called 'La, La, La', was admittedly very catchy if short on actual words and to Mrs Cobus the tune was bliss itself. She insisted on singing it every day for weeks on end in her wonderful voice.

'Laaaaa la la laaaaaaaaaaaa la la laaaaaaa la la laaaaaaa. La la laaaaaaaaaaaa la la laaaaaaaaaaaaaaaa la la laaaaaaaaaa-aaaaaaa.'

Have you ever had one of those songs you just can't get out of your head? 'Laaaaa la la laaaaaaaaaaaa la la laaaaaaa la la laaaaaaa' – STOP IT, BLESSED. WHAT WOULD BEETHOVEN SAY?

Anyway, on with the story of Clarence House. I freely admit that no amount of surveys, advice or quotes could have prepared me for what I was about to undertake, or how dangerous it was. I remember walking into the enormous hallway on my first day and within ten minutes I'd almost got myself killed. The entire ceiling of the drawing room, which was about thirty-five feet by thirty-five feet, needed removing (as did every ceiling) and because they were made of lattice wood and plaster I assumed that I was going to have to chip away at them all gradually and just grin and bear it. The ceilings in the house were all very high and as I ascended the stepladder for the first time tedium was already upon me. I reached the summit, took out my plasterer's axe and prepared to go into battle.

I figured the ceiling would probably be about five or ten inches thick and so when I first hammered the axe into the plaster I wasn't expecting anything to appear, save perhaps some dust. Instead the entire bloody ceiling started to come down and not surprisingly it took me with it, landing on my shoulders and knocking me off the ladder.

A second or so later, there I was standing in about three

feet of wood and plaster. I got away with cuts and bruises rather than a more serious injury because it was all rotten and so, despite the noise, the dust and the drama, the impact on the floor and the damage to yours truly had been quite minimal. What worried me more was the fact that it could have come down at any time and so with a bona fide death trap on our hands we'd have to move quickly. Or rather, I would, as to begin with I worked alone. The tenants, by the way, were gone by this time, and thank heaven for it.

Believe it or not the walls were even easier to tear down than the ceilings. In fact, you only had to shout at the plaster in the bathrooms and it would fall like leaves in the autumn. The rest of the walls were no problem whatsoever. A quick whack with my axe and that was it – thump! Obviously, I wore masks over my mouth and goggles over my eyes but because I used to become so submerged in all the dust and the soot I had to put a shower up in the garden. And believe me it got everywhere! I could have wrapped myself in cellophane and worn a deep-sea diver's suit and I still would have been digging it out from between my toes.

Over the coming weeks during 'Operation Rip Out' I removed over 700 tonnes of rubble from Clarence House. Seven hundred tonnes! Two master plumbers also joined me. I employed the finest electrician in the south east who on the first day was knocked flat onto his back by the faulty wiring.

'It'll all have to come out,' he declared once he could speak again. Thankfully all it took was a bit of a tug.

The woodwork was absolutely riddled with woodworm and was as soft as a sponge in some areas. The entire place resembled some kind of Georgian soft-play centre. Give me a good old-fashioned rotten interior any day of the week!

Because Fortnum and Mason had erected a lot of temporary rooms when they owned the place it was almost unrecognisable once I'd torn them all out and restored it to its original layout. The only thing that was operational in the house at this point was one of the toilets, but even this was far from ideal. Four of the rooms that had surrounded the loo had been erected by Fortnums and so I'd got rid. It was now the biggest cubicle in Britain with five doors leading to the lone latrine, only one with a lock. Privacy? This was open-plan pooing dear reader. Jimmy Ellis, who played Bert Lynch in *Z-Cars*, came over to see me one day and shouted down, 'You certainly get plenty of air, Brian. It's the airiest crap I've ever had!'

Eventually, once I was ready to start replastering, my brother Alan came down from Yorkshire to labour for me. His job was to mix sand, lime, cement and horse hair into mortar, then carry the plaster mix up the steep staircases on his shoulder in a massively heavy plasterer's hod. He was strong and used to work on building sites so he was game for anything, but he had hell keeping up with me. In my youth in Yorkshire I had been an exceptionally fast plasterer and now in my prime physically my speed was even greater. It's all in the wrist action, and if you ever bump into me, I'll be happy to show you.

Anyway, let's bring some more lovely animals into the equation, shall we?

One of the first people to come and see me at Clarence House once I'd started plastering was a chap called Percy Parslow. He later became a regular on the television show *Magpie* and was the country's first ever hamster farmer. He had thousands of them on his Hamster Farm in Great Bookham and bred 118 different varieties. He also had ferrets, rats, guinea pigs, canaries, peacocks, budgies, rabbits, donkeys, ducks and even a boa constrictor.

I was up a ladder plastering a ceiling one day when out of the blue the doorbell went. Fortunately, Mrs Bush was in attendance so I carried on.

'It's a Mr Parslow to see you,' said Mrs Bush a minute or so later. 'And he's got a hamster on his head.'

'Who's got a what?'

'It's a Mr Parslow,' she said, enunciating very clearly, 'and he's got a hamster on his head.'

When I got to the door there standing on the step was a middle-aged man with thinning hair that seemed to be home to a little brown rodent.

'I'm Percy Parslow from Parslow's Hamster Farm,' he said, holding out a hand. 'I hope you don't mind us calling unannounced but I've read all about you in the papers. You're an animal lover, I hear?'

'Erm, yes that's right. You say you have a hamster farm?' I asked him.

'Yes indeed,' he confirmed with a proud smile. 'In Great Bookham. It's about twenty-five miles away. I was hoping to persuade you to come and have a look.'

Talk about eccentric. This was right up my street! Over a quick cup of tea Mr Parslow, who even looked and sounded like a hamster, told me all about his farm. Apparently, he'd started off with just an outbuilding back in the 1950s and now had five fifty-foot barns all teeming with rodents. It was even open to the public and he had thousands of visitors throughout the year, not to mention breeders.

'People pay up to £300 for a hamster depending on the variety and I get enthusiasts coming from all over the world.'

'But how did you become interested?' I enquired.

My question seemed to sadden Mr Parslow slightly.

'I never really took to humans when I was a boy, Brian,' he said, putting a piece of biscuit onto his head. 'Hamsters make far better friends.'

After tea, Mr Parslow drove us down to Great Bookham so that I could have a look around his hamster farm, and what a place it was! The first four barns were housing just hamsters and he explained every single variety to me. He had cinnamons, honeys, chocolates, satins, mosaics, longhairs, sepias, piebalds, tortoiseshells, blondes and pinks. It sounds like a condom catalogue.

Every breed of hamster available was there in vast numbers and they all seemed to be in love with Mr Parslow. Each variety had its own cage and as he was giving chapter and verse he'd take a couple out, give them a kiss and then after allowing them to run around his shoulders a bit and nibble his neck they'd just climb onto his head and sit there quite happily while he spoke. It was the most extraordinary sight. He was just completely at one with them, and they him.

When we reached the fifth and final barn the first thing I saw on entering was a mynah bird perched on a box. I thought nothing of this until I came within about five feet of the bird.

'Have you had your bath?' it enquired, in a voice resembling that of Her Majesty the Queen.

'Yes, as a matter of fact I have . . . HANG ON A MINUTE!' I exclaimed, having to stop myself. 'You're a bird.'

As I laughed, the mynah bird, seemingly happy with my response, leant forward and affectionately nibbled my neck, ears and hair. This day was getting stranger by the second!

When I looked for Mr Parslow he was already at the far end of the barn removing what looked suspiciously like some ferrets from a large wooden cage. As with the hamsters he then gave each one of them a kiss before allowing them the Freedom of the Parslow. I was fascinated. The last thing I'd read about ferrets was that one had been deliberately put down the trousers of an over-trusting enthusiast resulting in it biting clean through his John Thomas. *Ouch!*

I flatter myself that the Blessed threshold of pain is

abnormal in its magnitude, and it has been tested over the years on many occasions. But be that as it may I still held little desire to have my old colonel bitten off by what translates into Latin as 'little thief' and so when Mr Parslow asked me if I would like to handle one of his inquisitive *furittus* I politely declined.

'I've got a breeder turning up in a few minutes,' said Mr Parslow putting back the ferrets. 'He's come all the way from Scotland.'

Sure enough, about fifteen minutes later a giant of a man arrived carrying a small brown box. He must have been at least six foot six tall and had bushy red hair, a huge belly and eyebrows that met in the middle – of his back. He was quite a specimen and made even me look like a featherweight. His voice, however, belied his impressive dimensions and if you closed your eyes it was like listening to a child.

'Hello, Mr Parslow,' he squeaked. 'Is he ready? I've got his box with me.'

Do all hamster lovers sound like their objects of desire? I mused. The two I'd met so far certainly did.

'He's all ready,' replied Mr Parslow. 'This is Mr Blessed, by the way. He's a famous actor.'

Overcome by modesty I forced a blush.

'Maurice Hibbard, very pleased to meet you,' he said shaking my hand. 'Are you a hamster man, Mr Blessed?' he asked.

'I am now!' I enthused.

My rejoinder obviously delighted the castrato-sounding

colossus and as the corners of his mouth curved north-wards what was left of his face reddened like a freshly slapped arse.

The hamster Mr Hibbard was collecting was about as rare as an Oscar ceremony without a Judi Dench acceptance speech and was honestly multi-coloured. I forget the name of the variety but when Mr Parslow presented the animal to Mr Hibbard he was very nearly in tears.

'Magnificent,' said the emotional giant. 'Truly magnificent. Here's your money, Mr Parslow. £900 wasn't it?'

Once Mr Hibbard had left with his new hamster in a coat of many colours I took him to task over the price.

'I thought you said they went up to £300? That colourful little chap was three times that.'

'Ah, yes Brian, but that particular hamster is quite special. It has taken me years to perfect the breed and Mr Hibbard has had to be very patient. He is the first person other than myself to own one of that colour.'

I was completely and utterly enchanted by Mr Parslow and when he started appearing on *Magpie* I would stop whatever I was doing so that I could get to a television and watch him. If memory serves me correctly, they used to film Mr Parslow's segments down at the farm and one of the most popular animals to appear on the show was his crow Winkle.

Mr Parslow had been very excited when he first introduced me to Winkle (thank God the sentence doesn't stop there!) as, according to him, he was the world's first and only talking crow.

'Because of the way they've developed, rooks and crows cannot speak, Brian,' he explained. 'Until now, that is. Follow me.'

Winkle resided in an outhouse next to Mr Parslow's home and when he saw us both entering he flapped his wings in welcome.

'Hello Winkle, I said. 'Mr Parslow's told me all about you.'

To be honest with you I was expecting him to give me a caw that sound like cabbage or something, but I was in for a shock.

'HELLO,' he said, in a clear, deep voice.

I couldn't believe my ears. It sounded just like Paul Robeson!

'Where did you get him?' I asked.

'I found him as a fledgling. He was on the ground under a tree looking a bit startled and we just hit it off.'

Winkle became an overnight sensation on *Magpie* and completely stole the show. All he could say was 'hello' but that was enough to keep me and the rest of the viewing public in raptures for weeks on end. Times were a lot simpler back then.

Of all the thousands of animals residing on Mr Parslow's extraordinary farm by far the most domesticated was a peacock named Percy. Peacocks are my absolute favourite birds and after seeing how I reacted to Percy, Mr Parslow suggested he come and stay with me at Clarence House.

'You mean to live?' I asked hopefully.

'Why not? Brian. You have such a beautiful garden. I think Percy would be very happy there.'

Mr Parslow had already offered me about twenty rats and hamsters but I'd had to decline because of the cats.

'Will Percy be able to handle a few cats?' I asked him.

'Oh, don't you worry. Peacocks are more than a match for any cat, I promise you.'

I felt tingly all over. I was so excited! I was a boy again.

Mr Parslow had a van for transporting animals and after packing up Percy and making sure that he was comfortable we set off back to Clarence House. Mr Parslow, who once again drove all the way sporting a hamster on his head, spent the entire journey advising on how to look after peacocks. I found it all fascinating.

'What male peacocks love more than anything else in the world, Brian, is a mirror.'

I was confused.

'You mean peacocks really are vain?'

'Vain?' he exclaimed. 'VAIN? Of course they're vain! Wouldn't you be with plumage like that?'

He had a point.

'He'll spend half the day looking at himself and the other half eating all the aphids off your plants. Honestly Brian, give a peacock some food, some shelter, a free rein and a mirror, and you'll never have to worry about them.'

Who was it that said, 'The surest cure for vanity is loneliness?' Well, that saying didn't take into account Percy.

Percy was a hit at Clarence House from the moment he

began strutting around the garden and with the surrounding walls being quite low he was able to fly up and then parade up and down them. This used to amuse the passersby enormously and when Percy's confidence had grown a little he would fly down into Patten Alley, pace its length and display his tail feathers whenever he had an audience.

And you think I'm a bit of a show off? I had nothing on Percy.

The good people of Richmond (or at least some of them) and Percy the peacock became so enamoured by one another that at the end of each day I would have to physically remove Percy from Patten Alley, just like my mother used to do to me when it was time for tea.

'I'm afraid it's Percy's bedtime now, ladies and gentlemen,' I'd say in a matriarchal manner. 'He'll be back again tomorrow, no doubt.'

Now you might be wondering how I managed to manoeuvre Percy from the alley back to the house. Well, this was one of the tips Mr Parslow gave me on the way home. You see, if you grab a peacock by its legs and then turn it upside down they instantly fall asleep. Did you know that? So, that's what I used to do. I'd walk down Patten Alley, take him by the legs and then deposit him on his perch in his little shed.

The only thing that could ever tear Percy away from either his mirror, which I rested against one of the garden walls, or adoring fans was rain. He hated it! All it took was a few drops and he'd be flapping towards his shed faster than Stirling Moss after a vindaloo. Vanity, vanity, all is vanity!

Mr Parslow had told me, on our journey back to Richmond, that at 7.30 a.m. every morning Percy would, in his words, 'Say good morning to the day'. Peacocks have a wide vocabulary of calls but the one reserved for the early morning is a kind of mewing sound lasting about three minutes and, in my opinion, not unpleasant to the ears. Unfortunately, not all my neighbours agreed and before too long I began receiving the odd letter.

Now, because Richmond is on the flight path into Heathrow you get aeroplanes passing overhead every few minutes and it wasn't that different in the late 1960s. In fact, if anything the planes were louder in those days.

'So what's your problem with one peacock then?' I used to ask. 'You bunch of namby-pambys!'

After all, his hooting was somewhat muted as he didn't have a peahen, and in comparison to the relentless rumble of the planes it was surely a small irritant. But it would seem that he took the blame for the whole cacophony of sound on his feathery shoulders. It was so unfair.

While we're on the subject of peacock calls, did you know that male peacocks make fake sex sounds to attract females? I read about this only recently, and in addition to exhibiting their plumage in order to get their end away these rather devious little Lotharios also make hooting noises that are normally only called out during the act, so to speak. This drives the peahens potty apparently and is just the right thing for getting them in the mood. There you are, avian sex lessons with Brian Blessed. Whatever next?

The most vocal complainants regarding Percy's call were those people associated with the two churches I mentioned which backed on to the garden. In addition to his morning glory Percy used to let out the occasional and rather moving early evening mew and it was this that used to have them all straining in the pews. In the end, the Anglican vicar, the Catholic priest and their querulous old flocks each started a petition about Percy that resulted in him having to leave Clarence House and go back to Mr Parslow's. They had the police, the lord mayor and all kinds of people whinging on to me and so in the end I had to give way. I don't mind admitting that saying goodbye to Percy the peacock saddened me enormously and according to Mr Parslow the poor bird sulked for weeks. I'd have my revenge though. By thunder yes!

The great poet John Dryden once said, 'Beware the fury of a patient man.' Wise words Johnny, my old chum. But how about a patient man with a hellhound by his side that made Cerberus the three-headed dog look like Lassie's maiden aunt?

Game on, my dear reader. GAME ON!

3

THE HOUND OF THE BLESSEDVILLES

Once Clarence House had a few rooms finished and there was no danger of the ceiling falling on their unsuspecting heads, I could finally introduce all my animal friends to their new home. The journey to and from Clarence House, which they'd made with me each day as I worked, was an event in itself as, instead of me taking them all in the car or putting them into some kind of ginormous carry-case, they simply followed me down Ormond Road and then along Patten Alley, just like Tibby had in Bolton-upon-Dearne. I must have looked like the Pied Piper! My brother Alan assisted me in this enterprise.

Only Fred, the Red Point Siamese, failed to catch on and so he had to be carried there and back. As I said, they'd bred all the brains out of the poor mite. Even when I was plastering, which could be a messy old business, the daft little cat would just sit there getting splattered. The fact he had no clue what was going on did make bathing him easier, I suppose, and while I attempted to remove all the plaster from his fur he'd just stare at me with his great big eyes and let out the occasional meow.

'Look at you,' I'd say enviously. 'Not a care in the world!'

With Percy no longer being in situ at Clarence House and with me not yet having fully moved in there I decided it was time improve the security. The place had already been broken into once or twice and on each occasion I had caught the burglar red-handed. I always let the poor terrified bugger go with a swift kick up the backside.

In the end, I sought the advice of the local constabulary, some of whom I'd got to know quite well.

'What you need is a trained dog,' advised a chap named Wilcott. He was a real bruiser of a man and had once fought Henry Cooper as an amateur boxer. 'We train all our dogs in a place near Bexhill. Not all of them make the grade though, so if you like I could have a word.'

'That really would be marvellous!' I replied.

Constable Wilcott went on to tell me that there were three kinds of trained Alsatian. First you have what is known as a barker, or stage one dog, which obviously looks very fierce but is trained only to scare you. After that you have a sleeve dog, which is trained to apprehend you. Finally, you have what's known as a fully balanced trained dog, which is trained to chase you, corner you and, if needs be completely overcome you. There's a bit more to it than that, of course, but at least that gives you an idea.

Anyway, what I obviously needed (or should I say,

wanted) was a fully balanced trained dog, known then as a stage three dog.

'They're very, very hard to come by Mr Blessed,' said Constable Wilcott. 'Most Alsatians are soft, you see, so very few make it that far in training. Then there's the cost, of course.'

'OK, how much.'

'About £375 for a stage three.'

'And how much for a stage one,' I replied.

'Oh, about £50.'

£375 was a tremendous amount of money in those days – the down payment on a house – but because of the sheer size of my new abode I could see it as being my only option. A barker might work initially but if anyone were ever to challenge the dog with a weapon they would realize it was soft. A stage three dog was just what I needed.

The police were marvellous and after finding me a suitable hound they then invited me down to Bexhill so that they could train me with him. This wasn't that long after I'd left *Z-Cars* so I was still a firm favourite with the boys and girls in blue and they couldn't have been kinder.

The dog lucky enough to be assigned to yours truly was called Sabre and when the people at Bexhill first pointed him out to me he was running through a field quite literally flattening people. Not biting, just flattening!

'Crikey,' I said to the man showing me around. 'He's a monster!'

'I bet you wouldn't like to get on the wrong side of him, eh Mr Blessed?'

'No I would not!' I replied. 'Look at those eyes!'

As the hellhound poleaxed yet another poor plod close to where we were standing I could see that his eyes were bright orange. Not only that, his teeth were like white miniature swords and as he lay claim to yet another victim he let out a snarl in triumph. What an animal! He was perfect. He looked like a large grey wolf.

'When can I meet him?' I asked.

'As soon as he's finished. This is his last session.'

The moment Sabre was brought to heel by the trainer he was a different dog.

'Mr Blessed,' said the trainer, leading him up to me. 'This is Sabre. Shall we all have an hour together?'

During the session Sabre and I became acquainted and although he was very obedient I was left with no doubt whatsoever that he would not be requiring much lovey-dovey patting. He had been trained to do a job – well, several jobs actually – and providing I fed him and treated him well and with respect he would carry on doing that job for as long as he was able and totally dedicate himself to yours truly.

After I signed the cheque, the trainer said, 'He is yours now, Brian, and will totally serve your needs.'

I opened the door of my Zephyr (Ford gave all the cast members their own Z-Car) and gave Sabre the freedom of the back seat. As we set off I somehow felt very safe with him behind me, yet at the same time quite vulnerable. This rather unsettling emotional dichotomy was brought into sharp relief within half an hour of the journey.

As we reached some traffic lights a car pulled up beside us but because it was perhaps just a little too close Sabre went ballistic. I had sweat pouring down the back of my neck at this point and while I desperately tried to placate the enormous barking beast I could see the innocent people in the offending motorcar were absolutely horrified by my hound from hell.

A short time later I'd almost forgotten Sabre was there, until, that is, we stopped at some more traffic lights. All of a sudden I could sense his presence and as I turned my head slowly around I saw his face was within about three inches of mine. I didn't feel threatened by this. On the contrary. I felt protected and at one with him – a magical feeling that was reinforced when he proceeded to cover my neck and face with loving kisses.

Sabre's trainer had given me a list of commands that we had to go through every other day – from sit, stay and heel to attack, bite and let go – and as this regime became the norm, and as Sabre and I began to forge a relationship, our devotion to one another became apparent. There were no pats on the head or cries of 'Aren't you a good boy. Yes you are!' There was just an almost tangible commitment to ensuring one another's safety. It was something to be savoured. Or should I say saboured.

As well as Sabre's training regime, the police at Bexhill had also given me a selection of signs to erect around the perimeter of the house warning people of what lay within, although in my opinion they were all far too understated. BEWARE THE DOG was the standard message most of the signs seemed to carry, when what they should have read was BEWARE THE HELLHOUND! When I was walking with him in Richmond he was as gentle as a dove and anybody could stroke him. Once he was back inside the grounds of Clarence House he was a formidable guardian.

The police also gave me a very long chain to which I would have to tie Sabre when I wasn't around. It could be fixed to a couple of metal swivels, one in the back garden and one next to the coach house, which was where Sabre lived – although he was allowed into the house as well and was friendly to Mrs Bush and Mrs Cobus. He got on with the cats too, and they'd all congregate in whatever room I was working in to watch me plastering with a kind of fascinated bemusement. Time after time I'd be up the ladder only to hear the splashing sound of Sabre drinking my bucket of water dry.

Once the heavy plaster work eased off I began the task of applying the finishing coat throughout, covering walls and ceilings with thistle, Keene's cement and a newly dis-covered plaster that contained thousands of particles of metal. Plasterers who were working on Chiswick House would pop in to see my technique. They were astonished when I used beeswax on the mouldings.

'God,' they exclaimed, 'that's not been used since the Pharaohs.'

For the first week or so after Sabre arrived I decided to stay over at Clarence House just in case there were any problems. I was due to move in there soon anyway, having served notice at Ormond House Cottage, and on the first morning I awoke to blissful silence. *This is just perfect*, I thought. Then, as I rolled over to look at my watch, I heard the front gates being opened.

Oh, god, I thought. *It's the postman!*

Without pausing to dress I got up and made for the stairs, but it was too late. Sabre had run out of the coach house, a deadly blur of fur and muscle, only to be pulled to a standstill by the chain. When I came down I found the postman cowering against a wall with the dog about twelve feet away baying at him.

'You could have told me you'd got yourself a giant wolf, Mr Blessed,' gasped the terrified postman.

Naturally I was very apologetic and quickly introduced him to Sabre.

'As long as I tell him you're OK, and as long as you're not threatening me, he'll be fine with you,' I assured him.

'There's absolutely no danger of that happening, Mr Blessed!'

Within the hour I'd warned as many of my regular visitors as I could and so, apart from the odd stranger here and there, Sabre had nobody to terrify.

Well, we'd have to try and remedy that.

The vicar in charge of the Anglican church at the bottom of the garden was – and may God forgive me – a right know-it-all and had a face simply made for slapping. Despite having been instrumental in having Percy evicted from Clarence House he still had the gall to ask me if I'd like to donate some of my garden to the church. Can you

Clarence House in Richmond, looking much the same today as when I left.

The extraordinary Nick Nyoka with Simba the lion.

Kali the panther.

Ladies swooned
at the sight of my
masculinity encased
in velvet and lace.
Playing Athos in
The Three Musketeers.

Juan as a baby, and as an adult at Chessington Zoo looking depressed as he sits by the concrete pool in his enclosure.

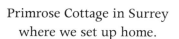

The beautiful Hildegard Neil in the early 1970s, around the time she rashly agreed to marry me.

Primrose Cottage in Surrey where we set up home.

Poodle Pants giving us a look.

With Hamish and Nick
at Primrose Cottage.

Hildegard with
Willy and Jessie in 1975.

With Rosalind and Hildegard in our conservatory at Primrose Cottage.

Cedars Lodge, our second home in Surrey, in 1986.

The nearby church with Jessie's favourite haunt,
the graveyard. Cedars Lodge is on the right.

A favourite picture of Jessie the compost dog.
Can you believe no one wanted her?

Buffy the Shetland pony working out how to escape in pursuit of his new love.

Misty, Buffy's lover. Sadly, he was not faithful to her.

Black Petra, who had a temper on her and took no nonsense from Buffy.

believe that? It was almost as if he believed he had the backing of some omnipotent being.

'You don't need it, so why not donate some of it?' he said with a disdainful sneer.

There was no please, or anything. In fact, it was almost like an order. God in heaven, he was so irritating. I told him to take a running jump or words to that effect. He claimed he wasn't used to being spoken to in that way, which surprised me.

For weeks after our confrontation he continued to be a rude little monster so I decided that war must be declared.

He may have had God on his side, but I had Sabre!

The wall separating the Anglican church from my garden was in a state of disrepair and because it was only just five feet high I could see right into the church grounds. During the summer, God's popinjay would conduct lectures and sermons there and if I was ever outside sunbathing or deadheading my roses I'd have to listen to it all. My God, he used to spout some crap. His parishioners thought he was marvellous though and would sit on the grass and marvel at his every word. Come to think of it, he'd have made quite a good actor – though had he played Noah I think the Ark would definitely have sunk!

Anyway, as my anger at the man intensified, and his at me, I decided to introduce the vicar and his followers to my lovely, cuddly Alsatian. He was waffling on about some rubbish one day, tossing in the occasional insult about actors being rich and spoilt, when I thought enough is enough. I walked around to the coach house, took Sabre off his chain, led him to the garden shed where we could not be seen and then pointed him in the direction of the throng.

'See 'em off boy,' I growled. They were of course protected by the wall.

By this time Sabre was absolutely seething and before you could say *Jack Robinson*, he was on his way to the wall sounding like Rin Tin Tin with a Catherine Wheel up his backside. The church garden now became a cacophony of loud protests and a lot of running about.

'Why can't you keep your dog under control, Mr Blessed,' shrieked the not-so-cocky clergy.

'He *is* under control,' I replied. 'In fact he's doing exactly what I asked him to.'

What larks Pip! What larks! Boy, I really did enjoy myself.

Once I'd called Sabre back and the Godly had taken their places again upon the lawn, I let him go again – and again – and again. Every time that vicar held an outdoor sermon, I would have Sabre baying at them all. Best of all there was nothing the vicar could do about it as it was the Richmond constabulary who had advised me to find a dog in the first place. I was merely following orders. Well, sort of. Eventually of course I let him off the hook.

I used to take Sabre all over Richmond and he never once attacked a human being or another animal. Get him inside the grounds of Clarence House, however (especially during a bit of outdoor evensong) and he was lethal. Grrrrrrrrrrrrrrrrr! The hound of the Blessedvilles.

One of my favourite neighbours in Richmond was the celebrated naturalist and broadcaster, Jeffery Boswall. As well as being all things to animal-kind, Jeffery was also in charge of the celebrated BBC Natural History Unit and had done some marvellous work with people like Peter Scott, who had his own series, of course, and was one of the founders of the World Wildlife Fund.

Jeffery had a contact at the Ministry of Agriculture and Fisheries, which were responsible for all animals within the UK, and once I had begun living in Clarence House full time he approached me about an idea he'd had.

'You have a big old place here, Brian,' he said to me. 'What's more, you are in residence almost all the time. How would you feel about the Ministry installing some cages somewhere so that you could take in a few animals before they send them back to their country of origin?'

'You mean like quarantine?' I replied.

'That's exactly what I mean. You'll have to apply for a licence, which I'll help you with, but I think this would be the perfect environment. You'd receive plenty of help, by the way, and the animals would never be here for more than a week. Two at the most.'

We had a terrible problem at the time with hundreds of wild animals being imported and put on sale to the public. Harrods used to boast that they could supply any animal in the world for the right price. And of course that cute baby leopard or lion you bought was more of a handful when fully grown. When the owners couldn't cope with the animal, or got bored with it, they'd often be persuaded to hand them over to the Ministry so that we could return them to their country of origin.

'What sort of animals did you have in mind?' I asked.

'Ultimately that's not my decision Brian, but because of the size of the place I'd probably recommend they go for ocelots, perhaps some Indian spotted cats and jungle cats to begin with.'

Sure enough, after applying for a licence and then jumping through all kinds of other hoops, the Ministry installed the cages complete with some imaginative vegetation inside. They must have been at least ten metres square and had several extra separate compartments inside them for whatever happened to be staying.

This was just madness! Wonderful madness, it has to be said, but madness all the same. All these creatures would stay with us for a while before being returned by ship or plane to their original environment.

Let's just have a quick recap, shall we?

I was in the process of renovating a dilapidated king's house and I've got Morecambe and Wise and all kinds of people talking about me on TV and popping in to say hello. I own several inbred cats, a wild dog who's been trained by the police and have just had an enormous cage installed so that I can house ocelots for the Ministry of Agriculture and Fisheries. Oh, yes. And I have a fatwa on my head courtesy of the local vicar.

Never – repeat – never, a dull moment!

The first animal to arrive at Brian's Animal Quarantine Centre was indeed an ocelot (which are also known as dwarf leopards). Ocelots usually measure about a metre from head to tail and weigh about thirty-five pounds. Salvador Dali used to have one as a pet and travelled everywhere with it. This one was a female and I named her Rima after Audrey Hepburn's character in the film *Green Mansions*.

Because Rima had been raised in captivity and was quite tame she could roam freely around the house and gardens before retiring to her cage in the evenings. Sabre didn't know what the hell to make of it at first, whereas the domestic cats were absolutely fascinated. They kept their distance, which was probably very wise, but they used to follow her around. I remember Mr Parslow popping in one day to give me an update on Percy and when his little head-hamster clapped eyes on the big cat it was inside Mr Parslow's jacket pocket as quick as a flash. If you've never seen an ocelot, Google one now. They are indeed just like small leopards but have a head more like that of a standard cat. Beautiful animals!

Just like Percy, the ocelot started wandering up and down the wall that backed onto Patten Alley and all the old ladies, who I assume were a bit short sighted, thought she was a tabby. 'Here, puss, puss, puss,' they used to call. Then, if Rima got close enough, they'd start tickling her nose and stroking her belly. They had absolutely no idea what she was or what she was capable of.

Unfortunately, Rima decided to get stuck up a tree one day and ended up in an awful state. Fancy a bad-tempered ocelot getting stuck up a tree! Anyway, in order to get the frightened animal down again I had to scale a ladder at least twenty feet high wearing a full beekeeper's outfit provided by Jeffery, who thought Rima was likely to lash out on being rescued. Personally, I thought this was a little bit over the top but as it turned out it wasn't nearly enough.

As I ascended the ladder Jeffery, along with two men from the Ministry, stood below holding a net. That wasn't for me, by the way. Heavens no. If I'd fallen onto it I'd have taken them all with me. This was to catch any falling ocelot. When I eventually reached the terrified creature, I tried to placate her by speaking a few words of comfort. After all, she knew me quite well by this time and so this seemed to make sense. Well yes, it would have made sense, if I hadn't been dressed up as Billy the Beekeeper. God only knows what the poor cat was thinking but I guarantee it wasn't, *Oh look, here's sweet Uncle Brian come to rescue me. Let me leap into his arms.*

In the end, I leant into the tree and grabbed hold of the animal. Although she was obviously against this course of action, I managed to get a grip on her all the same, but she still wasn't coming without a fight. The noise she made was deafening and that alone almost made me fall backwards. It sounded like a hundred cats all going ballistic simultaneously. This was one hell of an unlucky dip! By the time I'd pulled her out of the tree and dropped her onto the net (four or five seconds, maybe) she had ripped through the outfit and had lacerated my right forearm. Another few seconds and I wouldn't have had any skin left. This ocelot liked me, by the way! Imagine what damage a leopard could have done.

After that I'm afraid Rima had to be confined to her cage for the rest of her stay. This was for her own good, of course, but also for the good of the public, and especially the old ladies of Patten Alley.

The next animal to arrive was a jungle cat; these are native to the Middle East and southern Asia and have sandy-coloured coats and terribly long legs. This one had spent the last year or so as the pampered pet of an Arab gentleman who had become bored with it and wanted something bigger. Isn't that just appalling? I hope whatever he got bit him on the bloody arse! Although I didn't have a great deal to do with the animals (they were never here long enough and after the ocelot incident they had to remain caged), at least I felt like I was doing something worthwhile and observing them was a rather exciting privilege.

Every visitor we ever had at my makeshift quarantine centre was feline and as well as ocelots and jungle cats we had margays, Pallas's cats, golden cats from Asia and kodkods, which hail from Chile and have tiny heads and huge thick tails.

Apart from being feline, the other thing these animals all had in common was a love of milk and it seemed to have a kind of soporific effect on them. I remember we once had something called a marbled cat staying with us for a few days and they're considered to be the most ferocious cats on the planet. When Jeffery explained this to me I became quite wary of the animal, and it's a good job I did. Every time I went to feed the little tyke it would look at me with reddish eyes and then snarl viciously, which is what they do when they feel threatened.

'I come in peace,' I used to say. 'And I bring milk!'

Once this marbled cat, which was just the size of a domestic cat, had lapped up some milk it would start lolloping around as if it were drunk and within a few minutes it would be fast asleep! It happened with all my guests. The effect wouldn't last very long, mind you, and within ten or fifteen minutes they'd be back to their old selves.

One of the most beautiful cats that ever visited us was a sand cat. Have you heard of them? As well as being a mere twenty-five centimetres from head to tail they're the only cat that lives in the desert. Not surprisingly they're a kind of sandy colour and they have two dark stripes running around each of their front legs. If you've never seen one before, have a quick look on the interwobble. I guarantee you'll let out a great big awwww.

One of the many joys about living at Clarence House was that you never knew what was going to happen from one day to the next. One of my favourite memories from this time took place during the filming of the BBC's *The Three Musketeers*. A remarkable director and producer at the BBC called Shaun Sutton felt it would be marvellous if I played something totally different to a tough northern copper and therefore cast me as the extrovert Porthos alongside fabulous actors like Jeremy Brett, Richard Pasco, Mary Peach, Jeremy Young, Gary Watson and a marvellous director called Peter Hammond. So there I was dressed in orange velvet and breeches, sporting a beard and long hair, charging around on a white horse! It was a shock to the viewing public but they really loved it. We filmed at Chiswick House, in Dorset and, would you believe it, Richmond Park. Crowds would turn up to watch us filming and to my astonishment the ladies would faint in ecstasy at the sight of men dressed in lace and plumed hats. 'So masculine,' they swooned. I was the most flamboyantly dressed musketeer and therefore the most overwhelmingly sexy.

Anyway, my bold readers, back to Clarence House. One day I was upstairs when I heard the clip clop of horse's hooves. Sticking my head out of the window I saw the handsome Jeremy Brett ride into the forecourt of Clarence House on a powerful black charger. He was playing d'Artagnan and was dressed in royal blue and sporting a hat with a large yellow feather. There must have been at least a hundred people loitering by the gates, wondering what the hell was going on. Jeremy being Jeremy turned his horse to face them, took off his hat and bowed graciously. The crowd instantly applauded as Jeremy roared, 'Thank you, ladies and gentleman.'

He had been filming in Richmond Park and decided to pay me a visit. After dismounting, he swept into the hallway and stopped at the bottom of the elegant sweeping stairs at the very moment that Mrs Bush's niece appeared at the top. She was about seven years old and looked down at him with wide shy eyes.

'What is your name fair maid?' said Jeremy gently.

'Juliet,' she replied.

Jeremy then delivered the entire opening from Act II, Scene ii of Shakespeare's Romeo and Juliet. 'But soft! What light through yonder window breaks? It is the east, and Juliet is the sun. Arise, fair sun, and kill the envious moon who is already sick and pale with grief . . .'

On and on went Jeremy with his haunting magical voice echoing around the hallway. The little girl was enchanted and thanked him with wonder in her eyes. What an experience for her – something never to be forgotten.

Before I bring in the man after whom this chapter is named, I must just tell you about something that my father and I found in Clarence House.

Right next door to the kitchen in Clarence House there was a room that I had planned to turn into a laundry room. Like everywhere else, its interior above floor-level had been completely removed, but before I could start replacing everything I first had to see to the floorboards which were riddled with woodworm. There must have been millions of them inside these boards and they'd built little cities all over the place. Why they chose these particular boards I have no idea but when I first took the carpet up to take a closer look I could almost see them all sticking two fingers up at me. By getting rid of them I must have reduced the world woodworm population by at least half. The horrible little shits!

Anyway, when I started pulling up the contaminated floorboards I discovered what I thought was a well.

'Well, well, well,' I said. 'It's a well!'

My old dad was down helping me at the time and after we'd cleared all the timber that had sat directly under-neath the floorboards – which, of course, was rotten – I jumped into what I then assumed was a well to take a closer look. It was only about ten feet deep so I told my father to fetch a ladder so that he could come down and have a look too. On the wall of the well that was not a well but that looked like a well I spotted some rubber seals sur-rounding a section of brick work. On closer inspection, I discovered that they were sealing an opening of some kind and so, without even thinking, I ran up the ladder to fetch a ten-pound hammer.

'I'm not sure you should be doing this, Brian,' Dad said. 'There could be gases in there.'

Ignoring my father's advice, which, bearing in mind his knowledge of such things, was downright stupid of me, I began whacking the wall as hard as I could with my hammer.

'God,' I said, a second or two later. 'It's not a well at all, Dad, it's a tunnel. We've found a tunnel!'

Just then we started to hear what sounded like rodents of some kind and sure enough a few seconds later about a hundred rats scurried out of the opening and started trying to climb up our trouser legs and what have you.

They were nothing like Mr Parslow's rats, let me tell you, and quite a few of them had already started puffing their bodies up with anger and hissing at us. We were obviously trespassing!

Quick as a flash my father went up the ladder, chucked down a spade and then started trying to push them back through the hole. I did the same and within a minute or two we'd managed to force them back in. Fortunately I don't mind rats at all and being a former coal hewer my father had no fear of them whatsoever.

After blocking up the tunnel with some rocks and some pieces of wood we went out and bought some gas masks and some torches and the following day, accompanied by Mr Hatton my plumber and two of his lads, we climbed down to have a proper look. We managed to get rid of the rats by scaring them off with a couple of naked flames and, with the way ahead clear, we began to investigate. Those rats hadn't just appeared out of thin air and I was determined to find out where they'd come from.

At first the tunnel led downwards in the direction of Richmond Green. It was obviously very damp and the walls and ceiling had been lined crudely with some kind of stone. A few hundred yards further on we began to hear traffic moving above our heads and as the slope began to level off a bit I knew that we must have been close to Richmond Green. About fifty yards later the tunnel veered left and after walking about another 150 yards or so we came to a brick wall. This was obviously the start of Richmond Palace. My only guess as to why it had been built was that in the event of an invasion – probably by the French – the Duke of Clarence (later King William IV) could escape. How exciting. My own tunnel!

On the advice of my father we bricked up the tunnel the moment we got back and put down new floorboards, built as a trap door, and that was that. I have no idea if the present owners are aware that they have a tunnel running from their house but if they read this and then decide to open it up, for God's sake look out for the rats!

Because of the sheer size of its structure, Clarence House was constantly moving and it used to create the most astonishing noises. They were groans, mainly, which used to reinforce all the rumours about ghosts and things. The Colonel and Mrs Ommaney had been adamant that the house was haunted but this was all based upon things they'd heard as opposed to things they'd seen. The only person I ever took any notice of in such matters was the wonderful mystic Ruth Wynn Owen, but she too was convinced that we were not alone. Haunted or not, I simply didn't have time to become a ghostbuster. I was already an actor, a plasterer and an animal carer. If ghosts were present and wanted some attention they should make themselves useful and go and feed a cat or something!

One day my old pal Frank Windsor came to pay me a visit and because of the amount of physical work I'd been doing he said I looked exhausted.

'You need to relax a bit, Brian,' said Frank. 'Have you been to see that Nyoka fellow yet at Harrods?'

I must confess I had absolutely no idea what my friend was talking about, and I told him as much.

'He's an animal trainer with an extraordinary knowledge of wild animals,' Frank informed me. 'He's doing exhibitions in Pet Kingdom at Harrods for the next week or so. They've given him the entire fourth floor. Thousands of people have been already. He's amazing! A latter-day Tarzan in a leotard.'

Off I went to Harrods on Frank Windsor's recommendation to see Nyoka and when I arrived at Pet Kingdom there were literally hundreds and hundreds of people there. I couldn't believe it! Ninety-nine per cent of these were late middle-aged women and when Nyoka started the show I could understand why. It was all snakes. Hundreds of them!

These old dears wouldn't have seen anything this long and turgid in decades, let alone touched it. It was like the January sales, except this lot were hoping to grab more than a bargain. They seemed to find the whole experience very erotic.

The last time I'd seen serpents in such numbers was while I was doing my national service. I was on a forty-eight-hour pass and had been staying with my mentor Ruth Wynn Owen in Hoyland, Yorkshire. To say thank you I offered to take her daughters to a visiting funfair and she readily accepted. Ruth was a white witch, by the way, and in my next book I shall tell you all about her.

Ruth's daughters, Sally, Anne and Meg, were only slightly younger than me. Even so, we all ran off to the

fair like grinning school children. This was South Yorkshire in the mid-1950s so we weren't used to this kind of
entertainment. There were dodgem cars, swirling round-
abouts, Ferris wheels and helter-skelters. You name it,
they had it. It was wonderful. There were also side shows
scattered everywhere and one of these was being run by
a man dressed in a leotard. This hardy soul was also
sporting a very long pointed moustache that curled up at
both ends making him look exactly like one of those
old-fashioned circus strongmen. He was beckoning the
gathered hordes forward to see what appeared to be
an enormous terrarium and on closer examination I discovered that it was full to bursting with huge snakes.
One of these, a glistening Indian python, was already
wrapped around his upper torso and looked like it was
fast asleep. Sally and Anne were absolutely fascinated by
this and so quickly joined an enthusiastic band of laughing teenagers who were walking into the inner chamber
of the snake charmer.

'Are you coming, Meg?' I asked, turning round in
time to catch her horrified expression as she saw the
offending python. Petrified, she put her hands over her
face and screamed. I jumped like a freshly goosed vicar
but neither the strongman nor his reptilian friend took
any notice, seemingly conditioned to the reaction. Not so
the now rapidly swelling crowd who were all staring,
and so, before Meg could suffer any more, I put my arms
around her and led her away. That, I'm afraid, was the
end of the evening. Of course, many people have an

instinctive aversion to snakes, and interestingly, many monkeys dread them too.

The reason I mention this is because when I first saw Nyoka at Harrods he was wearing exactly the same outfit as the strongman – *and* he was carrying a reticulated python! I couldn't believe it. He must have been in his mid-forties at the time, and as well as the leotard was sporting slicked-back hair and a moustache.

Because my adventures at Clarence House had been generating so many headlines – and because I was one of the world's most beloved thespians – Nyoka recognized me immediately.

'You're the man with the ocelots, aren't you?' he said, allowing a rather grand-looking lady to fondle a large yellow snake. The entire floor was covered in snakes by this point. He must have had at least a hundred out there and they were all being held by fascinated old ladies from South Kensington. What a sight! Not one of them could let go for love nor money.

'That's right,' I replied. 'A friend of mine told me about you so I thought I'd drop by.'

'Hang around after I'm done, if you would,' he said. 'I'd like to have a chat.'

The demonstration itself lasted about an hour but it took him at least the same amount of time to get the snakes back again. The women holding the serpents were all so transfixed that Nyoka had to prise open their fingers.

Once the floor had finally cleared, Nyoka took me round and gave me chapter and verse on every one of his snakes:

where they came from, how dangerous they were and what they ate, etc. It was a real privilege. After handing back a particularly ugly hognose snake I enquired as to whether he had ever been bitten by any of the poisonous ones. This made Nyoka laugh almost uncontrollably.

'I'm sorry,' he said, 'but in a moment, you'll understand why your question amuses me.'

With that, Nyoka pulled his leotard down over his shoulders to his waist.

'Hell's teeth!' I exclaimed, taking a step back.

His torso bore the marks of what must have been at least 200 snake bites.

'You can't handle snakes without getting bitten occasionally,' said my new friend. 'I have 355 in total. And counting.'

'Really?' I replied. 'I'd say there were fewer than that.'

Nyoka chuckled once again. 'You can only see roughly half of them. They're all over my body.'

It turned out that Nyoka had become immune to certain snake bites because of the amount of times he'd been bitten. His blood was resistant to the venom.

'That doesn't mean to say it doesn't hurt,' he explained. 'Russell's viper, for instance, isn't the most venomous snake in the world but its bite is excruciatingly painful. It makes you sick for a very long time.'

Nyoka may well have been dressed like a showman, and to all intents and purposes he was. But that man was completely at one with nature and his animals came before anyone or anything. I had found a man who knew more organically about animals than anyone else I had ever met. Somebody I could ask question after question after question to and they would all be answered using first-hand knowledge. Nobody working with animals at the time – not even David Attenborough or Jeffery Boswall – knew as much as he did.

This may sound fanciful to some people but Nyoka told me that he communicated with his snakes psychically. These were wild creatures, remember, and Nyoka used this technique to keep them calm while they were being handled. They certainly responded to him as if they understood him and watching them all communicate was a mesmeric experience.

Over the next week I went almost every day to see Nyoka at Harrods and funnily enough so did many of the people I'd seen there on the first day. After each show we'd sit down and I'd quiz him for hours on end. I still knew so little about animals and I was desperate to learn. Desperate! I think Nyoka found my enthusiasm quite amusing (I tend to have that effect on people!) but like any good teacher he remained patient with me and tried to channel that enthusiasm into doing good.

About a week later I was plastering a ceiling at Clarence House when suddenly there was a knock on the front door. Dad was down helping me again and while he'd been mixing the thistle and I'd been slapping it on we'd been listening to the 'Ride of the Valkyries' on my gramophone. It inspired us to work more efficiently. *Dum de dum daaa daaa, Dum de dum daaa daaa, Dum de dum daaa daaa,*

Dum de dum daaa. Marvellous stuff! Anyway, as there was nobody else about I jumped down and went to see who was there. It was Nyoka.

'Hello Nyoka!' I said. 'Great to see you. Come on in!'

For some reason, he was standing behind one of the pillars and so I could only see his head. Then, as he started to move into full view I realized he had a friend with him.

'It's a black panther,' I whispered, amazed and awe-struck.

Nyoka looked down at the enormous feline. 'So it is!' he said, feigning surprise. 'I knew you'd be impressed. Quite striking, isn't she?'

'Striking?' I responded. 'Never in my life have I ever seen one. What's she called?'

'Kali. She's eight months old.'

'Would she like a saucer of milk?' I asked.

'I'm sure she wouldn't say no.' And he entered the house with her by his side on a leather lead. The moment was miraculous beyond my wildest dreams

I'd just invited a black panther into my house in Surrey. A BLACK PANTHER! I felt so pumped I could have run to Newcastle and back without stopping.

'Let me just go and warn my dad,' I said. 'Otherwise he might have a turn.'

'Who's there Brian?' Dad asked from a room at the top of the stairs.

'It's Nyoka, Dad, the fellow I've been telling you about.'

'Oooh, I've been wanting to meet him. Your mother will be very jealous. Has he got any snakes with him?'

'No, not a snake, Dad. But he has got a cat. A black one.'

'I remember your Tibby,' began Dad. 'What colour was he?'

'Red,' I shouted back. 'Come into the kitchen.'

A minute later Dad opened the door and yelped.

'My God, Brian, what a sight!' he gasped, putting a hand over his heart. 'That is a big cat!'

Kali the panther was something to behold. She moved with astonishing grace and had bright green eyes that were almost luminous. I'd never seen anything like it.

In the middle of the kitchen I had a huge Welsh table and apart from that and an old sink the only thing in operation was the Aga which also heated about five rooms in the house. After I'd given Kali a saucer of milk we all sat around the table. I needed to get my breath back! I was just about to say something enlightening when out of the blue the panther, who had finished her milk, leapt onto the table and started prowling in my direction. Time stood still.

'Nothing to worry about!' said Nyoka very quickly. 'I promise you she's only being friendly, she likes you.'

All I could think was, *I've got Bagheera from* The Jungle Book *at this moment on my kitchen table!* I was fascinated.

Nyoka put his hand into his bag and then handed me a brush.

'She wants you to brush her, Brian. Kali loves being brushed. Go on. If you don't she'll get very upset.'

Within half a second I was on my feet brushing Kali's back. '*Go on* Brian!' he said. 'She wants you to brush her, not tickle her.'

Nyoka was obviously playing with me a bit but what a game, eh? The brush was one of those you wrap around your hand and so taking my friend's advice I pressed down a little harder as I moved the brush across her back.

'That's it,' he said. 'Look at her now! She loves you Brian.'

Before long Kali started purring and purring; the sound got louder and louder.

After she'd had enough of the brush, Kali stood up and began patrolling all four corners of the large table. My word she looked impressive. She *was* a female Bagheera. Just to keep my father and me in check she'd let out a grunting snarl, which made me take a step back. Nyoka, once again, found this all quite comical.

'Don't be fooled by all the prowling and snarling Brian. That's all for show. She's actually just a big clumsy cat.' I couldn't see it at the time but after a couple of hours I knew exactly what Nyoka meant. In the jungle of course she would be poetry in motion but domestically she was a disaster. As Kali leapt from the table to explore the rest of the kitchen she was falling over everything. I didn't dare laugh, just in case she heard, but it was almost as if she had oil on her paws.

Nyoka and Kali stayed for the rest of the day and by the time they were ready to leave she and I were all over each other like a great big hairy rash. I had her leaping all over me and when I tickled her tummy she'd look at me with those intense green eyes and then growl and quickly roll over when she'd had enough. Panthers don't roar, by the way. They either hiss, growl or snarl.

For the next six months or so Nyoka brought Kali to the house at least twice a week and it got to a point when as he arrived he'd just open the back doors and she'd run inside! Mrs Bush never got used to her presence and would run up the stairs shouting, 'That bloody cat is here again! Get it out, get it out, get it out!'

Poor old Sabre didn't know what to do. The first time Kali arrived he just looked at her, as if to say *what the bloody hell are you?!* Then, once she became a regular, Kali would crawl up to Sabre while he was lying outside the coach house, poke him playfully on the nose and then roll over and try and look all sexy. It was marvellous to watch.

Incidentally, Nick Nyoka was quite a famous character back in the late 1960s and 1970s and if you do a search on the interwobble you'll come across some footage of him on the website of the East Anglian Film Archive. It's from 1970 and actually features Kali the panther. It's tremendous!

As I got to know him, he told me that his real name was Adrian Darley and he was born in 1921 in the slightly unexotic town of Stockton-on-Tees. He never really mentioned his early life but he did tell me that in the 1950s he began procuring wild animals for zoos and then after that became an animal trainer. Nyoka was best known for appearing with an enormous lion – the largest ever recorded, according to experts. Now, before you all start dusting off your quills and penning letters of complaint about keeping wild animals, please remember that we were at a different stage of progress and enlightenment back then. Even David Attenborough was making television programmes like *Zoo Quest in Paraguay*.

Rightly or wrongly, one of the most memorable evenings of my entire life was when my parents took me to the circus for the first time in Bolton-upon-Dearne. This too was way back in the mid-1940s and as we approached the big top I remember hearing the animals for the first time. These were sounds I'd only recently heard at the cinema and now they were here in South Yorkshire – live wild animals! I remember laughing at the clowns and then gasping at the daring acrobats, but when the elephants came out and then the lions and the tigers, I almost fainted. The lions, with their low moaning sounds, were astonishing!

These days there is absolutely no excuse for animal circuses to exist and for years now I've been trying to have them abolished. Many countries have banned them but Britain still lags behind. Do you remember the story of Anne the Elephant? It was only a few years ago. She'd been in a circus all her life and had been abused for years. And I mean abused! I think every single person in the British Isles was horrified.

It was awful to watch but a marvellous charity called Animal Defenders International managed to get some footage of Anne's ill-treatment and because of all the outrage it caused we managed to get her out of the lousy circus and into Longleat Safari Park. After that, we got a petition together asking for an outright ban of animal circuses and took it to Downing Street. I presented it. Why the government still haven't pulled the plug on them is completely beyond me and I think it's shameful. With all the media at our disposal, not to mention zoos that promote and undertake conservation work, why on earth do we still need animal circuses? It's unjustifiable!

The only thing that makes me angrier, and indeed sadder than the continued existence of animal circuses, is so-called 'trophy hunting'. We've all seen them, more's the pity: photographs of innocent and often endangered animals lying lifeless upon the earth, their very existences brought to a premature and often painful end. It's beyond comprehension, as is the endless slaughter of the noble elephant and rhinoceros.

I'm the world's biggest optimist – you all know that – and we will win in the end. I'm sure of it.

Anyway, rant over. Let's lighten the mood a bit.

The kitchen at Clarence House became known as the entrance to the Ark, for the simple reason that every week Nyoka would walk in with at least two different animals. When I heard his van arrive I'd stop whatever I was doing and run to the nearest window. *What's he got now?* I'd say to myself.

I will never forget the day I watched Nyoka climb into the back of his van wearing only the bottom half of his leotard and then climb out again carrying two baby tigers. I mean, how eccentric is that? I spent an entire afternoon playing with those two little rascals and was grinning like a fool for at least a week afterwards. It was sheer heaven! Their favourite trick was to hide behind doors and then pounce on me!

The only time I ever thought Nyoka may have gone too far was the day he turned up with a fully grown lioness. I was at the very top of the house finishing off a ceiling when he arrived and the moment he took Daphne out of the back of the van she started snarling and letting out a series of grunts.

I'd not seen a lion at close quarters since my trip to the circus and I admit that I had forgotten just how large and impressive they are. Despite being used to big cats this was on the top end of the scale and I thought twice about going downstairs.

When Kali had first arrived at Clarence House a feeling of hushed reverence had prevailed. With this new arrival, everything now became amplified by at least five, including the size of the cat!

'I'm only here for an hour, Brian,' said Nyoka. 'Don't worry, I assure you she's a big softie and one of the friendliest cats in the world.'

'She's also one of the largest,' I refuted him.

'Ha! Don't you worry. Just let her have a look around and then when she's ready she'll come and find me.'

Mrs Cobus and Mrs Bush had gone home by this point – probably to take some tranquillizers – and I was sure there was nobody else around.

'Yes, that's fine. Let's go and have a cup of tea, shall we?'

While Nyoka started telling me all about Daphne, who was now roaming freely around my half-built house, I sat in my chair feeling utterly captivated by the animal. Something was niggling me, though, and I couldn't for the life of me work out what. Just then, all became apparent as from the cellar there came a horrific, blood-curdling scream.

'Cyril,' I shouted, standing up immediately. 'I FORGOT ABOUT CYRIL!'

Cyril was a plumber who had come in to start installing the central heating and to my eternal shame I'd forgotten he was even there!

Quick as a flash, and with Nyoka close behind me, we ran out of the kitchen, through the hall and then down the cellar stairs. 'Cyril!' I shouted as I ran. 'Are you alright?'

The sight that greeted us, I'm happy to say, was the kind of thing you'd see at the end of a 1970s Disney film. Cyril, who had obviously tried to make a break for it, was now being pinned against a wall by Daphne who was busy licking his face. The petrified plumber looked at us imploringly.

'Help me, help me. Please!'

'This is what they do *before* they eat people Cyril,' I joked.

It took a while, but after a lot of reassurance from Nyoka, Cyril started getting used to being slobbered over and before too long his countenance had changed from

that of a petrified plumber into an enamoured cat enthusiast. Cyril was in love.

What a life though, eh? This is how mad it became at
Clarence House, boys and girls. I once had the Minister of
Agriculture and Fisheries standing in my kitchen stroking
Kali and telling me what a marvellous job I was doing and
all the while Jeffery Boswall's sitting at the table feeding a
couple of jaguarundi who had just moved in. Nyoka, who
was half-naked as per bloody usual, was walking about the
place brandishing an enormous boa constrictor, and while
Mrs Bush was on the stairs petting two baby tigers, one of
the electricians I'd hired was talking to Mr Parslow and
getting to know the ten Russian rats he'd brought with
him.

It was round-the-clock chaos, but somehow it worked.
The animals always got on well together. In fact, if anything, they looked out for one another. Sabre in particular
was extremely protective of them. We were all one very
big, unconventional happy family.

After about a year I gave Nyoka a key to Clarence
House so that he could come and go as he pleased. While
I was away filming he would move in and look after the
animals. Mrs Bush was OK looking after Sabre and the cats
overnight but things were a bit different now. We might
have jungle cats, margays, golden cats and clouded leopards ready to be transported to their country of origin.
Nyoka just adored being at Clarence House and like me he
seemed to revel not only in the peace and quiet there but
also the feeling of inter-species camaraderie. Every animal

lover who ever visited Clarence House, and there were a great many over the years, always commented on how natural and relaxed it felt. Which, when you consider who and what was living there and what went on day to day, should not have been the case. We had our challenges, of course. Luckily though, I had specialists on hand to advise me and happiness reigned supreme, swathing the house and gardens like an enormous blanket.

Incidentally, there were two animals in Nyoka's collection that he could never bring to Clarence House on account of their size. They were both kept at Colchester Zoo where he often worked and he once took Mr Parslow and me along there to meet them. The first one he introduced us to was the aforementioned Simba, who is still to this day the largest lion that has ever been kept in captivity. Nyoka had bought Simba as a cub on the Serengeti in 1959 and as well as weighing almost 850 pounds he stood four foot at shoulder height. Any adult no matter how large could have ridden Simba, although I wouldn't have advised it.

As Mr Parslow and I stared in wonder at Simba Nyoka asked me if I'd like to feed him some milk.

'Yes,' I replied, 'it will be a privilege.'

The bottle Nyoka handed me was enormous and held about four pints.

'He has at least two of these every day,' he said. 'Plus about twenty-five pounds of meat.'

That was about an eighth of me!

Although an absolute giant of a creature, Simba was a

real softie at heart and loved nothing better than a good old-fashioned hug. The sheer power at his disposal, however, prevented anyone other than Nyoka from being daft enough to give him one, and after pouring the half-gallon of milk down his neck and seeing the size of his choppers I quickly made my way back to safety. I simply adore animals but am acutely aware that I can only continue doing so for as long as I am alive!

The second animal Nyoka introduced us to was Cassius, a male reticulated python measuring a gargantuan twenty-five feet and six inches and weighing 240 pounds. Imagine that! That's over seven-and-a-half metres. The only thing I could think when looking at him was *Thank God Nyoka doesn't have a bigger van!* Otherwise he'd have had them over to Richmond. What a day out that was though.

While Cassius never visited, Nyoka would turn up with a boa constrictor called Bo Bo, which means friend. Boa constrictors are not nearly as strong as pythons and are much smaller, the largest growing to eleven feet long. Bo Bo was about eight feet long, quite old and terribly friendly – a bit like me now, really – and I freely admit that after a while I fell head over heels in love with him. I love all animals, and I mean *all* – but Bo Bo was one of the few who could melt my heart. Nyoka knew how much I adored him and after arriving one day he made an announcement.

'Bo Bo loves you Brian,' he said, wrapping the boa beyond compare around the back of my favourite kitchen chair. 'But he also loves your kitchen. For as long as your Aga remains on he'll be quite happy here.'

'You mean you're leaving him with me?'

'I am, Brian,' he said with a smile. 'I travel around far too much and Bo Bo needs to rest now. He also needs company, and he'll get plenty of that here.'

When not basking in the warmth of the kitchen Bo Bo lived in a vivarium Nyoka built at the back of the house and before he passed away about two years later he and I became as close as an animal and human can be. You perhaps wouldn't think it possible for a reptile but I swear to you that he used to purr and hum to me whenever we became entwined. It always started the same way. I'd walk into the kitchen, sit down in my chair and then slowly but surely Bo Bo would begin to wrap himself around me. Like a great many animals he adored having his neck tickled and that's when he'd start to hum and purr.

Whenever I went away filming poor old Bo Bo would become depressed and I used to worry about him terribly. I'd call Mrs Bush every afternoon just to make sure everything was in order and my first question would always be, how's Bo Bo?

'He's hardly moved since you went away,' Mrs Bush would often tell me. 'And he's off his food again' – which was mainly cooked chicken.

In the end, I used to take Bo Bo with me if I was only away for a night or two. I would put him in a large carryall and smuggle him into my hotel room, where he'd sleep at the end of my bed. I had to make sure the heating remained on, which meant it was like being in a sauna sometimes, but the fact that Bo Bo was happy allowed us both to sleep soundly.

During the summer when it was hot I'd take him for walks into Richmond Park. Once there I'd often lie on my back and stare at the sky while Bo Bo made himself comfortable lying over my legs and stomach. Having his weight upon me often used to send me off to sleep and whenever this happened Bo Bo, who must have felt me snoring, would make his way up to my face and start humming to me. It was the most wonderful way to be woken from one's slumber.

Shall I tell you something my sweet, patient reader? That time at Clarence House with Nyoka, Mr Parslow, Mrs Bush, Jeffery Boswell and all those beautiful animals is one of the happiest of my life. And one of the most surreal! You could make a film from this chapter alone, don't you think?

My adventures in Clarence House came to an end in 1972, after six years. My first wife, whom I had married when I was twenty-one and who would rather not be written about, had not lived with me for quite some time and when she decided to move into Clarence House, which we both owned, I decided to move out. These days my old makeshift menagerie is a Grade II listed building no less, and has a blue plaque on the front stating that the great Bernardo O'Higgins used to study there. I wonder if they'll ever put a plaque up for me one day? I think the most I can ever expect is a sign saying 'Beware the Blessed'! I wasn't in a position to keep the cats with me at first, so they went to live with a lovely old lady in Richmond who let me visit them as often as I liked. By the time I'd sorted myself out with a cottage, I could see how much they loved her – and she loved them – and so it would have been wrong of me to ask for them back. They were well cared for and happy, and that was all that really mattered. As for Sabre, well, he was a working dog not a pet, and he would have hated being cooped up in my tiny place all the time, and who would look after him when I was away filming? After worrying myself half to death I eventually contacted the police and, as it turned out, they knew someone who was looking for a Grade 3 hellhound with a big heart and so he went straight to a good home.

Nyoka, Mr Parslow, Mrs Bush and Jeffery Boswall are long gone now. As, of course, are the animals. That's the only problem with having animals. They will keep dying all the time! I do wish somebody would have a word with God and make them live longer. I feel incredibly honoured to have known them all and bringing those times to life again has been a source of great joy.

So, what is my legacy to my beloved Richmond then, apart from saving Clarence House and baiting its clergy? What have I bequeathed my sweet Eldorado? Well, there are two achievements which I would like to put forward; the first involving Mr Parslow and some pigeons and the second the birth of a baby.

Parslow and pigeons first.

One day, not long after I first met him, Mr Parslow came around to Clarence House with some pairs of white, yellow and black fantail pigeons. They were stunning to look at. After scaling one of my ladders and then putting up some houses for them in the trees, Mr Parslow took the pigeons out of the box one by one, whispered something to them, and then very gently released them in the direction of their designated home. It was impressive to watch and sure enough, in they all went. Percy Parslow the Pigeon Whisperer!

'They'll stay up there as long as they feel safe, Brian,' said Mr Parslow. 'You'll love having them around, I promise you. They make the most beautiful sound.'

The moment the words 'as long as they feel safe' left Mr Parslow's lips, I really should have smelt a rat. Or, in my case, a cat. Contessa the Siamese to be exact. She was the only one of my cats who made a habit of stalking birds and if she could catch one, all the better. By the time I started taking the cats to work with me at Clarence House I'd completely forgotten all about Mr Parslow's warning. What a berk!

I remember walking into the garden one day just to get some air when suddenly I heard a commotion coming from the pigeon tree. I looked up and there leaping in the direction of one of the white pigeons was Contessa.

'Oh no!' I cried running towards the tree. 'Get down here you little cow.'

Although there were no injuries to speak of (apart from one or two perforated eardrums) I'm afraid that the pigeons were gone for good. My loss, however, was most definitely my beloved township's gain and if you are ever passing Richmond Green and find that you're able to tarry a while amidst its splendid charms, try turning your eyes skywards for a moment. The pigeons, which are plentiful there, are just that little bit blacker and whiter and yellower than elsewhere. For they are Blessed pigeons!

How about that? I can turn the air blue and the birds yellow, black and white.

My second legacy to the town of Richmond took place at about eleven o'clock one morning in the late 1960s when I was jogging through Richmond Park. In the distance I suddenly spotted somebody lying on the ground under a tree. Had it been eleven o'clock in the evening I'd have thought little of it, but it was daytime and as a committed good Samaritan I ran over to investigate. As I got within about a hundred yards of the reclining figure I saw the person moving and could tell that he or she was in some distress. A few yards later the reality of the situation was upon me. It was a woman lying on her back and unless I was very much mistaken she was in labour!

It's the largest of the Royal Parks and a big old space, is Richmond Park – over 2,500 acres – and as I knelt beside the patient and looked around for reinforcements (preferably a doctor and a couple of midwives) not a soul was in sight. The poor lady was in terrible pain and when I tried to reassure her that everything was going to be OK she tried to speak.

'Aren't . . . you . . . on . . . the . . .'

'Yes, yes, yes, calm down,' I said. 'I'm Fancy Smith from

Z-Cars. Now for heaven's sake don't speak, just breeeeee-athe! That's it. In, out, in, out.'

Quickly cast your mind back to Goldthorpe, if you would. Remember Dr Morris who used to allow me to tag along as he delivered all those babies? I'd probably seen dozens of babies being delivered and so, as daft as it might sound, I had a rudimentary knowledge of what to do and – providing there were no complications – I thought we stood a chance. Just as well, as she was about to pop!

'Now, are you OK with me helping you deliver your baby?'

'Yes . . . that's . . . fine . . .' she replied.

With all systems now go I assumed the position, removed the necessary garments and advised her to breathe deeply. That's what Dr Morris always did. Just then, a dog walker came into view and after calling him over I ordered him to find a telephone box and ring for an ambulance as quick as he could.

The baby's head had already put in an appearance and then before you could say *Where do you stand on breast-feeding in public?* a fine baby girl was lying on the grass before me.

After picking her up I then reassured the mother that all was well. 'It's alright dear,' I said. 'You just relax.'

I had to free the child quickly and had forgotten my Swiss army knife so I tied a knot in the umbilical cord and bit through it. I remembered seeing Dr Morris do that – the knot-tying that is, not the biting. Once she was free I wrapped the baby up in my white T-shirt and cleaned her face with my vest.

By far the most singular act during this bizarre experience was handing the baby to the mother; something I will never forget. The look on her face was completely life-affirming.

Then, after first warning her of my intentions, I pressed down on the new mother's tummy to remove the clots and then the afterbirth. I was absolutely covered in blood, by the way. From head to knee!

The ambulance arrived thirty minutes or so after the baby and what a relief that was. Mother and baby both seemed to be doing well, which was a blessing, but they needed to be taken to hospital as soon as possible. After giving them both a kiss and then saying one final goodbye I helped them both into the back of the ambulance, closed the door and then waved them off. What a morning, eh? I never heard anything at all from her to this day.

Walking home through the park and then through Richmond itself was an even stranger experience than usual, especially as I must have resembled some kind of mad axe murderer. I was quite used to being stared at, of course, but by people wearing smiles usually, or looks of cheerful recognition. Not expressions of out-and-out horror, for heaven's sake! Now, I must have at least a million life experiences stored inside my scintillating old brain and any one of these could be called into my consciousness the moment somebody mentions something connected. It happens all the time with me and I'm forever interjecting with tales about this, that and, quite often, the other. Also, ladies and gentleman, I have a staggering memory and I'm not bragging, it's just a fact: actors and other professionals consult me regularly.

Well, I hadn't thought about this incident until, shortly after the publication of my last book (*Absolute Pandemonium* — have I mentioned that book before? I have! Oh, silly me. And what's that you say? It's still available? Well, I never . . .) I was on Radio 4's *Midweek* with the lovely Libby Purves and my fellow guest, Mark Harris the midwife, was chatting merrily away about the merits of male midwifery in the modern world when suddenly the memory appeared! It's a little tenuous, I suppose. It's a fascinating story though, and a part of my Richmond legacy. And, despite what you may have heard, it is one hundred per cent true.

Although I haven't lived there for the best part of half a century I still miss Richmond's manifold charms and it will always hold a very special place in my heart. So before I move on I'd like to express my appreciation to the town and its townspeople for playing host to what was one of the happiest phases of my life so far. And remember, you lovely virile Richmondites: if ever a dilapidated king's house comes on the market with enough room for a mad old man and his menagerie, just you give your Uncle Brian a call. I may not be as young as I used to be but with my plasterer's axe in my hand, animals by my side and the odd fellow eccentric popping by, I can achieve almost anything. Enjoy the tunnel!

4

HALCYON DAYS

It was July 1974 – a Saturday, if memory serves me correctly – and as the world went about its business listening to Charles Aznavour I was standing in the arrivals hall at Heathrow clad in some truly appalling clothing, shaking like a lorry load of alcoholic belly dancers. For a few months now I had been seeing an actress called Hildegard Neil. We'd first met in 1968, when filming a play called *Double Agent* for ITV. I was immediately smitten – obsessed even – by the beauteous Ms Neil, who liked me slightly in return. We went our separate ways when filming was over and, to cut a long story short, love didn't blossom until we met again six years later when we were both cast in the television series *Boy Dominic*.

Hildegard was coming out of an unhappy marriage and was having to start again from scratch. Looking back, a clean slate was exactly what we needed, but it was all a little bit daunting at the time and we were both quite nervous. Nervous in a good way, I should point out. After all, we were hopelessly in love and about to start a new life together. Money didn't matter one jot, just so long as we had a place to rest our heads.

As part of our clean slate we wanted to find somewhere new to live and so while Hildegard was away in South Africa visiting her family I found us a newly built three-bedroomed apartment in a building called Boundary House in Twickenham, south London. It was in a nice area and as well as the apartment being a reasonable size it was quite close to the river. *Bingo!* I thought. *Hildegard will love it*.

Now I don't want to get all Mills & Boon on you but I would still like to share with you the moment Hildegard arrived back at Heathrow, as this was the genesis of what has gone on to become of the most blissful unions on God's earth. Or at least in the Greater Bagshot area!

Whilst Hildegard had been in South Africa I had been busy preparing our new apartment and it was only when I walked into the arrivals hall at Heathrow that I realized what was about to happen. Finally here I was, about to meet, embrace and kiss the woman I loved more than anyone else in the world before taking her back to our new home. We were making a total commitment.

That realization hit me like a sack of coal and when Hildegard's flight eventually appeared on the arrivals board all kinds of *What if?* scenarios began racing through my mind. As the newly alighted passengers all started spilling into the hall I sat catastrophizing about what might be about to go wrong. We actor-explorers have incredibly volatile imaginations and can turn a random thought into Armageddon in about five seconds flat.

What if Hildegard's fallen out of love with me? I thought to myself. *She's had plenty of time to start having second thoughts. And what if she hates the apartment?*

I think you know me well enough by now to know that I do not scare easily, but by the time Hildegard appeared carrying her suitcases I had convinced myself that she'd changed her mind. Ninety-five per cent of the things we worry about in life never actually happen but that's the human brain for you. It can help us do all kinds of wonderful things but can also be an absolute nightmare!

The moment Hildegard saw me she stopped and put down her cases. She too was evidently petrified as I could see her entire body was shaking yet the smile that adorned her exquisite visage convinced me that she was not intending to about-turn. As Hildegard mouthed my name 'Bri! Bri! Bri!' tears began to appear in her eyes. I ran to where she was standing, took her in my arms and held her for all I was worth. It truly was the mother of all embraces and could have kept the entire romantic movement going for a decade.

As we arrived at Boundary House my nerves began to get the better of me once again. 'I do hope you like the apartment,' I said to Hildegard as we drove into the car park.

'I'm sure I will Brian,' she replied cheerfully. 'And I'm sure Nick, Hamish and the cats will too.'

'Oh dear!' I cried. 'The animals! I'd completely forgotten about them.'

'Well, as they're in Norfolk I've barely mentioned them. What's the problem, Brian?'

The problem was that within the terms of the lease I'd recently signed there was a clause that read – and I'm paraphrasing now – 'No pets allowed under any circumstances. And definitely not two dogs and two cats! Break it, Mr Blessed, and we'll cut your whatsits off!'

'Oh dear,' said the stunningly beautiful Miss Neil. 'What are we going to do?'

Hildegard and her soon-to-be ex-husband John had a house in Norfolk called the Nest and residing there were two Labradors and two cats. As they were in the process of selling the Norfolk Nest the animals, which John couldn't look after, would be coming to live with us.

'Don't you worry,' I reassured her. 'We'll smuggle them in after dark and then take them out for walks before it gets light. The Thames is just up the road and there are plenty of parks. They'll love it. The lease is only six months. We'll cope.'

We'd bloody well have to!

The apartment, which was in a block of about eight, was on the first floor and, despite being large enough to house a couple of humans, it was not really suitable for animals; save for a gerbil, perhaps, or a tin of salmon.

The Nest, conversely, was an animal's paradise and as well as being set in a few acres of land you could enter the property at ground level. The Labradors, Nick and Hamish, had, at John's insistence, always been kept in stables at the rear of the property. They really were tremendous fun and we hit it off immediately. Nick, who was black, used to hate living in the stables and so despite the obvious issues he was going to enjoy being indoors with us. Hamish, who was sandy coloured, had once had an eye operation and so always looked a bit skew-whiff but he too was delightful. They were like bookends, the two of them, and I've never to this day seen such devotion between two dogs.

Because they'd always lived in the stables, Nick and Hamish had been able to crap and pee at will, but this potential issue never occurred to either Hildegard or me until we were on our way to Boundary House. That's for later though. First we had to find the cats. A neighbour had been looking after them all these past few weeks and according to her they had gone out the previous evening and had not come back. As the feral felines were always free to come and go as they pleased, this used to happen regularly so Hildegard wasn't worried. They still needed to be found, however, otherwise, how could we leave. And so, armed with a bag full of treats, off we went into the woods.

Now, you may have noticed that I have not yet divulged the names of Hildegard's cats, and there are two very good reasons why: one, because of comic timing and effect, and two, because I can hardly bring myself to do so. Hildegard is quite skilful in choosing ridiculous names for animals and this was undoubtedly the zenith of my dear wife's efforts. As we began our search for the two of them she insisted that I shout them out.

'Do I have to?' I pleaded. 'What if somebody hears?'

'That's the whole idea, Brian!' snapped Hildegard. 'Now come on. You have the loudest voice known to man. Try putting it to some use.'

'Oh, alright then,' I said, suitably admonished.

I took the bag of treats from Hildegard, put my best foot forward and shouted as loudly as I possibly could, 'POODLE PANTS! TINY PUSS! WHERE ARE YOOO-OOOOOOOOU?'

Yes, you read that correctly, dear reader. Hildegard, who is the saner of us both, had decided to call her two cats Poodle Pants and Tiny Puss.

Now, that's all good and well if you are shouting for them in the privacy of your own asylum, but when you're out and about in rural Norfolk and possess stentorian tones such as I, then it might – just might – end up making you feel like a bit of a lemon.

'Shout it again,' requested Hildegard. 'They're bound to hear you eventually.'

'The whole of Norfolk's bound to hear me eventually,' I retorted. 'And what are they going to think?'

'Who cares! Now look. I'll do it with you, OK? They know my voice.'

For the next twenty minutes or so Hildegard and I sauntered through the woods calling out – nay, bellowing out – two of the campest names ever bestowed upon an animal.

'Poodle Pants! Tiny Puss! Where aaaaaaaare yoooooou? Here, puss, puss, puss.'

Can you picture it?

The ancient Chinese philosopher, Lao Tzu, once said, 'Being deeply loved by someone gives you strength, while loving someone deeply gives you courage.'

Well, that just about sums it up really because, mark my words, strength and courage were essential in those bizarre moments.

When at long last a Russian Blue and a black and white cat sauntered out of the undergrowth my heart leapt like a gazelle being chased by a cheetah.

'Here they are,' said Hildegard relieved. 'Come here you two. Let's get you in the car with Nick and Hamish.'

The journey up to Norfolk had taken us a good four hours and so the journey back again was always going to be interesting.

'Nick breaks wind all the time,' Hildegard warned me as I assumed my position behind the wheel of my recently valeted car. 'He also tends to shit quite a lot so we might have to stop once or twice.'

As we set off I began to consider Hildegard's words of warning.

'What do you mean we might have to stop once or twice?' I asked suddenly. 'Is Nick going to inform us when he needs to go to the loo?'

In between the Nest and Boundary House I was peed on three times by Poodle Pants, who insisted on travelling on my lap, while Nick did his business all over the back seat. The smell was unbearable! In the end, Hildegard and I just sat there in silence and allowed nature to take its course. There was no point getting annoyed with them as it wasn't their fault and asking them not to do it was like asking a black nimbus cloud not to rain. Nope. We just had to sit it out and try not to vomit.

By the time we finally arrived it was dark and with most of the residents being early-to-bedders we had no problem smuggling the animals in. The problem was how to housetrain them all before they needed the toilet again!

It became obvious that the Russian Blue, Tiny Puss, was an extremely clever and cunning cat, while her daughter Poodle Pants was sweet but thick.

Hamish was heart-warmingly affectionate and from the word go I fell head-over-heels in love with him. We seemed to have a connection somehow and this was proved on the very first night. Hildegard and I were lying in bed when suddenly Hamish came into the room and began pushing his face into mine. Instinctively I knew that he was trying to tell me Nick was about to misbehave and so I jumped out of bed, raced into the living room, grabbed Nick and then ran down the stairs and out of the building. Sure enough, the moment the door was closed behind us Nick made a deposit. The sixth that day, as far as I could make out.

'Well done, Hamish!' I said when we went back inside. 'Aren't you a good boy?'

Well yes, he was, until it came to his own toilet time. For some reason, Hamish's early warning system was wired up to Nick's bowels and this did cause one or two minor issues. Nothing compared to Nick Vesuvius, mind you. Hamish had still saved us from a fate worse than death.

Considering what was deposited inside the apartment there was no escaping the smell leaving it and we spent hours and hours trying to prevent the place humming like a public convenience; not to mention a shed load of cash. Shares in Airwick must have gone through the roof and we used to get the strangest looks from the other residents. In fact they regarded me with suspicion even before Hildegard and the animals moved in. Then, once the apartment became home to the secret six, the looks of suspicion intensified somewhat and were now fortified by repugnance. We were not popular.

How we managed to get away with keeping the animals there is beyond me. I mean, having one pet in a first-floor flat where none are allowed is always going to be risky. Especially when you're surrounded by lots of other people. But keeping four there? The cats were obviously allowed to come and go as they pleased and the Lord alone knows how they were never spotted coming in through the kitchen window via a nearby tree. Smuggling Hamish and Nick out for walks was hilarious, especially if one of them started to bark. While they were in the apartment this wasn't a problem as being quite obedient dogs they tended to quieten down when told, but out on the landing anything could happen. If one of them ever did decide to let out an excited bark whilst we were wending our way out for walkies you could bet that within a second or two somebody would be coming to investigate.

Hildegard and I were always ready for this and could be out of the building within five seconds of closing our door. Once out, we'd then edge our way around the side of the building so as not to be spotted through any net curtains. It was a proper game of cat and mouse – or elderly resident and sneaky thespian, if you want to get technical.

Once free, we would take the dogs up to Richmond lock on the Thames and then either walk up towards Kew Gardens or down towards Richmond. The dogs used to absolutely adore these walks and because it was safe to let them off the lead they were as free as they had been in Norfolk. We used to walk for hours and hours so they were, without doubt, some of best exercised dogs in London.

Sorry for lowering the tone once again ladies and gentlemen but while we were out on these walks the only place Nick would take a crap would be on a front door mat. It was completely bizarre. We could walk for miles and then all of a sudden a house would appear and off he'd run. If there wasn't a mat he'd move on but if there was and he was able, he'd squeeze one out. We didn't dare own up and tell the residents. We just grabbed him and scarpered. They must have thought the pooh fairy had come to visit them.

Because of my almost off-the-scale virility Hildegard fell pregnant soon after we moved in together. This had always been the plan and so when it was confirmed we were absolutely delighted.

'I'm going to be a dad, Dad,' I roared, when I called up my parents. 'Isn't that marvellous!'

I acted as if Hildegard and I were going to be the first people ever to procreate and spent the next few months boring people to death about what was to come. You can forgive a little exuberance though, surely? The only thing that stopped me from driving my friends and family mad was the fact I had to find us somewhere else to live and so together with acting work that came along, that's what kept me busy.

'Do you think we should live in the countryside?' I asked Hildegard.

'Have you ever lived in the countryside, Brian?' asked Hildegard.

'No, never. But I know I'd like to.'

'You mean you *think* you would. It gets terribly dark at night in the countryside, Brian, and that can become quite disconcerting if you're not used to it.'

'What would you suggest then?' I asked.

'How about Surrey?' she replied, smiling. 'That's almost all countryside and still only a short journey from London.'

Bingo!

'Surrey, it is then.'

After travelling the length and breadth of this fine English county we settled on the area around Bagshot, Lightwater and Chobham, which is on the M3 corridor.

Once that was decided I then registered my interest with all the local estate agents. This was always enormous fun as the moment I entered such an establishment everyone present would stop what they were doing and stare at me open-mouthed. Then, once I was on my way, I'd quickly look back and you could guarantee that everybody would be on the phone. 'That wild man Brian Blessed's moving into the area!' is what they were probably saying. 'Time to sell up!' I say this only partly in jest, ladies and gentlemen. You see, living next door to the Blesseds, circa 1976, was not for the faint hearted as with a new house came, not only a new human being, but also some new animals. Lots of animals!

When I gave notice on Boundary House I quickly realized that if I wanted to get my deposit back I would have to ensure we had satisfied certain criteria; i.e. leaving the flat in the same condition as when we had moved in.

Visually, this was not a problem as although our residency had afforded the apartment a certain lived-in quality (you can say that again!), I went to great lengths to ensure it had been returned to its original condition. A day and a half painting and cleaning, no less!

Alas, it was one of the other five senses that left me fretting with fiscal foreboding – namely, smell. It didn't matter what I did or what I put down, I could not get rid of the animal aroma that had been permeating the place since we moved in. In fact, I must have used at least fifty gallons of pine disinfectant trying to shift it, but instead of the place smelling like a nice forest it just carried on reeking of dogs and cats!

What saved me was the fact there was a gap between us leaving the apartment and the owners taking repossession. I think it was about three weeks, and before we went I made sure that one of the kitchen windows was left open. Sure enough, a few weeks later I received a call from the agents.

'I'm sorry to bother you, Mr Blessed, but we've had a complaint from the owners. Apparently, the place smells of animals.'

'ANIMALS?!' I cried incredulously. 'But that's impossible. The only creature in residence during our tenure that could have been considered an animal is me, and I have quite a nice odour, so I'm told.'

May the good Lord forgive me dear reader, but the agent looking after Boundary House was a fan of mine (I'd signed some photos for him when I collected the keys) and so I knew that, providing I had an excuse, I could probably get off scot-free.

'I've got it!' I cried. 'I left one of the kitchen windows open to help air the place. Some cats must have got in and sprayed everywhere. They're buggers for that.'

'That must be it, Mr Blessed. No harm done. I'll call the owners and tell them.'

'Thanks, Send them my best if you would.'

What a performance! Laurence Olivier himself would have been on his feet shouting '*bravo!*' and uncorking the sherry if he'd seen it. It was a genuine *tour de force*, as the critics say.

Anyway, enough of this modesty. We must away to Surrey.

Whilst still at Boundary House and mulling over where to live I received a call one day from one of the estate agents. We'd looked at dozens of places and after what had seemed like an age we'd managed to narrow it down to just three properties.

'We've just taken on a new cottage, Mr Blessed,' said the estate agent. 'I think you should come and have a look at it.'

'No, no,' I said hastily. 'No more cottages, I beg of you.'

'You did say you wanted somewhere with character, Mr Blessed, and this place is awash with it.'

'Alright, I submit. Take us to it!'

The following morning, Hildegard and I met the long-suffering estate agent in a place called Brick Hill, which is equidistant between Sunningdale, Windlesham and Chobham. It's nothing more than a small collection of cottages really but as we arrived I remember feeling as though I'd stepped back in time.

'Who on earth lives around here?' I asked the agent.

'Well, apart from some gypsies who have a camp at the top of the road there, they're mainly original Surrey people.'

'How do you mean original?' I asked.

'Their families have been living here for centuries,' said

the go-between. 'What's more they tend to speak using the delightful Surrey dialect.'

'I wasn't aware there even *was* a Surrey dialect?'

'It's not too dissimilar to the West Country dialect. Hardly anybody uses it these days. In fact, the people of Brick Hill are probably some of the last ones.'

I couldn't believe it. Surrey had an indigenous population!

'I've never met a native Surrovian before,' I quipped. 'Let's have a look at the property, then perhaps we'll meet one or two.'

'It's called Primrose Cottage. This way.'

Brick Hill had felt like a time-less enclave right from the off, yet the moment I knew it was populated by gypsies and by people whose families had lived there for eons I was as good as hooked. The cottage, which was about a hundred years old, did indeed have bags of character and was overflowing with charm. It was all set on one floor and had three bedrooms, one bathroom, a good-sized kitchen and a large living room. There was no central heating but with an Aga in the kitchen and a fire large enough to roast a pig over in the living room, I wasn't too worried. Outside there was about a third of an acre of land and the entire place was surrounded by trees. Brick Hill reminded me of the film *Brigadoon* in which a group of houses appears every hundred years.

'You do realize we're in paradise,' I said to my beautiful wife-to-be.

She nodded to me, beaming. We were absolutely besotted with the place.

After thanking the estate agent for suggesting it we made an offer for the place there and then. £25,000, I think it was. Fortunately, this was accepted by the owners, a Mr and Mrs Fosbrook, and after sorting the mortgage we were able to move in almost immediately.

Although we didn't get to meet any during the visit, it didn't take long for us to get to know our neighbours at Brick Hill and they were just as interesting as the estate agent had suggested they might be.

To the rear of our garden was Miss Snooks who lived in a tiny two-room cottage. She was a bit of a rural eccentric and used to wear a long trench coat that was done up with a safety pin. Every day she would set off across Sunningdale golf course to do her shopping and would spend the rest of her time sitting in front of her fire. She didn't talk much but because she was quite old we used to look after her and always made sure she had enough coal. Living right next door to Primrose Cottage was a spinster in her forties called Mad May. I've no idea who started calling her that but she would ramble on and on about anything and everything which used to drive people round the twist. Then, without warning, she'd stop and remain silent for days on end.

Other neighbours included Mr and Mrs Smith, who had four children. They became great friends of ours. Then there was Mr Tedders, the coal merchant. I spent an absolute bloody fortune with him but he always looked after me with an extra bag or two. That's what everybody was like in Brick Hill. It was a true community.

The gypsies, whose camp was at the top of our road, were as much a part of this unique community as anyone else and they were all great characters. Their leader, a man called Gregory, was better known to the population of Brick Hill as Gregory of the Roads, on account of the fact he was a road mender by trade. He had an unorthodox way of acquiring his raw materials. What he'd do first was find out where the council were digging up a road and then go along with his horse and cart. After offering the council workers a cigarette and then engaging them in a bit of witty repartee he'd offer to take the old tarmac away. Once back at the camp he'd melt it down and voilà! A brand-new road just waiting to be laid. There are literally hundreds of private roads in that area so he was never short of work. The only problem was that the tarmac was so weak that after about ten weeks thistles would start appearing through the cracks!

But Gregory wasn't the only one who enjoyed getting one over on the great and the good of Surrey. I too used to dabble in this particularly pleasing pastime on occasion, and although what I did could never be described as being a trade, I used to positively enjoy it.

Allow me to explain.

The vast majority of these executive byroads used to be inhabited by decent people who'd break bread with just about anybody. They still are. There was one exception, however. I'm afraid I cannot identify the road in question as I don't want to upset anybody (I've already done that!). Suffice to say, there were a dreadful bunch of snobs who lived in Sunningdale and used to have a go at Gregory whenever they saw him passing in his horse and cart.

'I say! Did you see what your horse just did? Who's going to clean that up? You do know this is a private road? Clear off now or I'll call the police.'

Although these roads were indeed private, a lot of locals used them as shortcuts when on foot and nobody seemed to mind. All except this lot. I don't know what it was about them. They were simply odious. But because Gregory was such a placid gentleman he had no trouble ignoring them. If only I could have done the same!

They say, so I'm told, that revenge is sweet. Well, you can't get much sweeter than sugar, can you? Every couple of weeks or so if I saw him outside the pub I'd slip Gregory a fiver. Then, once he was ensconced in the saloon bar I would empty my pockets of sugar lumps. These I would then feed to Gregory's horse, and you know what sugar does to a horse, don't you? It turns it into a manure factory.

Once Gregory was suitably refreshed he would then leave the pub, untether his nag and then stumble home via millionaire's row. This was a shortcut to the gypsy camp and because it was so late at night nobody used to have a go at him. They were probably either asleep after overdosing on Complan or busy throwing their car keys into an ashtray at a swingers' parties. Either way, Gregory and his horse always went unchallenged after closing time and would deposit enough horse manure on that road to grow a hundred roses. Success!

Come the morning the residents would go ballistic.

'Oh, my God! Jeffrey, call the police! That awful gypsy person has allowed his horrible horse to defecate all over our road again. I don't want it outside my lovely house!'

Nevertheless, when no one was looking they would gratefully scoop it up and place it around their roses so it did provide a free service.

I think it's fair to say that life in Brick Hill was bordering on being perfect. Although small, Primrose Cottage was to die for and it just epitomized cosiness. The ceilings were all quite low and because the cottage had a bit of age to it everything was slightly higgledy-piggledy. None of the doors seemed to fit exactly and the floorboards squeaked. It was almost as if the cottage was alive, if that makes sense, and seemed to be thriving on the energy of its inhabitants. I freely admit that I often used to pinch myself when I got up in the morning and I'm sure the animals did the same. They all adored living at Primrose Cottage and seemed to be on a kind of permanent high. This was, in no small part, down to the surrounding area and the cats in particular were like children during the summer holidays: out at the crack of dawn and you wouldn't see them again until tea time. You could see their eyes widen in happiness as they set off on their daily adventures.

When it came to walking Nick and Hamish we were

spoiled for choice at Brick Hill and when the leads came out and you shouted 'walkies', mayhem would ensue immediately. Our favourite walk – or should I say *their* favourite walk – was over the M3, which was just a few hundred yards away from the cottage, and then straight on to Chobham Common. This is one hell of a place and comprises of no fewer than 1,400 acres of lowland heath. That's a lot of heath for two Labradors to explore! They had a good go though, as did I. You see, as well as taking Nick and Hamish for a walk I did a lot of my Everest training on Chobham Common so it's served us well over the years.

Second to Chobham Common in the walking stakes was Sunningdale golf course which is to the north of Primrose Cottage just across Chertsey Road. I used to go jogging there quite a bit and always took Nick and Hamish with me. Those boys were in their element and ran around in circles of happiness. Day in, day out, Nick, Hamish and I were like a mad threesome having limitless fun. The golfers smiled patiently and tolerated our wild frolicsome behaviour.

The only time I ever encountered anybody superfamous on Sunningdale golf course was when I was out on a run one day with the boys. They were probably fifty metres or so ahead of me at the time and suddenly I heard a rumpus. They'd either found a rabbit or had disturbed a golfer and as I approached the melee I prayed for the former. Alas, I was not in luck. Nick and Hamish had indeed disturbed a strolling golfer but despite them obviously ruining the poor man's shot he seemed to be taking it very well. So well, in fact, that when I arrived at the tee the dog's quarry was on his knees stroking his attackers.

'What beautiful dogs,' he said in a broad American accent. He had short golden hair and seemed to be about my height. 'They certainly took me by surprise.'

Now I'm no golfer boys and girls but even I knew who this was.

'God in heaven, you're Jack Nicklaus!' I proclaimed. 'What are you doing here?'

Now if ever there is a prize given for the most fatuous question ever asked you have my permission to submit this. Jack Nicklaus, the most successful golfer of all time, is on a golf course. I wonder what he could be doing?

'I'm here to have a game with my son,' replied the God of Golf, kindly ignoring my stupidity. 'Haven't I seen you somewhere before?'

'*I, Claudius?*' I replied. 'I play Caesar Augustus.'

I wasn't being arrogant or presumptuous. It's just that *I, Claudius* had recently begun its first run on the BBC and in the USA, where it was very popular, and even without the wig and the makeup people had been stopping me all the time.

'That's the one!' said my new friend. 'I've been watching it in my hotel room. I hope you're not as ruthless in real life, Mr . . .'

'Blessed. Brian Blessed.'

'Nice to meet you, Brian. Tell me, have you ever played golf?'

When I answered Jack's question in the negative, he

said simply: 'Well don't start. It'll ruin your acting career.' And then he strolled off. What a lovely chap though.

One of my favourite jobs at Primrose Cottage was making the fire in the living room. There was something enormously gratifying about this task and, as well as deriving a slight sense of achievement from the proceedings, I also loved the fact that it used to accentuate the cottage's homely quality. Ask anyone who does it and they'll tell you there's an art to it. Screw the paper up too tightly and the fire won't be able to breathe. Put the coke or the coal on too quickly and it won't catch. Everybody has their own procedure, of course, but once you have honed your technique and it has become second nature, it is a joy. Let's not forget I'm the son of a coal miner!

Being complimented on your fire is not unlike being complimented on a performance of some kind and produces the same feelings of pride and satisfaction. Ask somebody who has an open fire and they'll tell you. We don't have one anymore and it's something I miss terribly. Cleaning out the cesspit, on the other hand, was not quite so magical, but that's country living for you. It's all character building!

A few years later, while I was appearing in Andrew Lloyd Webber's *Cats,* this came up in conversation one day with my old friend Her Majesty the Queen. Well, if you're going to drop a name, drop a big one! She'd been attending a performance of the show and had asked to meet some of the cast afterwards. It's always an enormous pleasure meeting Her Majesty and I was looking forward to a royal chinwag.

After punching me on the elbow, which she does to attract my attention and is the reason I call her 'Knuckles', the Defender of the Faith spoke: 'Tell me, Mr Blessed. What do you actors do during the day? I've often wondered.'

'Well, Your Majesty, today I have been cleaning out the cesspit.'

'You have a cesspit at home, Mr Blessed?'

'I do indeed, Ma'am.'

'We don't have that problem at the palace,' she said, a touch of commiseration in her voice. 'Thankfully we are on the mains.'

We've had some bizarre conversations over the years, Her Majesty and I.

Anyway, back to the mid-1970s. We'd only been in situ at Primrose Cottage for a matter of weeks, and as well as having a veritable sea of boxes scattered about the place the garden was badly in need of some TLC. Being a frustrated horticulturalist I'd already committed myself to administering some of this and so, from the moment I leaped out of bed in the morning until the moment I donned my jimjams and took the short ride to Bedfordshire, I'd be either digging, hoeing, planting or simply luxuriating in mother nature's bower.

Shortly after lunch one day I was digging out one of the flower beds when suddenly I heard a car pull up outside the cottage. Hildegard had popped to the shops some time earlier and so I assumed she had returned and after sinking my spade into the freshly tilled soil I turned round to greet my wife. But instead of a radiant temptress brandishing a shopping bag, I was surprised to see a male middle-aged casting director brandishing a cine camera.

'Jimmy Liggat,' I roared. 'Lovely to see you but what are you doing here?'

Jimmy had worked on some of the biggest films of the sixties and early 1970s and was best known for his work with the great Stanley Kubrick. He'd cast *Lolita*, *2001: A Space Odyssey* and *Clockwork Orange* and I'd known the delightful gentleman for years. The poor chap looked exhausted. He was sweating profusely and his face was as red as a ripe tomato.

'Thank God I've found you,' he said, almost collapsing onto the front garden fence. 'I've been trying to find this place for hours. I take it you're not on the phone yet?'

'Any day now, apparently,' I replied. 'What's with the cine camera?'

'What indeed,' said my fatigued friend. 'Before I tell you, could I have a glass of water please?'

'Yes, of course,' I said, before helping him to his feet and giving him a big hug. 'Come into the kitchen.'

After I'd brought him back to life, Jimmy explained that he was working on a new film with Stanley Kubrick called *Barry Lyndon* and had come to see me about a role.

'Why on earth didn't you just go via my agent?' I asked.

'Stanley insisted I come and see you personally,' said Jimmy. 'And, if possible, get you on film.'

'Doing what?' I asked.

'Reading the part, of course. I've tried telling him you're not right for it but he's obsessed by you. There's no time for an audition as he's up to his ears filming so he asked – sorry, told – me to film you reading a page or two.'

'Well, it sounds a bit unorthodox I suppose, but I've no problem with it.'

'You might when I tell you about the part,' said Jimmy, slowly lowering his head.

'Go on,' I said, cautiously.

There was a long pause.

'He wants you to play a very short gay man,' he eventually whispered, staring at the kitchen floor.

'Come again?' I said.

This time Jimmy raised his head and started at me piteously.

'HE WANTS YOU TO PLAY A VERY SHORT GAY MAN,' he said as loud as his quivering voice would allow.

I'm not sure how Jimmy was expecting me to react exactly, but he was obviously fearing the worst. As it was, I simply sat down at the kitchen table. For the first time in my life I was completely speechless. Eventually I managed to repeat Jimmy's request aloud.

'He – wants – me – to – play – a – very – short – gay – man,' I said slowly.

Poor Jimmy just stood by the sink, nodding his head.

'How on earth am I,' I began after getting to my feet, 'standing at about six feet tall and weighing seventeen-and-a-half stone, supposed to turn myself into a gay dwarf?'

'He is supposed to be a baddie,' said Jimmy hopefully.

'I couldn't give two hoots! Goodie, baddie, lass or laddie, I am not right for it!'

'Look,' said Jimmy. 'I've been telling Stanley that ever since he came up with the idea but he's adamant you're the right man for the role. He's a huge admirer of yours.'

'Really?' I cooed, my ego getting the better of me for a second.

'Yes, really. He thinks you're the best thing since sliced bread.'

'But on film I specialize in playing tough guys and rogues,' I said. 'Not only that, the camera makes me look twice the size I actually am. I can't think what he might have seen me in that would convince him that I'd be ideally cast as a tiny person? Are you absolutely sure he hasn't got me muddled up with somebody else?'

'Like who?' inquired the exasperated Jimmy.

'Well, from the sound of things, Quentin bloody Crisp! This has got to be a joke, Jimmy. It's not April the first is it?'

'No, Brian,' Jimmy responded. 'Stanley passionately wants you to play the part.'

I genuinely did wonder whether the all-powerful Kubrick had mistaken me for another actor and, as pleased as I was to see my old friend Jimmy, I was unable to treat the approach seriously. I simply couldn't stop laughing.

'This is crazy,' I roared. 'Look, Jimmy, tell Stanley that I'm flattered he thought of me, but I really do think he should try and look for somebody else. I'm all for a challenge as you know, and I've played giants, yetis, wizards of all kind – my range of parts is astronomical – but this particular one is beyond me.'

'You mean I can't even persuade you to read a few lines?' he said beseechingly.

'Not on your nelly.'

After giving him another glass of water I wished Jimmy all the best and then sent him on his way. *What a strange encounter*, I thought to myself.

For the rest of that day I tried to imagine myself playing a munchkin. I repeated the story to Hildegard when she came home and she collapsed into a heap with laughter. How about you, dear reader? Can you imagine a pint-sized me, mincing menacingly about the place? Well of course you bloody can't!

About a week later I received another visit from Jimmy, armed once again with a cine camera and, this time, a look of complete hopelessness.

'You haven't come about the gay dwarf again, have you?' I asked him as he approached the cottage.

'I'm afraid so,' he replied. 'Stanley's adamant. I knew there'd be no point calling you or going through your agent so I thought I'd try you again, face-to-face.'

Poor Jimmy, I felt so sorry for him. Even so . . .

'Well, you've got two chances, Jimmy,' I said sticking my chin in the air. 'Fat chance, and no chance.'

Jimmy looked disappointed, but not surprised.

'I thought you'd say that,' he groaned. 'Is there nothing I can do to make you change your mind?'

'What's the budget for the film?' I asked him.

'About eleven million.'

'Not even for that,' I said grandly. 'Anyway, why on earth can't your director just accept my decision?'

'Because Stanley Kubrick is used to getting his own way,' said Jimmy. 'Look, would you at least come and meet him. Perhaps then he'll realize you're not suitable and move on. Oh, please, Brian. For me! He's giving me hell.'

Poor Jimmy really was at the end of his tether.

'Well, I suppose I could,' I said, succumbing to his plea.

To be honest, I was becoming intrigued by the idea of meeting Kubrick now. After all, he was a cinematic genius and the whole film world – directors, producers and actors – bowed to his greatness.

'Where would I have to go?' I asked, warming to the idea.

'We're shooting in Somerset. I'll send a car.'

The following week the car arrived as arranged and after a few hours I found myself alighting by some fields in the middle of nowhere. You should have seen Jimmy's face when he saw me. It was like he'd just won an Oscar!

'Brian! Thank you so much for coming. Stanley can't wait to see you.'

I was being treated like royalty! I couldn't believe it.

I flatter myself, boys and girls, that I have worked on some pretty big films over the years with some mightily impressive sets, but this really did take the biscuit. It was in a field that must have been at least a hundred acres and, as well as having legions of extras in attendance all dressed as soldiers, there were literally dozens of caravans and lorries, enough lights to illuminate the entire county, and at least a thousand sheep. And as for the crew! Well, I'd never seen anything like it. There must have been hundreds of the buggers, all scurrying around like ants. It was like the Great Yorkshire Show!

'What the hell's going on Jimmy?' I asked.

'Don't ask!' he whispered. 'We've been here for weeks.'

As he led me over to the business end where all the equipment was, I spied Stanley Kubrick sitting behind the main camera. Time stood still, along with everyone else. No one dared move!

'He's going for a take in a few minutes,' said Jimmy in a hushed voice.

At that moment Stanley Kubrick slowly turned his head and looked at me. He had dark hair and eyes like black pools set in a pale face. For a second I saw a hint of a smile.

'Hello, Brian,' he said in a quiet, measured voice. Then he returned his focus to the crew. 'OK, are we ready to go?'

'Yes, Mr Kubrick,' said the assistant director.

'Tell the sheep handlers I'll cue them a few seconds after we go.'

'Yes, Mr Kubrick.'

The tension was palpable. I got the feeling that everyone present was scared stiff of Stanley and you could have cut the atmosphere with a knife.

'OK, ACTION!'

As opposed to watching what was going on in front of the camera like everyone else, I kept my gaze firmly on Mr Kubrick, and about ten seconds into the take I saw him move his index finger upwards by about half an inch.

Nothing happened.

'CUT,' he said. Then he covered his face with his hands. After half a minute of silence, he shook his head in quiet despair.

'Why the hell didn't the sheep go?' he asked the assistant.

'We were waiting for your signal, Mr Kubrick.'

'But I gave the signal about ten seconds in. Didn't you see it?

Kubrick then repeated what he'd done with his finger to the assistant.

This bloke's hard to please, I thought to myself.

After giving his assistant a lesson in how to make hundreds of sheep move across a field, Kubrick turned around and looked straight at me.

'Brian Blessed,' whispered the great man. 'Is it really you?'

'In the flesh,' I assured him, adopting a similarly muted tone.

'It's so good to see you at last,' he said, shaking me by the hand. 'Let's go for a walk, shall we? We've got a lot to talk about.'

After instructing his assistant to tell the crowd to remain where they were until he returned, he led me away.

'Now look,' I said. 'Before we go any further I want you to know – sorry, I mean I *need* you to know – that I will not play a tiny gay gangster. I admire you as a director and I'm sure you're a terribly nice fellow, but it simply is not for me.'

Again I made the point that the camera made me even larger. Kubrick said nothing at all and we just kept on walking. Then, after about ten minutes, he stopped and sat down on the grass. I followed suit and for the next hour we both waxed lyrical about a vast range of subjects. I flatter myself that I was able to keep up with his extraordinary mind. My knowledge of astronomy intrigued him, and the conversation soared from there to philosophy and on to Soviet film makers such as Sergei Eisenstein.

'You are a male Scheherazade,' he said, staring at me with eyes that seemed to glower – not in a sinister way but with a probing intensity. Kubrick was fascinated by Konstantin Stanislavski, the great teacher and author of *An Actor Prepares*. He used many of his techniques when directing his films. At this point I interrupted him by saying, 'You are renowned, Stanley, for demanding dozens of takes.'

'Yes, Brian, that is true. I am constantly striving for perfection. I sense that some people have a feeling that I am a bit of an ogre. Not so! I love actors and I love working with them. Filming for me is at its best when I am shooting actors in close up. Faces, faces, faces. I love actor's faces.'

His own face shone with a strange haunting dark quality when he was excited but he never smiled. When I was being funny his eyes would water with amusement but his expression otherwise did not change.

'You don't smile or laugh, Mr Kubrick,' I said. 'Shall I tickle you?'

He shook his head in response and his eyes filled with moisture again. We discussed the fact that when filming *Barry Lyndon* he had obtained lenses developed by Zeiss for NASA to enable him to film scenes under natural candlelight. I was completely gobsmacked when he told me that. It was then that I fully realized what a privilege it was to be in the company of such a genius. Oh I had a ball. I am delighted to say that I thrilled him with my tales of adventure. He would positively shake with excitement.

On and on we went as we discussed his films such as *Paths of Glory, Doctor Strangelove, Clockwork Orange, Spartacus* and, of course, *2001: A Space Odyssey*.

'You know that scene where William Sylvestor as Professor Floyd is travelling to the moon and falls asleep in a chair with a judo match going on in a TV screen in the background?' I said.

'Yes, yes of course I do, Brian.'

'Well,' I continued, 'you see a black belt woman throwing a blue belt with Doug Robinson, the sixth dan, refereeing the match. That black belt woman was my first wife. She was a perfectionist like yourself. Doug Robinson said she had a right go at you. Words to the effect of, "For God's sake, make your mind up where you want me to throw her!" Apparently you employed great diplomacy and handled the situation like a true gentleman.'

He looked visibly shaken by the reminder, but then almost laughed, saying, 'Yes, Brian, your first wife was quite a handful. Very dramatic. Tell me all about Kilimanjaro.'

'I beg your pardon?'

'I read in an interview once that you like mountains. Tell me about Kilimanjaro.'

Never one to pass up the opportunity of delivering a mountaineering monologue, I regaled the celebrated director with everything I knew about the famous African mountain, including the tale of the leopard of Kilimanjaro, which was found frozen on the mountain at over 18,500 feet. The animal was later immortalized in the opening paragraph of Hemingway's *The Snows of Kilimanjaro*, and nobody has ever been able to explain why it was roaming at such high altitude.

After completing my lecture, I lay back on the grass and waited for my audience to show his appreciation.

'Do you know how I think the leopard got there?' he said eventually. 'MARTIANS! I think they put the leopard there.'

Obviously, I thought this was a joke but as I sat up and attempted to conjure up a witty retort I realized that Stanley was being very serious. His statement was so strange and childlike that it bordered on the banal. For an infinitesimal moment he appeared to be a boy of about six. For a genius like him, it sounded almost unimaginative.

It turned out that Stanley was indeed a firm believer in Martians, little beings who lived on Mars but liked to visit earth occasionally and put leopards on top of mountains.

All this time, by the way, the entire cast and crew had remained in place, including the sheep, and we'd been gone for well over an hour. As we arrived back on the set, Kubrick told his production team to break everybody for lunch. He then cordially invited me into his luxurious caravan where we were joined by Ryan O'Neal, a delightful, warm lad who was completely devoted to Kubrick.

'Every day it's a miracle working with him, Brian. I'm learning so much,' he said.

Ryan and I had worked with film director Arthur Hiller – he of course in *Love Story* and I in *Man of La Mancha* – and were just discussing this over a cup of coffee when Kubrick slowly placed his face within inches of mine and whispered, 'Brian, tell me about boxing.'

His request made me smile with surprise. With Ryan also nodding at me, I needed no further encouragement to reveal my knowledge of the noble art. For half an hour I held their attention. They were astonished when I related how I'd met the great heavyweight, Jack Dempsey, known as the Manassa Mauler, in his restaurant on Eighth Avenue and 50th Street in New York. On that momentous day he introduced me to some of the greatest world heavyweight champions of all time. Ezzard Charles, the Cincinnati Cobra, Gene Tunney, the Fighting Marine, Rocky Marciano, the Brockton Blockbuster, Jersey Joe Walcott, and the great Joe Louis himself, the Brown Bomber! I then covered my life in South Yorkshire when I was a youngster, where we all boxed and mixed with champions. I ended my story by saying to my two enchanted listeners, 'Have you ever been in a red corner? Have you been in a blue corner?'

They both shook their heads and then remained still. Finally Kubrick stood up and said, 'You must come to my home, Childwickbury Manor. I wish to discuss a boxing film with you. You see, boxing is one of my greatest passions.'

'Well, I never would have thought that,' I replied. 'So that's why you invited me onto your set? It wasn't about me playing a tiny man who's gay?'

Kubrick suddenly, surprisingly, let out an enormous laugh. 'You, Brian, a small man who's gay? What a ridiculous idea.'

Several hours later I was back home planting my tomatoes. In retrospect it was one of the most bizarre experiences of my life. I never saw or heard from Kubrick again!

By the time we had made ourselves at home in Primrose Cottage, Hildegard was heavily pregnant and becoming quite nervous. We both were! She'd carried on working for as long as she'd felt able and had recently appeared in a series called *The Early Life of Stephen Hind*, with Michael Kitchen. Once at home, however, Hildegard had nothing to think about except the birth and, being in her mid-thirties, she was aware that there could be complications. These days it's perfectly normal to have a child at thirty-six but back then that wasn't the case.

Hildegard had decided to have the baby at Wimbledon Hospital and as the time drew near I did my best to reassure her that everything would be alright. I must have seen dozens of women in their thirties have babies while I was following Dr Morris around in Yorkshire and didn't remember one complication.

'Don't you fret, my love,' I whispered. 'You'll sail through it.'

Because I was bushy bearded and overtly masculine, everybody – and I mean everybody – was convinced we were going to have a boy. I remember Hildegard's agent at the time, a lovely fellow named Vernon Conway, coming to see her one day and after putting his hand on her tummy he stood back and announced, 'Yes, there's no doubt about it you two. It's definitely a boy.' Thank you, Nostradamus. Where would we be without our agents!

In truth, I was desperate to have a baby girl. I already had a daughter from my first marriage but for reasons I won't go into here we didn't see each other and it pains me to say that we still don't to this day. Anyway. These things happen. I don't know why I wanted a baby girl but for some reason the thought of having a son never grabbed me. I expect a psychologist would be able to furnish you with a reason.

The only thing that wasn't going according to plan in my life was the fact that I was appearing in an absolute stinker of a play. It happens from time to time. The travesty in question was entitled *The Exorcism* and was being staged at the Comedy Theatre in London, which is just off

Leicester Square. Despite *The Exorcism* being a thriller this was the perfect venue as during the previews we got more laughs than a Brian Rix farce. It was terrible! My co-stars in the play were the actresses Honor Blackman and Mary Ure. Poor Mary had been suffering all kinds of personal problems at the time, including a battle with alcoholism, and after the opening night, which was a disaster, she went home, took one too many sleeping pills and passed away. It was a tragedy. Poor, poor Mary. She was a wonderful lady and an incredible actress.

My one saving grace during this particular professional nadir was a black Persian cat with orange eyes called Comedy who used to visit me in my dressing room. He was a theatre cat, like the character Gus in T. S. Eliot's *Old Possum's Book of Practical Cats*, and had been wandering round the Comedy for years. I'm pretty sure what with Health and Safety that this tradition no longer exists in the West End – Alas, poor Tiddles, I knew him well – but back then there were dozens of cats and some were quite famous. Comedy the cat must have weighed at least three stone and because he wasn't very nimble on his feet he was forever getting into trouble on the roads. Panton Street's a bit of a one-way rat run really, and so you've always got cars, motorbikes and black cabs whizzing along. It's no place for an overweight feline, let me tell you.

I became so worried about Comedy that I ended up putting him in the car and taking him home with me. I couldn't possibly leave him to be run over on Panton Street and thought it best to give him the freedom of Brick Hill.

Fortunately, the big black cat got along famously with Poodle Pants and Tiny Puss, although the latter liked to play tricks on him and in particular to leap on him when he was fast asleep. Being a sweet cat, Comedy never bore a grudge against the little madam. And Nick and Hamish thought he was just terrific, as did Hildegard.

Straight after breakfast the three felines would be out into the garden. Poor Comedy would usually run out of steam by the time they got to the garden fence but at least he was now happy, safe and well cared for, as all domestic animals should be. The only time Comedy ever expended any energy was when I went out with the dogs, but even then, only occasionally. I think he trusted me and so when he saw me and the boys strolling off towards Chobham Common he'd meow, as if saying 'Wait for me!' After that he'd follow us over the bridge, onto the common and would just trot along minding his own business. I don't know what it is about cats who like following humans but I do seem to attract them.

When Hildegard eventually went into labour I got her in the car and we made our way to Wimbledon. I don't remember very much about the birth, except that it was a terribly emotional experience and afterwards Hildegard's entire body was shaking. The result was Rosalind, who has been the apple of my eye ever since. Not even *The Exorcism*, which unbelievably was still going, could chuck a spanner into these works and our lives, which were already beatific, now felt complete. It was fascinating to observe Hildegard at this time; she appeared to be experiencing absolute bliss.

Before Hildegard and Rosalind had arrived home, I'd spent a good week or so cleaning up the cottage, decorating the nursery and sprucing up the garden. I'm no Monty Don but that garden looked a picture by the time I'd finished with it and when I got them home Hildegard was thrilled with my efforts. Fathers can often feel a bit useless during pregnancy so it was nice to be able to contribute something. I also arranged for us to have an au pair, a delightful young Scottish lady called Elizabeth, as I was spending so much time away, so that meant there was now nine of us living in Primrose Cottage.

My knowledge of babies and how to care for them came in very useful right from the off, but not just for practical reasons. The sheer responsibility of having to look after a newborn baby had worried Hildegard and so having somebody close by who was confident with them and who just got on with it seemed to temper that fear somewhat.

The day we arrived back at Primrose Cottage with Rosalind is one that I shall remember till my dying day. When I got out of the car I opened the back door, lifted Rosalind from the car seat and then passed her to Hildegard. Just then the welcoming committee appeared, comprised of Nick, Hamish and Comedy, Poodle Pants and Tiny Puss. Hamish in particular appeared to be terribly excited by the new arrival and when we allowed him to have a peek at Rosalind, who was fast asleep, he all of a sudden became very quiet and still, as if trying not to wake her. Over the coming weeks and months, Hamish very rarely left Rosalind's side and assumed a very fatherly role. Dogs do that sometimes and Hamish was a marvellous third parent. Of course it is always said a dog gives more than it receives.

After being at home a few days it became apparent that poor Hildegard was suffering from exhaustion. The latter stages of the pregnancy and the birth itself had taken their toll and she seemed to become weaker as time went on. One of the first problems she encountered was sleep – the bane of almost every new parent – and it was at this point our calm au pair came to the rescue.

'If Rosalind wants to sleep, let her!' she advised. 'When she sleeps, you sleep. It's as simple as that.'

Even with the sleep issue sorted, Hildegard was still not operating at full capacity and so I decided to say no to TV, film and theatre for a while and put all my efforts into looking after Hildegard, Rosalind and the animals. At this time I even had to gently entreat Hildegard's friends to give her breathing space; no telephone calls please!

Every morning at about 6 a.m. (which is the middle of the night for an actor) I would leap out of bed, don my pinny, bound downstairs and then set about making cups of tea, feeding animals, bathing babies, lighting fires, walking dogs, kissing cats and watering plants. I was in my element! Once I get going I'm like a whirling dervish and for a good three months or so Primrose Cottage was in an almost constant state of perfect pandemonium. It was effective pandemonium, in that we all got fed and nobody died, but it was pandemonium all the same. Absolute bliss!

Hamish was my right-hand man and when Rosalind was asleep he would follow me about and await instructions. At dinner time, I'd say to Hamish, 'Go and get the cats, boy. Round them up.' He'd then run out into the garden and when he'd found them all he'd issue a series of quick barks. Two minutes later I'd have three hungry cats in the kitchen, all weaving in and out of the table legs waiting for their dinner.

'Now bring me the bowls, boy!' I'd cry. 'Bring 'em here.'

One by one, Hamish would then pick up each bowl in his mouth and carry it over to where I was standing. Then, once I'd finished filling them, he'd carefully put them back on the floor. This boy made Lassie look like a fat bungling amateur.

It was around this time that Hildegard said something to me that completely knocked me for six and made me re-evaluate my entire relationship with animal kind. I'm not sure how the conversation came about but I remember it as if it were yesterday.

'You have quite a romantic relationship with animals, Brian,' she began. 'You like the *idea* of having animals and to a certain extent you follow that through. But there's something quite ritualistic about how you behave with them. It's a quixotic relationship. You don't know anything *about* animals, Brian. You don't understand them. I mean, how could you? Look at Clarence House. How many lions, panthers and ocelots did you house? That's all fine if you want to pretend to be Tarzan, but at the end of the day that was all about you, not them. I don't think you love animals Brian, completely. Not like you say you do.'

At first Hildegard's words cut through me like a knife. I considered myself to be one of life's true animal lovers, yet the more I considered her bombshell the more I realized it to be true. It wasn't that I *didn't* love animals, I just hadn't fully committed and my relationship with them had indeed been partly romantic. The goings-on at Clarence House had, if I was being honest, been as much about me fulfilling a childhood dream as they had been about helping or connecting with animal kind. It was the archetypal rude awakening.

'What if I don't have it in me to really love animals?' I asked her anxiously. 'What if I am just a charlatan?'

'You're no charlatan Brian,' Hildegard reassured me. 'And of course you have it in you. Just listen to them, Brian. Talk to them. Not like you do now. I mean *really* talk to them. Try and connect with them. Don't talk at them.'

Unlike me, Hildegard had been surrounded by animals ever since she was a baby and that was something that had never changed, regardless of where she had lived. She's never claimed to be so, but Hildegard was and still is a true animal lover and from that moment on I began watching her like a hawk. Sure enough, her manner and behaviour were the opposites of my own and on a totally different level. I was very loving and playful with the animals – lots of kisses, fur ruffling and pats on the head, etc. – whereas Hildegard held them in her arms and made eye contact. It was like comparing a couple of old theatrical acquaintances to a mother and son. I cared for them whereas she cared *for* them, if that makes sense. One quite passive and one active. It was a completely different dynamic and what affected me most was how they responded to Hildegard compared with how they responded to me. They responded to me in exactly the same way I treated them; on a fun but ultimately superficial level. I was somebody who took them for walks, patted them on the head and fed them from time to time. Like a favourite uncle or a grandparent. Hildegard, on the other hand, was a parent. They were attentive with her and they trusted her implicitly. Most importantly though, they loved her. That was completely apparent. And why did they love her? Because she loved them unconditionally and they *knew* she did. Many of you reading this will know exactly what I'm talking about and will be no doubt be nodding away like donkeys. That's what animals need, isn't it? In fact, that's what we all need. Unconditional love!

To this day, thanks to Hildegard, I have made it my mission to offer all animals I meet just that. BIG LOVE! Crocodiles don't seem to be all that interested but I can't help that. It works a treat on the rest. What you receive in return is beyond price but that's not why we do it. We do it because it is the right thing to do and because we love them. Am I right? Well of course I bloody am! The fluffy stuff's all good and well but if you want to make an animal feel truly secure you simply must go the extra mile. The upshot from a welfare point of view is that because the relationship is deeper, you are better able to recognize things like illnesses. This has paid dividends in our house over the years and as well as helping to prolong the life of many beloved animals and save them a lot of pain it has kept a multitude of vets in business! I daren't tell you how much I spend on vets' bills every month but my God it's money well spent.

Hildegard's revelatory pep-talk was without doubt one of the most significant conversations I have ever had as it changed my life immeasurably. I will always be incredibly grateful to her.

When Rosalind was about eighteen months old we had a visit from our family doctor. He'd been looking after Hildegard ever since the birth and had once commented on Hamish's devotion to Rosalind.

'It's not healthy having dogs so close to babies,' he'd said. 'They can give her all kinds of diseases. In fact, you should try and keep her away from animals, full stop.'

We took absolutely no notice of the good doctor's counsel, on account of it being complete and utter nonsense, and this was rudely brought home to him during this particular visit. After he'd given Hildegard the once-over I asked him if he'd like to say hello to Rosalind.

'Yes please,' he replied.

'OK. Follow me,' I said. 'She's in the garden.'

The image that greeted us as I opened the back door

makes me smile even to this day. Rosalind, who was sitting right in the middle of the lawn, was holding a large ice cream and was being looked after by Nick and Hamish. The expression on the doctor's face as we stepped out into the garden was one of total disapproval. That quickly changed, however, to one of out-and-out horror when he realized how Rosalind was distributing the ice cream.

Pushing it towards Nick, who was sitting to her left, she said, 'One for you.' Right on cue the dog licked the ice cream and began wagging his tail contentedly. 'And now it's Hamish's turn,' she said, very firmly. 'Here you are Hamish, have a big lick.' With the ice cream no more than about an inch from his mouth Hamish did exactly as he was bade and then wagged his tail, à la Nick. 'And now, one for me!' Rosalind concluded, with an air of cheerful achievement.

The doctor, who was quite pale by this point, politely refused his turn for a lick and removed himself from the premises forthwith. I know it's not everyone's cup of tea sharing food and the like with animals, but we've never come to any harm. Rosalind's still alive and as fit as a butcher's dog.

By this point, Hildegard and I were both back at work and so at last we could try to establish some kind of nor-mality. I say normality, in truth, there was nothing at all normal about our family, and thank heaven for it. Being an actor is hardly a run-of-the-mill profession, and at the time I was also trying to find my feet as a mountaineer and explorer. Find my feet! What an awful pun. We were just beginning to achieve an equilibrium, however, and life couldn't have been more idyllic. I was appearing in all kinds of marvellous things, such as *I, Claudius*, *Space 1999* and *The Basil Brush Show*, in which I portrayed Captain Hook for the very first time.

The great American poet, Henry Wadsworth Longfellow, once said that 'into each life some rain must fall.' Well, not long after finishing an episode of *Space 1999* one day Hildegard and I experienced a bit of a monsoon.

I'd arrived back home from Pinewood Studios full of beans. I adore working there and after completing a good day's filming I'd been itching to get back home and start hugging the hordes. Unfortunately, the sight that met me as I walked through the front door couldn't have been more at odds with the serene one I'd left some hours earlier. Hildegard, who was sitting at the kitchen table, had her head in her hands and was sobbing uncontrollably. As I went to hold her and ask her what was the matter I suddenly saw Hamish lying motionless on the floor just outside the back door. Rosalind was sitting next to him and as she tried to lift his head up I could see that he was dead.

'What on earth has happened?' I asked, turning Hildegard around and then taking her in my arms.

'He was run over,' she said, barely able to speak. 'I ran to him in the road and he just looked at me Brian. He was asking me to help him. Asking me to stop the pain and I couldn't. I couldn't help him. He was terrified Brian. Terrified!'

At that point, Hildegard broke down completely.

Not Hamish, I said to myself, gazing at his lifeless body. He's my right-hand man. My deputy dad. As if in a trance, I ran my hands up and down his body hoping by some miracle to bring him back to life but Hamish was no canine Lazarus. In fact rigor mortis had set in.

Fortunately, Rosalind was far too young to appreciate what was happening and when I picked her up and carried her indoors she whispered, 'Hamish sleeping Daddy. Shh-hhhhhhh.'

'That's right sweetheart,' I said, giving her a big kiss. 'Let's leave him, shall we? Leave him to sleep.'

The following day I dug a grave for Hamish in the corner of the garden. He had adored looking after Rosalind there and for as long as she continued playing in the garden he would be able to carry on caring for her. As I stood holding Hamish, I squeezed him, very gently, one last time. His body was lifeless, of course, but still familiar. I'd probably spent weeks hugging and tickling him over the years and knew every inch of him. After saying my own goodbye I then handed him over to Hildegard. She seemed to have been quite calm just prior to the burial, but as she slowly took his body from me and held it in her arms her tears started flowing and she let out a terrible cry. It was incredibly distressing. She just howled and howled and howled, the sound echoing around Brick Hill.

The one who suffered most in the long term was Nick. He and Hamish had been like bookends ever since they were puppies and had a love like nothing else I'd seen before. Although he couldn't comprehend what had happened, Nick was lost without his friend and spent the rest of his life looking for him. Watching this broke our hearts in two, but instead of standing there sympathizing we had to try and divert his attention and give him something fun to do. To be honest that wasn't too difficult as Nick was so full of fun.

At the end of that year, which would have been 1976, I had to visit the RSPCA one day to get some advice about Nick's eyes. He had an infection of some kind and whenever I had a sick animal and couldn't get hold of a vet I used to pop in and ask for their help. Hildegard and I already had a good relationship with our local branch and would reciprocate by donating money or helping with an appeal. The day I popped in for Nick would have been just after Christmas but the inspector who was on duty was feeling far from festive.

'What's up?' I asked. 'You look fed up.'

'We've had over twenty dogs since Christmas Eve,' lamented the inspector. 'And it isn't even the new year.'

I felt for the poor man.

'It must be demoralizing,' I sympathized.

'It's infuriating!' he countered. 'Last Christmas we had fifteen in total and have managed to rehome all but one. Over twenty is going to take some doing though. And we could end up with thirty.'

'All bar one?' I probed, my heartstrings already beginning to strain slightly.

'That's right. The only one left is Jessie.'

'Well what's wrong with her?' I asked him.

'Nothing,' he replied. 'In fact, she's perfectly fit and healthy.'

'Then why couldn't you rehome her?'

'I'll show you. Follow me.'

With that, the inspector led me towards the kennels and after passing what seemed like a multitude of canine cuties we at last reached the final cubicle.

'This is Jessie,' he said sorrowfully. 'Look at her. Poor old thing.'

There, sitting before the inspector and me, was an animal that looked like a pile of mouldy compost.

'Jesus Christ!' I whispered. 'She looks like me first thing in the morning.'

'Not exactly cute and cuddly, is she?'

'Well, she does have lovely ears. And those eyes. She could melt a thousand glaciers with those.'

'It hasn't worked so far,' said the inspector. 'It's the rest of the body that puts them off!'

It was true though. At first glance Jessie – who was some sort of medium-sized terrier – did indeed look like a relative of Fungus the Bogeyman. Look for a second longer, however, and you could see the real Jessie: A warm, honest animal that was simply crying out for love.

'Do you know,' I said to the dumbfounded inspector. 'I think she's an absolute stunner.'

The longer I stayed in Jessie's company the more she seemed to realize that there was perhaps a chance of her being rehomed and after twenty minutes she was running around her kennel like a whirling dervish. This alone almost broke my heart as she obviously knew what rejection was and had experienced it many times. When Jessie eventually stopped running around in circles, she looked at me beseechingly, her eyes almost crying out in desperation.

'Please take me with you,' she was saying to me. 'Nobody's ever wanted me. Please!'

How could anyone resist that.

'Put her in the back of the car,' I said to the inspector.

'You, my girl,' I added, dropping to my knees and giving Jessie a cuddle and a great big kiss, 'are coming home with me!'

I honestly believe Jessie knew that I'd asked if I could take her and I will always remember her reaction. She was almost rigid with excitement, like a child on Christmas morning, and when the inspector began collecting her toys and her bowl she was all the time chivvying him along. 'Get on with it man! Some of us have a new home to go to!'

When I arrived back at Primrose Cottage, Hildegard immediately came out to meet me.

'What did they say about Nick?' she began. 'Did they give you anything for . . . Good God, what's that on the back seat?'

'This,' I announced, 'is Jessie. The newest member of our family and until about fifteen minutes ago one of the RSPCA's longest-serving residents.'

'Look at those eyes,' cooed Hildegard. 'Let me get Rosalind and the others.'

Jessie fitted into our family seamlessly and it didn't take long for us to realize that as well as being a little bit mad she was also as slow as a tortoise with dodgy knees. Jessie was only capable of four things: eating, sleeping, going to the loo and fetching, and the latter used to have us all in stitches.

Although fetching was Jessie's life, she wasn't very good at it. From the moment she got up in the morning until the moment she went to bed, Jessie would spend her entire day trying to persuade humans to throw things for her. It didn't matter who they were or what they were doing, if they had at least one good arm Jessie would be on at them from the moment they walked through the door. What the poor old thing almost always failed to appreciate, however, was that in order for the popular game of fetch to realize its full dynamic potential and give satisfaction to those participating, the object that is being propelled must be of sufficient weight and size to A) reach a distance that is worth pursuing, and B) be visible to whoever – or whatever – is doing the throwing. Unfortunately, Jessie continually failed to grasp this point and so rarely got past first base.

I remember a plumber came to do some work one day and from the moment he arrived Jessie was by his side.

'I've always had a way with dogs,' he proclaimed, almost bursting with pride. 'I don't know what it is but they just seem to love me. Look at this one here. Can't take her eyes off me.'

What the plumber didn't realize was that at his feet was a piece of wood about two inches long that had been put there by Jessie and that all she wanted him to do was pick it up and throw it. She wasn't saying 'You're marvellous and I love you.' She was saying 'For heaven's sake, throw the bloody stick!'

'She certainly has taken to you,' I concurred. 'I've never seen her like this before. It must be love at first sight.'

If we had a guest in the house I'd always give them a stick to throw, but if it was a paying guest – as in me paying them – I'd always keep my mouth shut and claim that she was besotted with them. The tradesmen got a bit of an ego boost and I got a smaller bill.

Jessie even used to leave bits of cardboard, silver paper and leaves at people's feet and would pester their lives out to throw an object that half the time people couldn't even see. She was so adorable, though, and so full of love that no one minded her obsessive behaviour.

5

THE COUNTRY BUMPKIN

Although we've started a nice new chapter there's a quick tale about Jessie I simply must tell you. I can't believe I've only just remembered it!

A month or so after she arrived at Primrose Cottage I had to go away filming for a few days. According to Hildegard, this had unsettled Jessie somewhat as she had already become quite devoted to me, and I to her. Subsequently, the very next evening when I phoned home the first thing I said to Hildegard was, 'How's Jessie?'

'You mean Jessie and her seven pups,' Hildegard replied quite casually.

'I beg your bloody pardon,' I replied. 'Seven pups? But how?'

'How do you think? She was obviously pregnant when you adopted her.'

'The randy little madam. I didn't think they allowed that sort of thing at the RSPCA. And I thought she might have problems finding a boyfriend!'

When I returned home the following evening I was

excited to see Jessie and her new brood. 'Where are they?' I whispered as I came through the front door.

'They're in the bathroom,' said Hildegard shaking her head.

'What are they doing in the bathroom?' I asked, still in hushed tones.

'That's where she decided to have them. Probably because it's warm.'

Although I was now quite used to co-habiting with various different species, the one thing I had not encountered thus far was a litter of any kind. My God, I was excited. It was like Rosalind arriving all over again, just with far less travelling and fewer people.

By the time we reached the bathroom door I was quite literally bubbling over with excitement. If memory serves I was even doing a little dance.

'Now look, Brian,' Hildegard said, 'Jessie's doing well but she's a bit nervous. She needs quiet and calm so behave yourself.'

This talk often happened just prior to events requiring either tact, composure or sensitivity, and I always tried to pay attention.

Satisfied that I wasn't going to make a Tarzan call or start swinging from the light fitting, Hildegard slowly opened the door to the bathroom. I will never, ever forget the sight that greeted me. It was nature at its magnificent best: a doting mother and her beautiful new brood. As soon as Jessie saw me at the door she immediately began wagging her tail, and if I'd had a tail I'd have done the same for her. Instead, Jessie had to make do with the broadest of smiles and a few words of congratulation.

'Now then, you randy old tramp,' I cooed, and then slowly knelt down in front of them. 'Aren't you going to introduce me to your little ones then? They're stunners, aren't they?'

For a few moments she covered her pups protectively. With great care, I went to stroke Jessie and the moment my hand touched her fur I could feel her start to relax. 'There we are old girl,' I whispered. 'All I want to do is give you a big hug and a great big kiss. Well done, Jessie. Well done.'

Within minutes I was knee-deep in puppies. I cuddled them, rolled around on the floor with them, showered them with kisses and even sang them all silly songs. I do believe a tear or two might have made an appearance, but I couldn't say for sure. Once again I was a father, and as I sat cross-legged amid the litter like a large bearded Buddha, I had pride and euphoria seeping from my pores. Life was very much affirmed that day, I can tell you. Just a few weeks earlier, Jessie had been nothing more than an unwanted peculiarity; enduring rejection on an almost daily basis. And now look at her. She was in her own home tending to her brood and was simply wallowing in love and hair. Just like me.

Once her little rascals became mobile we decided to build a small enclosure for them and sat Rosalind in there with them. Naturally she was in seventh heaven being set upon by seven miniature licking machines and the only noises you ever heard emanating from the pen were high-pitched barks, giggles and squeals of unbridled delight. She'd normally need a new dress after being in with the puppies but my God it was worth every stitch.

Once word got around that Jessie had given birth to a litter we had visitors by the dozen, not to mention offers of homes for the pups – which had all taken after their adoptive father and were pretty little things. It seemed that everyone in Brick Hill wanted to have one of Jessie's young 'uns and the fact that they'd all remain local was just marvellous. Like all litters, each one had its own unique character and after watching their personalities develop for a while we named them all accordingly. One of the puppies I remember most was Walter the Waiter, so called because all he ever did was wait by doors, for some inexplicable reason. The one we kept for ourselves was named Bonzo, although I can't remember why. Perhaps it was after the Bonzo Dog Doo-Dah Band? He was black and white and loveable.

By now I was beginning to see myself as a bit of a country bumpkin. Not a squire or a lord of the manor – I hail from far too big a gene pool. I was more of a Pop Larkin really, with a hint of Heathcliff. We may have been just a few hundred metres from the M3 and only a few miles from Londinium, but Brick Hill seemed as pastoral as the Yorkshire Dales and all I saw before me was countryside. I simply revelled in it. It's been the same ever since.

One of my great joys at the time was growing vegetables and with a little bit of land at my disposal I was hell-bent on becoming a bona fide 'son of the soil'. Self-sufficiency was becoming quite popular then, what with *The Good Life* and what have you, and I'd often heard that there was something incredibly satisfying about growing your own produce. And, of course, eating it. In fact, if you've got enough room for a vegetable patch in your garden but don't have one, why not sow yourself a turnip or two? You won't regret it. Get out there and dig, you masters of time and space.

You remember I said earlier that when I do something I tend to give it my all? Well, growing my own veg was certainly no exception and after planting as much as I possibly could in my patch at Primrose Cottage I went in search of fresh fallow. Fortunately, one of our neighbours, a delightful lady in her seventies named Mrs Millard, had a very large vegetable garden which she wasn't able to utilize and so she very kindly offered me half.

'Grow whatever you like there, Mr Blessed,' she said, in that delightful Surrey dialect. 'It's good ground, especially for tayters.'

This was music to my ears! I probably burn at least 12,000 calories a day and so carbohydrates are an essential fuel for the Blessed combustion engine.

'Thank you, Mrs Millard,' I boomed, taking her hand and planting a great big kiss on it. 'And if you ever need any help tending your half, you just let me know.'

What a mistake that was.

Mrs Millard, who was obviously after a free gardener, took me up on my offer and had me running around like a slightly less buxom Charlie Dimmock. No matter though. It was a small price to pay for being able to grow my own spuds and it was a good arrangement.

Mrs Millard lived two doors down from Primrose Cottage and in the middle was Mad May. To get to Mrs Millard's I would have to pass through Mad May's garden and some days she'd come out for a chat. I swear on my life that I could never understand a single word May said as her indigenous drawl was the broadest of them all, and the fact that she spoke at about 200 words a minute didn't help matters. After clambering over the hedge that separated us I'd then creep towards the other side of Mad May's garden as quietly and quickly as I could. Please don't come out, please don't come out, please don't come out, I used to say to myself as I scurried along with my head bowed.

Nine times out of bloody ten she'd see me and if May was in the mood for a natter I'd had it. She would be an hour at least. I would smile and nod and shake my head sympathetically and think to myself, *Ah this is karma and will score me points for the next life*. After all, one must be aware that we often meet angels unknown.

Sometimes, when I'd finished avoiding May or was tired of digging potatoes, I'd pop in to see old Miss Snooks, whose garden backed on to ours. She was the one with the trench coat that was done up with a safety pin, remember? Miss Snooks was one of life's true eccentrics and although she was clearly a hardy old girl there was something quite vulnerable about her. She was a total recluse and was frightfully shy. The reception I used to receive when I arrived at her cottage was distrusting to say the least and she would simply curl up in a ball. No matter. She was on her own and had no family so I felt it my duty to make sure she was OK. When he was delivering coal to Primrose Cottage in the winter, I would always ask Roy Tedder to leave me a few extra bags and then once or twice a week I'd take some down to Miss Snooks' cottage and leave them by her fire.

As I said, Miss Snooks barely said a word to me during these visits but instead of me assuming that her behaviour was that of a rude old lady, I always got the impression that the company of others simply made her feel uncomfortable and that expressing herself did not come naturally. She was frightened, not ill-mannered. Everybody has a past, of course, and I always had an unfortunate feeling that Miss Snooks' was a sad one. I certainly didn't enjoy making her feel uncomfortable in her own home, but you should have seen the state of the place. There was a hole in her roof that must have measured a foot square and in the winter of 1977 – probably late January – I had to insist on her allowing me to mend it. The cottage, which was all one level, only had a bedroom, a sitting room with a galley kitchen, and a bathroom, and because the hole was in the living area Miss Snooks was in danger of either drowning or freezing to death, or both.

'I'm sorry, Miss Snooks,' I said to her. 'I'll be as quick as I can but I'm afraid I have to mend this roof. Here's two bags of coal. I'll fix the roof, make a fire, and then I'll leave you alone.'

Any excuse to light a fire! If you ever see me carrying some kindling stop me and I'll show you what to do.

A few months later, in the spring, just after Rosalind's second birthday, we unfortunately experienced what is any parent's worst possible nightmare. Rosalind had appeared at the back door one morning and had said to Hildegard, who was busy feeding the dogs, 'I'm just going for a walk Mummy. I won't be long.' Hildegard thought absolutely nothing of this as Rosalind often informed us that she was going for a walk. Normally this would comprise of a few laps around the back garden but unbeknownst to Hildegard she planned on going further afield this time. A few minutes later, when Hildegard went to find Rosalind and bring her back inside she was nowhere to be seen. I was in the living room at the time reading a script and I can remember clear as day Hildegard calling to me.

'Brian, come quickly. I can't find Rosalind!'

'What do you mean? I saw her go into the kitchen about ten minutes ago or so.'

'She said she was going for a walk and I assumed it was around the garden. I've just been outside and I can't find her anywhere.'

Within a couple of minutes Hildegard, myself and our best friend, Mavis Smith, were all scouring the area trying to find Rosalind. Many of you reading this will have experienced something similar, and I hope to God that whoever went missing was found safe and sound. It induces the most incredibly powerful thoughts and emotions and the longer she was missing the worse they became. It was almost overwhelming.

As word got around that Rosalind had disappeared more and more people began to join in the search and one of the first to volunteer was Miss Snooks.

'Is it true your baby's gone missing?' she enquired. It was the longest sentence I'd ever heard her speak.

'I'm afraid it is, Miss Snooks,' I replied.

'Well don't you worry, 'coz I'm going to find her, alright?'

'Thank you, Miss Snooks,' I said. 'Thank you.'

It's funny but when she said she'd find Rosalind she was so resolute that I somehow believed her.

About fifteen minutes later Miss Snooks, who'd gone searching down one of the lanes with the heroic Mavis, was true to her word and delivered Rosalind back to us safe and well. In fact it was earth mother Mavis who found her sitting under a bush but the brave Miss Snooks was by her side. It was such a special moment. Our beautiful yet increasingly intrepid daughter was safe, and as well as our wonderful neighbours coming to our aid and reminding us how lucky we were to be part of such a close-knit community, Miss Snooks, who none of us really knew, but who we cared about deeply, seemed to have come out of her shell a bit. It was a good day, she actually smiled.

The next addition to the Blessed menagerie – or should I say, additions – arrived while I was making *The Little World of Don Camillo* for the BBC (it was all filmed in the

Po Valley in Italy by the way). What a fine series that was. Have you seen it? It's yet to be released on DVD for some reason but it was very well received when it came out and was great fun to make. It's based on the books by Giovannino Guareschi and tells the story of a local Catholic priest who is at loggerheads with a bombastic incumbent Communist mayor. I played said mayor, who is called Peppone, and the whole thing is an absolute riot. The Italians are very good at writing comedy, especially satire and farce, but in a scene in *Don Camillo* they took the phrase 'toilet humour' rather too literally, as while Peppone is standing outside Don Camillo's house one evening, causing a rumpus, the priest pours the entire contents of his commode out of his window and straight onto the mayor's head!

Anyway. During a week-long break in filming I was walking towards Sunningdale Golf Course one day when suddenly I heard a very loud meowing sound somewhere in the distance. Given the number of cats in the area I normally wouldn't have paid attention, but whatever was generating the noise was obviously in distress and so I immediately went in search of its source. As far as I could make out it was coming from the vicinity of a small track situated next to the bridge that stretches over the M3. It's only a few metres long and is lined with one or two trees.

Further investigation revealed that underneath one of these trees was a large white box. As I approached the abandoned container I heard the now familiar meowing sound once again, but it certainly wasn't coming from the box. It was coming from the tree. I looked up and there crouched on a branch before me was a black and white cat. The poor little mite looked petrified, but before I could do anything to assist it, my attention was diverted back to the box. It was now moving slightly and I started hearing some higher-pitched versions of the sounds my new friend had been making. *It must be kittens*, I thought to myself. Sure enough, when I slowly opened the lid of the box I discovered a litter of five perfect miniature moggies. The cat up the tree was a male, so perhaps he was the father? Whatever he was, some bastard had obviously abandoned the lot of them and so before I could draw another breath I put the cat under my arm, picked up the box and took them all straight home. What on earth possesses somebody to do something like that? You probably know what I'd do with them. It involves a chin, and my bloody fist!

Fortunately, the litter and the fully grown cat were all given a clean bill of health from the vet and so the moment he had gone we set about making them all feel at home. We named the adult cat Peppone, which only seemed right, and what a cheeky little burglar he turned out to be. Yes, I said burglar. We obviously knew nothing of his background, but it was as though he had been delivered by Raffles himself. He was fed at home the same as any domestic cat. In fact, with my propensity to throw scraps from the table and administer treats every five minutes, he was probably on at least half as much again. That didn't matter though. If we left anything out in the kitchen, whether it be sausages, fish, bacon or even cheese, Peppone would have it. He wasn't daft enough to eat it there and then, however. Oh no, he'd just pick it up and take it outside somewhere. He reminded me of Cousin Wildcat in the Brer Rabbit stories.

After he'd got to know the surrounding area a bit better he started waging war upon our neighbours' larders and in next to no time had become a one-cat crime epidemic. He was a nightmare! If any one of our neighbours ever left a window ajar while they were out shopping or what have you, he'd be in there like a rat up a drain pipe. Complaints came in almost daily but what on earth could we do? Send him to a correctional facility? The problem was that if Peppone couldn't find any food in the house he'd take a nice leisurely tour instead and because he was such a clumsy oaf he'd always end up knocking over a vase or something. The heightened sense of awareness that felines are so famous for always seemed to desert him on these occasions and although Peppone was never caught in the act, so to speak, he was often seen making his escape from the premises.

'Mr Blessed! That cat of yours has had it away with my Harry's dinner again.'

'Has he! Just you wait till I get hold of him. I'm so sorry! Have a turnip.'

Whenever I saw him after one of these visits I'd give him a comical telling off.

The looks he gave me back always seemed to say the same thing: 'I hear what you're saying governor, but to be quite honest with you I enjoy rampaging in people's kitchens.'

Come to think of it, I should have renamed him Macavity from *Old Possum's Book of Practical Cats*.

Despite now being a bona fide son of the soil, I was also one of the known universe's most popular actors – thank God I am modest – and so adaptability was my byword. That and booming! One day I'm a vegetable farmer, sowing sprouts and chewing straw, and the next I'm on horseback as King Richard IV shouting things like, 'Let blood, blood, BLOOD be your motto. Slit their gizzards!' at Peter Cook, which I did for several episodes of *Blackadder*. It was quite a contrast, but not an unwelcome one.

I wasn't the only one being offered work at Primrose Cottage. Hildegard was too. And therein lay a bit of a problem. If Hildegard and I were ever away simultaneously, who would look after the animals? Young Rosalind would be cared for by the nanny, so that was a relief. But what about our menagerie? Mavis from up the road was always happy to help, but asking her to do more than a few hours just seemed unfair. Looking after one dog can take it out of you, but three dogs and nine cats? That's a job for a professional. Or a nutcase. There was only one thing for it: If Mohammed couldn't look after the mountains, the mountains would have to come to work with Mohammed.

After thinking it through and then making a few enquiries I ended up buying a second-hand caravanette, together with an old Ford Cortina. From now on, the animals and I would be mobile, and if work required me to be away for a few days, there'd be nothing at all to worry about. Well, not for me or the animals at least. The Cortina, which I purchased from a neighbour, was older than Methuselah, but he assured me that with a whack in the right place, it was guaranteed to start.

'See this rubber hammer?' he said. 'Well, before you try and start the engine you must always remember to hit the car with the rubber hammer, just here.'

With that the hopeful vendor hit the car alongside its engine.

'What does that do?' I asked him.

'It will get the bristles rotating. The bloke I bought it off told me to do it and I've been whacking it ever since. Hasn't let me down yet.'

'Well, if it's good enough for you and the last bloke,' I assured him, 'it's good enough for me.'

And with that I shook the man warmly by the hand and then gave him the five pounds he was asking. He was right though. It may well have been a bit of a banger, that old Cortina, but it kept going for years.

When it came to the caravanette, once again I ended up going to a neighbour. This chap used to deal in them so I was well looked after. When I told him what I wanted it for he howled with laughter.

'You're not going to sleep with them all in there, are you?' he said aghast.

'If I have to, yes,' I replied resolutely.

'I don't know who to feel most sorry for,' concluded the merchant. 'You or the animals.'

'We don't need your sympathy,' I laughed. 'Just a script, a codpiece, some grub and the open road!'

It was true. The animals and I had an absolute ball on the road together and ended up journeying the length and breadth of the entire country. So content were we in our charabanc, in fact, that even when at home I would drive us all up to Chobham Common so that we could alight a while and frolic collectively. I didn't always take the younger cats, as they may well have gone wandering off, but I still had Nick, Jessie, Bonzo, Poodle Pants, Tiny Puss, Comedy and Peppone with me. Just the seven, in all. What a sight we must have looked, tearing down the motorway on our way to yet another fabulous starring role. The cats and I in the Cortina looking like something out of the *Wacky Races*, and the dogs in the caravanette, sticking their heads out of the window so that whenever I looked in a wing mirror all I could see were flapping tongues. It was bliss and God was in his heaven. Halcyon days!

I think we had the caravanette for about eight years in all and one of the most memorable trips I ever took in it was in 1983. I'd decided to surprise Hildegard with two Labrador puppies called Willie and Benji. These two tearaways obviously couldn't be left on their own and so the caravanette was used more than ever. God only knows what it must have smelt like! I think Hildegard and I had become immune!

Willie was a yellow Labrador, by the way, who was

delightfully thick, and Benji, who was black, liked to swim all the time and was as quick as lightning.

Anyway, the journey in question was only twenty-five miles and involved a casting at Pinewood Studios. Rosalind was at school by this point, which was a blessing, but with Hildegard away filming I still had the welfare of six dogs and three cats to consider. Mavis wasn't around unfortunately and so after exhausting every other avenue there was only one thing for it, the lot of them would have to come with me.

I'll tell you what, while we're here, shall we have a bit of a roll call? Just to refresh your memory? Yes, why not! Well, we had the aforementioned Willie and Benji, of course, who thought going away with all the big boys and girls was the best thing ever. Then we had Jessie and her brood, who were all now grown up. The three who'd stayed with us were Bonzo, Walter the Waiter and Sheila. I haven't mentioned Sheila yet but she was a very loving dog who specialized in cuddles and big licks. She was a carbon copy of her mum, really, but with less matted hair! Last but not least we had Nick, of course, who, despite being very elderly, was still able to clamber aboard the caravanette and keep order. God bless him.

Up front with me were Poodle Panties, Tiny Puss and Peppone, who couldn't be left alone under any circumstances!

Now, a fifty-mile round trip might not seem like much but with ten animals in tow it can get a bit complicated.

The journey up to Pinewood was jolly to say the least.

The dogs, when they weren't furiously barking at passers-by, were all trying to push their heads out of the windows. I think they thought they were going for a walk. The cats, on the other hand, simply meowed a great deal and periodically relieved themselves around my person.

The casting in question was for a new major television series called *The Last Days of Pompeii*, which eventually starred Laurence Olivier and Ernest Borgnine and many other big stars, and it had a budget of many millions. Luckily for me, the two people in charge of casting it, Lesley De Pettit and Maude Spector, both knew me of old and when they saw me standing in the doorway in my gardening gear neither batted an eyelid.

'Brian! Thank God it's you,' said Lesley De Pettit. She sounded absolutely exasperated and poor Maude Spector looked almost in tears.

'What the matter?' I asked. 'And what's up with that lot?'

Sitting on some sofas at the other end of the office were a succession of actors and actresses – some of whom I knew – and about half of them were in a state of shock.

'It's the producer, David Gerber,' began Maud. 'Columbia have sent him to oversee casting and he's being very difficult. He's virtually murdered every single actor or actress he's seen so far and is treating Lesley and me appallingly.'

David Gerber was one of the biggest names at Columbia Television and I think they even have a statue of him outside their studio. He had won endless Golden Globes and Emmys.

'I want you to go in there, Brian,' continued Lesley de Pettit, 'and I want you to thump him on the chin and knock him out.'

'I can't do that, Lesley,' I said, a bit taken aback. 'Basically I am a gentle soul. Can I go in now?'

'I don't see why not,' said Lesley. 'He's a bit deaf so you might have to shout. Give him hell though, Brian! Honestly, he's been rude to everybody. Actors have been leaving in droves, absolutely traumatized.'

With that she pointed to the door leading to Gerber's office and after giving it a quick knock, I entered.

'Afternoon, Mr Gerber,' I boomed. 'My name is Brian Blessed. According to the girls out there you've been insulting everybody who's walked through your door. Can you hear me because apparently you are a bit deaf?'

Mr Gerber, who was sitting in his chair, looked shell-shocked. I think it's safe to say that he hadn't encountered anybody like me before.

'In all my years as a producer, nobody has ever talked to me like that before, Mr Blessed,' he said.

All of a sudden, a look of surprise and recognition began to light up his face.

'Oh my God,' he said gazing at me. 'I don't believe it.'

'Don't believe what?' I said.

'Where are my eagles?' he said. 'WHERE ARE MY EAGLES!'

'What are you talking about,' I asked, becoming quite bemused.

'WHERE ARE MY GODDAM EAGLES! YOU WERE AUGUSTUS CAESAR IN *I, CLAUDIUS*!'

'Aaaah,' I said. 'Now I get you! Yes that was me.'

I, Claudius had been a huge hit in America and at the end of one episode, after losing a battle, I shout to a messenger, 'Tell Quintilius Varus, WHERE ARE MY EAGLES!' Which, of course, feature on the Roman standard.

Suddenly Mr Gerber and I were the best of friends and his testy belligerence faded away.

'I can't tell you how many times I have watched that show, Mr Blessed,' he said. 'You British can't make films for toffee, but when it comes to television, well, you're just about the best there is.'

I decided to let him off the film comment, as I could tell that he was about to offer me some money.

'I'd like you to play the senator and Governor of Pompeii for me, Mr Blessed. How does £50,000 sound?'

'I can't play the senator,' I said. 'For a start, he's fat and it'd mean me having to shave my beard off. No, no, no. I'd be perfect for Olinthus, a cross between Samson and St Peter. I'd be great in that part.'

'Oh, I agree, Mr Blessed. That part could have been written for you. The problem is that it has already been offered to Gregory Peck.'

'Well, in that case I'm afraid I can't help you,' I said, and then got up to leave.

Mr Gerber's jaw dropped. 'You mean you're going to turn down £50,000?' he said incredulously.

'I don't want to play a fat man, and that's that. Sorry. It's Olinthus or bust!'

Mr Gerber was now in full-on panic mode.

'It's out of my hands, Mr Blessed. The backers want Peck and I can't overrule that.'

'But you're the number one bigshot,' I replied passionately.

'I know, Mr Blessed,' he said, 'but the backers decide everything. Jesus, I wish it was otherwise.'

As I walked down the side of his office towards my mobile menagerie, the rest of Mr Gerber's round windows began opening, his head poking out of each in turn like a succession of identical busybodies as he tried to persuade me to play the senator. The trouble was that just a few metres away the dogs had their heads out of the caravanette windows and were barking madly. I couldn't hear a damn thing! They wanted me to give them a walk and Mr Gerber wanted me to play a morbidly obese Greek politician. I'd never felt as wanted in all my life!

The journey home was far less eventful, thank God, as not long after feeding the animals they all quietened down and went to sleep. Even so, my day was far from over. In fact, I had a performance to get to. I was playing Old Deuteronomy in Andrew Lloyd Webber's musical *Cats* at the time and had to get back, clean up, and get to the West End.

A week or so later I received a telephone call from Mr

Gerber. Gregory Peck had turned down the role of Olinthus and so it was mine if I wanted it.

'How the hell did you manage to persuade them, Mr Gerber?' I asked him.

I was under no illusions, ladies and gentlemen. The backers wanted a big film star and that wasn't me. I was a good all-rounder, but not a film star.

'With great difficulty,' he replied.

A few months later I was talking to that marvellous actor Ned Beatty, who ended up playing the senator in the *Last Days of Pompeii*. He had heard Mr Gerber suggesting me as Olinthus to one of the backers one day and the conversation had had Ned in stitches. He had been chatting to Mr Gerber on the telephone about something and when the backer had entered the office Ned had been asked to go on hold, except that Mr Gerber had obviously failed to press the right button. I'm paraphrasing now, but the conversation went something like this:

Backer: Who do you suggest for Olinthus now that Peck's not interested?

Gerber: I'd like to suggest Brian Blessed.

Backer: Who the hell is Brian Blessed?

Gerber: He's a British actor.

Backer: Never heard of him. What role's he playing at the moment?

Gerber: He's playing a cat.

Backer: A what?

Gerber: A cat.

Backer: Let me get this right. As a replacement for

Gregory Peck, one of the biggest film stars of all time, you want me to suggest an unknown British actor who is currently pretending to be a cat?

Gerber: Erm. Yes.

How the hell Gerber managed it I'll never know, but I'm damn glad he did. It was a marvellous role and for once I ended up playing the hero! And the role ended up coming with a salary of £100,000, which in those days was big money.

Anyway, by this time we also had Hildegard's mother living with us, and, despite the age-old cliché, we actually got on very well together. Josie was her name and what a fantastic woman she was; tremendously clever. A real powerhouse! She always lived life to the full and had a voice that could take bark off the trees. She was like a female version of me I suppose. She was as deaf as a post too, bless her, and moved over here from South Africa when Hildegard's father passed away. Josie used to suffer awfully with the hot weather and so it seemed like the sensible thing to do. We gave her a nice room, stuck a gigantic TV in it, and she was as happy as Larry. Tennis or Rugby Union was her thing and so back then it was BBC 2 all the way. I've never known anybody get so excited by a tennis or rugby match as Josie. One minute she'd be sitting there silently glued, and the next she'd be on her knees screaming at the umpire or whoever it was who'd incurred her considerable wrath.

Although she was full of spunk, Josie wasn't a particularly well woman and every four or five months or so she would have a seizure, during which her heart would pack up. Fortunately I was always around when this happened and discovered a technique that would get her going again in next to no time. I say discovered. In actual fact it was all instinct really.

The first time it happened at Primrose Cottage Josie was in her bedroom. I was in the kitchen juggling some cats when all of a sudden I heard an almighty thud. Quick as a flash I raced into Josie's room where I found her lying on the floor doing the death rattle. I'd seen this before and I knew I hadn't long. I also knew Josie had a heart condition, so without any further ado I picked her up by the legs, so she was hanging upside down, and I started shaking her like you would a duvet that you're trying to get into its cover. Don't ask me why I did this. I just did!

'LIVE JOSIE,' I demanded. 'LIVE!'

Anyway, after shaking her for a while and ordering her not to die, I lifted her onto her bed and began giving her what's known as an external cardiac massage. This is quite different to the usual CPR and is performed by an exertion of pressure and relaxation on the chest bone, at the rate of about 100 per minute It's pretty extreme stuff but it works and within a couple of minutes she was back with us. Once her organ was pumping again I went to the kitchen and made her some very strong black coffee with spoonfuls of brown sugar. Once again, this was done through instinct, but after pouring some of it down her neck she immediately sat up.

My beautiful pond,
home to my collection
of Koi carp . . .

. . . until the Great Duck
Invasion. I don't know
where they came from but
they were here to stay.

This was taken in 1990 prior to my Everest expedition.
The dogs, from left to right, are Willy, Bodger, Peanut, Benji and Suzy.

Ducks! They got everywhere.

Duke, who liked to give me a nip!
He looks as if he's about to go
for my ankles again.

Stephen Gittings, my agent, who's animal-crackers,
riding a horse called Hud. You can see Buffy lurking.

Rosalind aged fourteen.

My old Exmoor pony, Poppet.

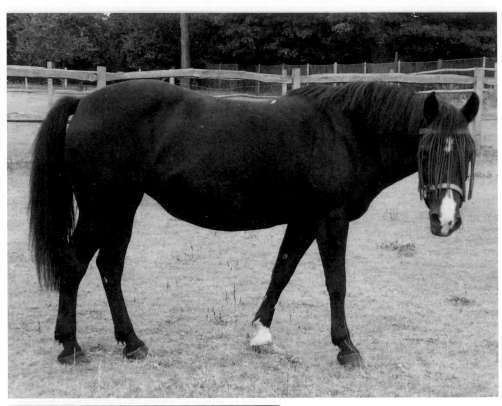

Rosalind's horse Bessie.

Tilly, who was abandoned
near our house.

Bodger, who was brought
to us in a terrible state.

Duke after the food.

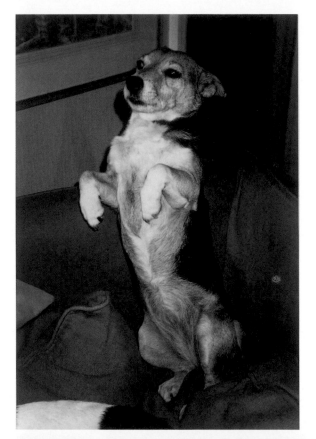

Suzy, who was always
Hildegard's dog.

With my friend
Virginia McKenna.

A life-affirming encounter with Baby the elephant.

Misty, who lit up my soul.

In my cabin with Misty,
discussing Buzz Aldrin.

Misty liked to pee on the statue
of Buddha every morning.

'Oh I thought I was a goner. Brian, you have amazing hands? What's on BBC 2?'

After a couple of years I had this ritual off to a tee.

One of the things that used to make me laugh most about my marvellous and clever mother-in-law, and believe me there were quite literally hundreds, was that she refused to believe that Dame Edna Everage and Les Patterson were A) the same person, and B) fictional characters. It didn't matter what we said or how we said it, she was having none of it. And my God, did she hate Les Patterson.

'You're talking rubbish, Brian,' she used to say. 'How can that disgusting looking man also be such a beautiful woman. It's impossible.'

'But that's not a woman at all, Josie. It's Barry Humphries! He's a comedian.'

'I don't believe you, Brian,' she responded.

Years later after Josie had passed away we were asked by the RSPCA to house a Yorkshire terrier called Bobo. She too had a bit of a dickie ticker and the first time it gave out on us I decided to give her the Josie treatment. I picked her up by her hind legs, shook her about a bit, put her on the bed and then massaged her chest. The only thing I didn't do was give her the black coffee! It worked though and had I been a fully paid-up Buddhist I'd have believed she was Josie II.

While we're on the subject of the BBC, which we were, just a moment ago, they once put me on the brink of a full-blown acoustic catastrophe one day thanks to a last-minute change in scheduling. Allow me to elucidate.

We're going to have to jump in my time machine briefly as this took place in about 1978, although the scene is still Primrose Cottage – the living room, to be exact – and it was late afternoon. Rosalind and her chums were sitting on the sofa waiting for their favourite television programme to start and as Hildegard was out shopping, I was in charge. The television programme in question was *Paddington*, which I also used to enjoy. As the start time neared an air of anticipation gripped the room. The children's legs, which were dangling over the front of the sofa, began to waggle like dogs' tails and as the previous programme came to an end the enthusiastic toddlers started nattering about what was to come. They were about three years old.

'Due to the late running of our previous programme,' said the continuity announcer, 'I am afraid we will be unable to show *Paddington* today. But don't worry children, he'll be back tomorrow."

I looked at the girls, they looked at me, and then we all looked at the television again. The silence that greeted the announcement was deafening, but not nearly so as the cacophony that followed it. As the realisation that Paddington wasn't coming out to play gradually hit home, bottom lips starting quivering like small pieces of jelly, heads went back, and after what looked like a giant collective breath, the grieving infants began to wail. But these were no ordinary wails. They were the kind of shrieks and howls that only wronged toddlers can produce.

'WAAAAAAAAAAAAAAAAAAAAAAAAAAAAAAAA AAAAAAAH!'

It was impossible to comfort them.

'Don't worry girls,' I said desperately, '*Paddington* will be back tomorrow, just like the man said. There's no need to cry.'

Not surprisingly, my words of comfort held no comfort at all and only seemed to add to their grief.

The looks I received too, were like daggers in my chest. I was the devil incarnate!

'WAAAAAAAAAAAAAAAAAAAAAAAAAAAAAAA AAAAAAAH!'

In a fit of desperation I called up the BBC and asked to speak to the Director General. I remember the phone number was Shepherd's Bush 2000.

'This is an emergency,' I said. 'It's Brian Blessed and I simply must speak to him.'

Fortunately I knew the DG, a chap called Ian Trethowan, quite well and when his secretary eventually put me through I came straight to the point.

'Can you hear that, Ian?' I asked, pointing the receiver towards the girls. 'That is the sound of several toddlers mourning the loss of an episode of *Paddington*. BBC 1 said they couldn't broadcast it because they were running over and this is the upshot. I've got three-year-olds who are heartbroken. You simply MUST help me!'

'Calm down, Brian, calm down. I'll see what I can do.'

I forget which programme was on, but after it had finished I sat there literally praying for *Paddington* to start. The girls were still inconsolable and it was heart-breaking.

After whatever it was had finished we were once again treated to the calming tones of the continuity announcer.

'Well, boys and girls, it seems that we are able to bring you that episode of *Paddington* after all, so here he is now.'

'OH, THANK GOD FOR THAT!' I sighed, as a beautiful calm descended on the room.

The girls were transfixed by Paddington, as was I. Of course his programme only lasted for five minutes, during which time, as far as I can recall, he simply made some toast and spread a bit of marmalade on. The little ones loved it.

Not long after we finished filming *The Last Days of Pompeii*, which is an absolute cracker, he said modestly, my time in *Cats* also came to an end. I'd been starring in this fabulous show ever since it first opened but after two-and-a-bit years playing Old Deuteronomy I really needed a rest. How the hell they managed to keep me interested for so long I will never know, but being part of such a groundbreaking production is something I will always be tremendously proud of.

On my last night in the show the company presented me with, what else, but a cat! They all knew that I was animal crackers and after spending over two years pretending to be one, what else could they possibly give me? The feline in question was an absolutely ginormous Angora and, because he looked like one, we decided to call him Rug.

But Rug wasn't the only animal to accompany me from the stage door of the New London Theatre in 1983. He was certainly the most corpulent, but he was by no means the first. That particular accolade went to a completely deaf Jack Russell who, as well as being a snappy little devil, had one red iris and one blue. Peanut had been wandering around the dressing rooms for months and the more I got to know her the more I fell in love with her.

She belonged to a colleague of mine called Jeff Shankley, and because of her age Peanut could no longer be left at home. Jeff, who is lovely man and a wonderfully gifted actor of great repute, played the part of Munkustrap in the show and used to enjoy teasing me about my rather ungainly shape.

'My word, you are quite a size,' he'd say during rehearsals. 'Trevor, would you mind asking Brian to stand at the back on his own please. If he moves he's in danger of knocking us all over.'

Cheeky sod! How he's still working I'll never know.

Jeff lived in a houseboat on the Thames and poor Peanut, who was also partially blind, had started falling in all the bloody time. Jeff was in despair, bless him, and so as opposed to him having to drag Peanut around with him all the time I offered her a home at Primrose Cottage.

Because Peanut was deaf she only reacted to physical gestures and over the years Jeff had developed a kind of doggy sign language. It was terribly clever and before I took Peanut home with me I asked him to produce a dictionary for me. They had signs for everything: jumping up, lying down, walkies, going to bed, and even one for fetching Jeff's newspaper. My favourite was the one to stop Peanut barking. You simply put your hands over your ears!

Instead of informing Hildegard that I had accepted yet another lodger, I decided to leave it as a surprise. Or a shock. I wasn't sure exactly. But I was confident that love would find a way and as I walked into the living room with Peanut in my arms I couldn't have wished for a more amusing, and ultimately enthusiastic reaction. Hildegard had been trying to watch television for the past hour but had been constantly interrupted by the dogs. By the time Peanut and I neared entering the room she was in full voice, and, it appeared, on the edge of a nervous breakdown.

'No Jessie! I am not throwing cardboard now. And will you all stop sitting in front of the television! Oh, for heaven's sake.'

'Hildegard,' I said quietly, poking my head around the door. 'I think I have exactly what you need.'

As she turned around and caught sight of Peanut her visage changed from a maddened matriarch to a besotted dog lover.

'Awwwwwww,' she said holding out her arms. 'Tell me she's staying, Brian.'

After breathing an enormous sigh of relief I confirmed Peanut's status as the newest member of the Blessed family and as the two of them continued their maiden love-in I sat down and told Hildegard who Peanut was, and from whence she came.

Moments later the rest of the brood swarmed around to see what was occurring and, like Hildegard, they were thrilled by the new arrival. The entire cottage was now alive with the sound of excited canines declaring love and undying friendship and if Peanut had been on the floor she would have been lost forever amidst a sea of tongues and wagging tails. Hildegard and I were outnumbered roughly eight to one that evening (that's not including the cats) and as the spirited throng continued vying for Peanut's attentions I sat back in my chair and just luxuriated in the moment. To this day I don't think I have ever witnessed such a joyful and optimistic occasion. Cacophonous maybe, but simply sodden with all that is good.

The thing that had attracted me most to Peanut while she had been patrolling the dressing rooms of the New London Theatre was her bossy manner. What a little madam she was! It didn't matter who you were or how big your dressing room was. If she wanted you to move she'd tell you, and she'd carry on telling you until you did as you were told. Some dogs enjoy chasing things, like Jessie, and others enjoy telling humans what time of day it is. Peanut may well have been deaf and blind in one eye but that little dog had enough confidence to rule an army. Although she wasn't quite as despotic at Primrose Cottage she most definitely ruled the roost. She was crazy about Hildegard but I'd get the odd nip if I didn't fall in line.

Poor old Rug, on the other hand, had to leave us after just a few weeks. Don't worry, I don't mean she died. No, no! She was just too bloody furry. All Angora animals have the most amazing coats but they have to be cared for meticulously. Whilst we were just about able to manage a daily brush-athon I'm afraid Rug still used to get all kinds of things stuck in her fur. In order to remove the detritus we often had to cut bits away and she was starting to look rather strange. We were advised by the vet to have her rehomed somewhere quieter and with fewer animals.

'A rustic existence doesn't suit Angora cats,' he said. 'She needs to be a pampered pussy.' Fortunately we had a neighbour who had been mad about Rug ever since she had arrived, and when we asked her if she might be interested in giving Rug a home she was cock-a-hoop. She was a widow, I think, and with no other pets in the house she was free to pamper Rug and brush her as much as she liked.

Not long after leaving *Cats* I was offered a part playing Long John Silver in the Disney television series, *Return to Treasure Island*. I won't go on about how marvellous it is, suffice to say that it's the best thing I have ever done and if you have half a brain you will order it on DVD, buy a 50-inch television and then revel in my wonderfulness.

The filming schedule began with two weeks in Wales, which was lovely, and was followed by several months in Jamaica, which was even lovelier. Poor old me, eh! It's a hard life but one must carry on as best one can. After Jamaica we had six weeks' break before filming in Spain so I immediately set off for home.

As I entered the garden of Primrose Cottage, there to greet me was an astonishing sight. In amongst the usual melee of dogs and cats were two Shetland ponies who were both helping themselves to my begonias.

'Hildegard!' I cried. 'What the hell is this?'

'Wonderful to see you darling,' said Hildegard, emerging through the back door and planting a passionate kiss on my lips. 'The white one's called Misty and the black one's called Buffy. I was going to tell you on the phone but I thought I would surprise you.'

I was surprised all right.

'I've always wanted Shetland ponies,' said Hildegard, smiling happily.

'Really?' I replied. It was news to me. Then I had a thought.

'Where are they sleeping?' I asked, suspiciously.

Hildegard said nothing but went very red, very quickly.

'You haven't?' I cried. 'Not in my cabin!'

Not long previously I had built myself a lovely wooden cabin, or what is commonly known these days as a man shed. I had an aquarium in there, a big television, a huge chair and a kettle. I still have a cabin to this day and as well as giving me somewhere to plan my expeditions and write my books it gives Hildegard somewhere to banish me to.

'I didn't think you'd mind. They're quite clean and I'm sure they'll be happy sharing it with you.'

'Yes, I'm sure they will. They'll be chuffed to bits, especially if they like television.'

After helplessly watching the ponies devour some of my carrot tops I entered my cabin and looked inside. The entire place was covered in straw.

'Your aquarium's still there, and I've fed your fish,' Hildegard pointed out. 'What more do you want?'

To be honest I was more bothered about my vegetables than I was the cabin, but generally we rubbed along quite nicely. The ponies were usually out during the day, feeding on the lawn and what have you, and so if I still wanted to escape for a while, I could.

It turned out that one of Hildegard's friends had persuaded her to take the ponies. This friend also had a couple and had managed to convince Hildegard that she too was a pony person.

After a couple of weeks, Misty and Buffy, who were lovers, had been through my garden like a plague of locusts. 'It's no use,' I said to Hildegard one day. 'I'm going to have to find a field nearby to keep them in during the day. 'I haven't got a flower or a vegetable left.'

Unfortunately, the only fields nearby were occupied and so after wracking our brains for a while we decided we'd have to move. We'd had some unbelievable times at Primrose Cottage but with new animals arriving almost by the week we'd simply outgrown the place.

After about a week of searching Hildegard came across a house in Windlesham called Cedars Lodge. Windlesham is about a mile from Brick Hill and, until we moved in, it was known as being quite a sleepy little place. The house has eight bedrooms, and as well as having some lovely stables at the back it came with about three acres of land. It's situated right next door to the local church, which I rather liked, and overlooks the graveyard. That's obviously not everyone's cup of tea but it's one of the few places where you're guaranteed a bit of peace and quiet.

The only thing I found a bit disconcerting was the price. We'd paid just £25,000 for Primrose Cottage and when Hildegard told me how much we'd have to pay for Cedar's Lodge I took in a deep breath. 'It's £240,000,' she said. That was big money in those days, but with the family growing at such a rate and us having a policy of never turning any animals away, we had no choice.

I remember taking Buffy and Misty down there for the first time and when we let them go in the fields Hildegard was rapturous.

'There,' she cried. 'Isn't it worth the money, just seeing them both happy like that?'

Round and round the paddocks they ran in celebration. I didn't say a word. I couldn't. Thank God I had many offers of work accepted and still coming in.

Oh, did I mention the horses we inherited from the house's previous owners? Just the three! Because they were moving to a smaller place they were going to have to have them all put down and we could not bear the thought of that. Two of them were ex-racehorses I think and the other was an old Exmoor pony. Hildegard and I were both dumbstruck when they informed us what they had in mind.

The two ex-racehorses ended up going to some girls we knew in Brick Hill. They were both horse mad and we knew they'd look after them. The Exmoor, who was called Poppet, stayed on with us. He was a gorgeous dark bay colour and had a deep chest, a broad back, smallish ears and a large head. A typical Exmoor, really. Despite his great age, Poppet was a hard so-and-so and although he and the two Shetlands always got on well, there was no question as to who was in charge. Any nonsense and Poppet would give you a shove, a bite, a kick or all three.

The first person to attend to Poppet was the blacksmith. He was like a male version of Mad May, in that he spoke with a very broad Surrey accent, and the moment he saw Poppet he began to smile.

'Aaaah, kicks like a mule, this one, if you let him. I knows him of old, I do. If you upset him he snorts like a pig and gives you a tasty bite.'

This blacksmith was terribly calm, I have to say. Then again he was obviously used to dealing with aggressive animals and despite Poppet becoming agitated when I went to fetch him, the blacksmith seemed prepared for what was ahead.

'I knows how to deal with this one, Mr Blessed,' he said. 'Just you watch this. Putty in my hands, he'll be.'

After lifting up one of Poppet's feet the blacksmith paused for a second.

'Now look 'ere young man,' he said. 'I'm going to be working on your boots for a while, so there's no use you pushing and shoving. I got a few treats in my apron so the quieter you are, the more you get.'

Once the blacksmith set to work he then began singing a little tune. It's impossible to replicate here of course (unless you've bought the audiobook, in which case you're in for a treat!) but the only word he ever used was O-di-boots, which, although not a real word as such, must have had something to do with what he was doing. 'Oh, those boots,' might have been an accurate translation.

O-di-boots, O-di-boots, O-di-boots, O-di-O-di-O-di-boots.

In between verses of O-di-Boots he'd give Poppet a very candid running commentary.

'Right then Poppet. I'm just giving you some new shoes, easy does it.'

He'd ramble on for a minute or two and then go back to singing O-di-boots once more.

This course of action was complemented by treats being administered every few minutes and it worked an absolute treat. He was finished in next to no time.

'That's amazing,' I said to him. 'I thought he was going to be an absolute nightmare.'

'Naaaaaaaa. He's a pussycat compared to some of 'em. Probably mellowing in his old age.'

The relationship Poppet and I developed was as close as anything I've ever had with an animal and as a consequence he was always incredibly gentle with me. At the end of each day I'd open all the gates that led to his stable and then, when I was ready, I'd call for him. Poppet would always be right at the far end of the three acres and the moment he heard my voice he'd start galloping home. Exmoors are incredibly powerful animals and I used to adore leaning on the fence and watching him dash through the fields. When he was about fifty metres away Poppet would start greeting me by making a funny whinnying noise. It's almost impossible to describe really but it used to make me feel marvellous. The moment he started making the noise I'd greet him.

'Poppet, my old chum!' I used to shout as he approached me. 'How's your day been then? Let's get you inside and get you fed, then you can tell me all about it.'

Once he was safely in his stable Poppet would put his head forward in my neck, and then I'd do the same to him. That was our 'hello hug', if you will. When it came to food, he was an absolute pig. Besides his hay net I would spoil him with lots of carrots, apples and the like.

After letting Poppet eat I'd scratch him for a while. It was obviously heaven to Poppet though and he used to hate it when I stopped. I'd usually do this for about half an hour and would try and cover his entire body. If I ever missed a leg or something Poppet would lift it off the ground as if it were injured. He wasn't daft! As I scratched, his eyes would start to close and if he was really enjoying it his tongue would start lolling out of his mouth. It sounds fabulous, doesn't it? I must get somebody to try it on me one day. God we were so happy together.

Although animals dying is always hugely upsetting, what I've always found even more distressing – in the short-term at least – is when they get themselves injured. It's the animal's inability to communicate what's wrong that pulls on my heart strings and I always become desperate to make them well again.

I think the most dramatic example I have to offer is the

time Poppet pulled a large iron gate off its hinges. What a palaver! We'd had a couple of friends staying with us and for some reason they'd ended up tethering Poppet to this gate and then forgetting about him. They hadn't abused him or anything. They'd simply forgotten to untether him again. Anyway, after a while the poor lad became so agitated by being left that he managed to remove the gate from its post. Exmoors are enormously strong remember, and he'd created so much momentum pulling to and fro that instead of the iron gate falling onto the ground it had fallen on top of him. I think I'd been out shopping that afternoon and by the time I arrived home he'd been lying under it for over an hour.

'We don't know what to do,' Hildegard said. 'The vet isn't available and whenever any of us go near Poppet he starts to panic. He's terrified, Brian.'

When I eventually arrived at Poppet's side and saw him lying under the gate I was knocked sideways by a tidal wave of horror. This is what I mean about not being able to communicate. My beloved Exmoor was obviously petrified yet he couldn't tell me a thing. He wanted to say, *I'm scared Brian. Please help me.* But he wasn't able.

I knelt down by his head, kissed him on the nose and then told him what I intended to do.

'OK then Poppet,' I began. 'Very slowly, and I mean very slowly, I'm going to lift the gate off your body. OK? When I do that I don't want you to move. Do you understand? You can't move until I've had a look at you.'

After kissing him on the nose again I grabbed the gate

and then slowly started lifting it from his body. There were quite a few cuts I could see but as far as I could make out, nothing serious. It'd all be down to whether he'd had any bones broken. Once Poppet was free of the gate I rested it against the fence and then went back to examine him.

Instead of staying put he'd got to his feet and was now busy trotting around and shaking himself down. It was marvellous that he was obviously feeling OK but I could see he was in shock so I whispered loving words to him and sang a gentle song whilst soothing him all the time.

After giving each other a hello hug I led him up to his fabulous stable so that I could treat his wounds. The vet would be here the following morning but in the meantime he needed cleaning up. He may not have been in any danger but he was still in a lot of pain and I worried that he may even have broken a rib or two. It was my job to make him feel as safe and comfortable as possible and so I set about my business.

The first thing I did was give him some of his favourite food. Then, as he began eating, I told him I was going to clean his cuts and that it might just hurt a little. I then applied some thick green unction onto his wounds which took the pain away. Fortunately Poppet didn't seem to mind at all, and so once I'd bandaged him up and he'd finished all his food I placed two hay nets in his stable which he ate joyfully. When he was totally calm I left him. I think I checked on Poppet at least four times that night and carried on doing so for a week afterwards. Fortunately he hadn't broken any bones but I kept dreaming up different problems he might be having, such as delayed shock, and the moment one of these popped into my head I'd go running down to make sure he was OK. I couldn't rest until I knew for sure that he was going to be OK.

When we moved into Cedars Lodge I found myself once again living right next door to a church. Because our house was closer to the church than the vicarage, people used to knock on our door expecting to find his reverence. They got the shock of their lives when they were greeted by me.

'Good heavens you're that actor! We were expecting to see the vicar.'

'You can always be blessed by Blessed if you wish,' I would offer cheerfully.

More of a nuisance was the fact that next to the church was a graveyard – and that unfortunately offered Jessie the compost dog the opportunity to take up a new hobby. Jessie, who by this time was about ninety, used to enjoy jumping into graves before they were filled in and this presented me with two sizeable issues. The first was her inability to extract herself. Before we became aware of her obsession we would simply assume she had gone missing. Once we realized that she would probably be sitting on top of a freshly buried coffin I would trot over with a ladder and rescue her. She always seemed surprised to see me but would allow herself to be scooped up, tail wagging happily.

The second issue was more to do with timing really and used to send the vicar off his nut. You see, Jessie didn't always wait for the burial service to finish before jumping in and this used to cause mayhem. It always started off with a scream from the congregation, I remember, and ended with me apologizing profusely whilst extracting the offending animal. It used to happen regularly.

Just think of it though. Granny's gone, God bless her soul, and as you and your fellow mourners gather solemnly around the grave, the vicar, voice trembling, sorrowfully commits her body to the ground.

'Earth to earth, ashes to ashes, dust to . . . GOOD GOD, WHAT'S THAT?!'

But I think my greatest gift to Windlesham church, and especially its lady parishioners, has to be Buffy's chopper.

Yes, you read that correctly, boys and girls. I forgot to mention it earlier but Buffy, who was the brown Shetland pony, had a todger that at times appeared bigger than himself and he would use it whenever he got the chance. No wonder Misty was so devoted to him!

On the other side of our paddock was a field belonging to our kindly neighbour, surrounded by strong fencing as far as the eye could see. In this field, munching contently, were several large female hunters. Buffy found them irresistible and day in and day out he strove with body, mind and soul to get at them. He burrowed like a giant ferret, loosening the bottom part of the fence so he could gain access to his heart's desire. All hell would break loose with the hunters screaming and running in circles to avoid him. In truth, he'd have been lucky to get up as far as their ankles, but that made no difference to him. Shag first, think later was Buffy's motto. He certainly had the right tool for the job. He just needed longer legs. Thank God our dear neighbours were understanding!

It took hours sometimes to catch him. Buffy was a sweet character but on these occasions he would turn into a raging demon. He would have been perfectly cast in *The Exorcist*. It must have looked as if we were trying to re-enact a scene from *The Lone Ranger* as I stood with a strong mountaineering rope trying to lasso him. Once I had succeeded in getting the rope round his neck and my hand onto his head collar he would still drag me all over the field. He was incredibly strong and even though at the time I was pressing 400 pounds, I was no match for him. He would drag me to the four corners of the field, his fiery eyes bloodshot with lust and his chopper looking like a fifth leg. I'd have to circle him round and round until I managed to subtly head him towards the exit gate. Once outside I would lead him along the tiny road back to the stable where he would eventually calm down . . . Poor Buffy!

We would reinforce the fencing to protect the female hunters but just when we thought we had solved the problem he would find a weak spot and chaos reigned again! Consequently his reputation grew by the day and people flocked to see and feed him carrots and apples.

Every Sunday the church would be packed. The vicar was called Jeremy and he held sway over his flock with inspirational sermons and readings from the Bible. It was always a moving service and yet many of Jeremy's parishioners had their minds elsewhere. As soon as the service was over they'd pour out of the church and head straight to the narrow lane that led past our three-acre field. There they would cluster together and excitedly observe Buffy's fifth leg.

'Just look at it,' they would comment, 'it almost touches the floor.'

On one occasion when I was grappling with him and being dragged around, sweating and cursing, a couple of old ladies shouted, 'Grab his whatnot, Mr Blessed, that may help.' This was followed by hoots of laughter.

To try and divert some of the attention away from Buffy's boner we decided to take on yet another Shetland pony. Black Petra was her name and she had a right temper on her. She also had no interest in Buffy whatsoever and whenever he became amorous, which was often, she'd end up chasing him. Poor Buffy didn't know what to make of this as it was usually him doing the chasing and I think it may have emasculated him slightly. Thank heaven for that!

After about three years we decided to leave Cedars Lodge. As well as being mistaken for a vicar all the time, everything was just a little bit grand for us and it never really felt like home. Because of its sheer size and situation, we'd been asked to hold village fetes and all kinds of things there, but playing Lord and Lady of the Manor was never really our thing and when I found out Hildegard was also becoming down on the place I was thrilled to bits. I think we prefer snug as opposed to grand and fortunately for us we found the right place very quickly.

6

NO FREEDOM
FOR JUAN

Before I go on to describe our new home, I want to jump back in time to describe how I met an animal whose fate still haunts me. In 1968, while I was well into my renovations at Clarence House, I was invited down to Chessington Zoo, which is about ten miles south of Richmond. These days it is known as Chessington World of Adventures and has all kinds of things going on, but back in the 1960s it was just a home to about 1,500 exotic animals. The zoo first opened back in 1931 and during the Second World War it tried to evacuate its animals to zoos in areas less at risk of being bombed. One of these was Paignton Zoo in Devon, which managed to take quite a few, but for the ones which had to stay it remained a perilous time. Indeed, between 1939 and 1945 the zoo was bombed no fewer than twenty-one times and as well as three zoo keepers, over a hundred animals lost their lives. Damn you, Hitler! If he were here now I'd chin the moustachioed little bastard and then feed him to my foxes.

Anyway, the fellow who invited me down to Chessington was called Eddie Orbell. He was in charge of the big cats down there and we got along famously. Unfortunately, Eddie moved from Chessington up to Scotland a few months later but I remained in touch with Chessington and got to know many of the staff well.

Not long before Eddie left he called me up to tell me about a baby orangutan that had recently arrived from Borneo. His parents had been tragically murdered by some hunters and the poor mite had been left traumatized.

'We're trying to bring him out of his shell a bit, Brian,' said Eddie. 'And he needs to see as many friendly faces as possible. I think he'll like you.'

Why Eddie thought he'd like me I've no idea. I was delighted, however, and made my way down there as quick as I could.

I think there's no denying the fact that all baby animals are cute. Even some humans! But you'll be hard pushed to find one as cute as a baby orangutan. Because of the way their hair sticks up they tend to look like they've just been given an electric shock and their huge eyes shine like beacons of love. Like all young creatures, baby orangutans simply exude wonder and innocence and they can melt hearts at fifty paces.

When I arrived at Chessington Zoo to see their new arrival I was taken to a building near the monkey enclosure. In the corner of the building was a large cage with some straw in the corner but for the life of me I couldn't see an orangutan. I should say now, ladies and gentlemen, that my opinion of zoos has changed dramatically over the years and these days, unless it's a question of either conservation or preservation, wild animals should remain just that – wild.

'Has he escaped?' I asked the zoo keeper. 'I can't see him anywhere.'

'Hang on,' he said opening the cage door. 'I'll call him.'

'Juan. There's someone here to see you. Come on, Juan. Let's have a look at you.'

Suddenly the pile of straw moved slightly which confirmed that something was indeed there.

'Juan,' I called, joining in with the zoo keeper. 'Please come and say hello. I've come all the way from Richmond to see you.'

Just then, very, very slowly, a tiny dark hand appeared from beneath the straw.

'That's it,' I said encouragingly. 'I won't hurt you. In fact, I've got a nice bottle of milk here for you.'

Slowly but surely the little hand moved the straw aside to reveal Juan, the most exquisitely loveable creature I have ever seen.

On the zoo keeper's command, I sank very slowly to my knees. 'Hello there,' I said, almost in tears. Honestly, these things can turn mountaineers into Marys. 'Why not come and give me a great big cuddle?'

With that, I held out my arms and before I could say another word Juan had crawled across the floor and wrapped himself around my neck. All I wanted to do was kiss him and so for the next ten minutes or so I held him tight and did exactly that. I absolutely smothered the little bugger and told him a thousand times how beautiful and special he was. I must say I have never received such a reception before in my life, except this was no performance. I meant every kiss and every word. No young animal should ever be alone and I wanted Juan to know he had a friend.

'I love you to pieces you beautiful little man,' I kept on saying to him. 'Look at you! My God I could eat you up. Now come here and give us another kiss!'

All Juan wanted was to love and be loved and a few rounds with Uncle Brian was exactly what the little mite needed. And me, come to think of it.

Over the coming weeks and months, I visited Juan as often as I could and the moment he heard my voice he'd be on me like a shot. It was always the same routine; he'd go straight up to the top of my head, then down to the back of my neck, across the shoulders and then round on to my chest. Once there he would stare at me and our eyes would lock. Then, after a moment, I'd grab him and start kissing him. Although Juan was quite receptive to this behaviour it was not the same as kissing and hugging a human baby. In fact, it always turned into a bit of a playfight as opposed to a petting session and as he became older the kisses stopped and we would spend most of our time playfighting.

Because there were no other orangutans at Chessington I think Juan came to view me as a kind of patriarch. I was certainly the closest thing he had to a relative. I mean, look at me! Young orangutans usually never leave their mother's side until they are about seven years old so the poor thing had never experienced any of the love, guidance or protection that one received from a parent. Everything was instinct.

After spending time with Juan, I always went next door to see the gorillas. Do you know, until the late 1950s gorillas had an appalling reputation as violent brutes who'd kill humans on sight? It was only when the admirable George B. Schaller published *The Year of the Gorilla*, which detailed how he observed the animals for two years in east and central Africa, that we realized they were gentle giants. Anyway, the gorillas at Chessington used to gravitate towards me for some reason and if the man in charge was there I'd always be allowed into the enclosure to say hello.

The ones who showed the most interest in me were the four female gorillas (naturally), two of which were adolescents and so just at the stage where they were becoming quite powerful. My word, those girls were full of mischief! If they knew you weren't physically very strong they'd play with you. I took a friend of mine in there with me one day who was quite tall and thin and they threw him all over the enclosure. Not to harm him, you understand. They were simply playing. It was marvellous to watch. Well, for me at least.

The two other females, who were the girls' mothers, used to discipline them by tapping them on the nose, so whenever they became naughty with me I'd tap them on the nose and say 'Ah-Ah', which is the universal sound for stop. No animal likes being hit on the nose and these girls were no exception. The effect of my tap used to last about two minutes, after which they'd become rumbustious again. Many years later I hit a polar bear on the nose. There was no wrestling to be had there, thank God!

While we're here I may as well tell you about that because it's become the stuff of legend. A few years ago I was on an expedition to the magnetic North Pole and one morning while I was packing up my tent I suddenly noticed some footprints around the camp.

'Bloody hell,' I said to a colleague. 'They belong to a polar bear. He or she must be tracking us.'

The first question that popped into my mind was, 'I wonder when they'll make their presence known,' and that night, I got my answer. At about 8 p.m., three of my fellow explorers and I were having something to eat in our tent when all of a sudden this huge white nose began to appear through a hole in the flap.

Without even thinking I dived forward, shouted 'Ah-Ah-Ah' and then slapped this nose as hard as I bloody well could. Fortunately for us it beat a hasty retreat and was never to be seen again, but I don't mind admitting that it almost gave me a heart attack.

Large animals like lions, tigers and bears simply hate being slapped on the nose. So, if you ever come face to face with one, you'll know exactly what to do. You can always trust your uncle Brian to advise you on life's little dilemmas.

One thing that isn't often said about female gorillas is that they are exceedingly sexual and if you ever sit next to some, like I have, and are the male of your particular species, you'll have a hell of a job keeping your trousers on. First, they will try and pick your pockets – and believe me they could teach Fagin and the Artful Dodger a thing or two. For animals so large they are incredibly deft and will be riffling through your wallet and pulling out your dry cleaning ticket before you even realize it's gone.

Once they've been through the contents of your pockets they'll then start on the contents of your smalls. These four flirtatious females used to quite literally fancy the pants off me and the same thing would happen every time I visited. After giving them all a hug and then having a wrestle with one or two of the males I'd sit down in the corner of the enclosure and chat to the keepers. After a few minutes two females would wander over, ever so casually, and then sit themselves down either side of me. The feigned nonchalance used to have the keepers and me in stitches as when they moved in for the kill they would actually look around as if they didn't know I was there. The only thing they didn't do was whistle!

Slowly but surely, a black hairy hand would appear above my flies and then start reaching for the zip; the owner of the hand still looking around as if following the flightpath of a fly or something. By this time the zoo keepers and I would be crying with laughter and just as the zip would begin to slide down I would tap the offending hand and say, 'Ah-Ah-Ah-Ah! Come on girls, stop it now.' Suitably admonished, they would then sit there embarrassed. They would actually look shamefaced! It was marvellous. Two minutes later exactly the same thing would happen, just with a different hand. They'd have fitted in very well in South Kensington!

That's the thing though. You see, despite male gorillas weighing about thirty stone and having shoulders like mountain ranges, their cocks are like bloody lipsticks! I don't know how they manage to fertilize the females with appendages like that. The average size of an adult gorilla's penis is four centimetres, which is less than two inches, so no wonder they look grumpy all the time. They're nature's fool. Destiny's plaything.

Humans, on the other hand, have enormous penises compared with gorillas. I won't name the fellow here, but years ago I used to play celebrity football matches with a chap who had a cock like a fully grown pygmy, just without the spear and the ceremonial dress. He used to call it Fred. I think the female gorillas could see which side I dressed on and they simply wanted a closer look. I should have allowed one of them to get hold of it just to see what they thought. That said, they'd probably have yanked it off. I SAID YANKED!

At about this time I got to know the now-late zoo owner and gambler, John Aspinall. He had several mountain gorillas at his wildlife park in Kent and one day he invited me down to meet them. These days John's family, and in particular his son Damian, run a foundation that is committed to returning gorillas to the wild, but even then, his father always insisted on housing them in large open spaces instead of cages.

The largest of these mountain gorillas at Aspinall's zoo was called Gurges. He was about six foot three, which is slightly taller than average, and because I was a black belt in judo and got on very well with him we used to wrestle every time I visited. Under normal circumstances gorillas and human beings would probably not engage in such activities, but that would be as much the gorilla's decision as it would be the human's. Gorillas are normally quite passive creatures, whereas humans reek of aggression and this unnerves them greatly. It's hardly surprising though, that after thousands of years of war-making and killing we make other animals feel nervous. Subsequently, there are three things you should never do in the company of gorillas: first, do not make eye contact. Not unless you must. Second, do not show your teeth, not even with a smile. And third, do not approach one with an open hand. These are all signs of aggression. The best thing to do if you're alone with a gorilla is rub them on the cheek with your knuckle and then make lots of soft OOOOHING noises. That's what my wife does with me of an evening and it works a treat.

Wrestling with Gurges was obviously not the same as conventional wrestling, either in terms of style or technique, but it was enormous fun all the same. I used to get him in all kinds of holds – very slowly, mind you – and he would willingly fall into them and then laugh. Gorillas, not surprisingly perhaps, laugh very heartily and very deeply, and mark my words it is a joy to watch and hear. Did you know that gorillas laughed? They do indeed, as do most apes. What's more they simply adore being tickled. I probably wouldn't advise you giving it a go as there's a knack to it, but I for one have delighted dozens of great apes with a quick tickle here and there. Tremendous fun!

During one of our wrestling bouts one day I allowed Gurges to get me on the ground. He was always very careful not to hurt me and despite the argy-bargy (and the fact that he could have ripped me apart in a moment) I always felt very safe with him. Anyway, once he had pinned me down I made a noise as if I was hurt. You know the kind an ape makes when they're annoyed or distressed? They scream 'HAA HAA HAA HAA HAA' very quickly. Well, no sooner had I started HAA HAA HAA-ING than all the female gorillas stopped what they were doing, ran over to where I lay and started hammering Gurges both physically and verbally. What a commotion! The poor primate didn't know what had hit him, and neither did I. I'd never witnessed such a torrent of physical and verbal abuse. Wow!

After they'd finished demolishing my fellow combatant, the girls then picked me up off the ground, sat me down on a stool and started stroking me and playing with my ears. Then, once they had lured me into a false sense of security, down went their hands and they were in for a lucky dip. I must say it made me feel terribly wanted. Poor old Gurges though. Take my word for it boys; being henpecked by a spouse or a mother-in-law is nothing to being set upon by a pack of randy female gorillas.

Bloody hell fire! I've become so diverted by sex-mad gorillas that I've completely forgotten about little Juan. Sorry about that ladies and gentlemen. Let's get back on track.

Because Eddie Orbell and I got on so well together I managed to persuade him to allow me to take Juan home with me to Clarence House once or twice. In hindsight, this was not a good idea as orangutans are not very sociable creatures and despite it being done with the best of intentions I'm afraid it rather unsettled Juan and temporarily damaged our relationship. It confused him. One minute I was taking him out of his cage and allowing him to experience freedom, and the next I was putting him back in again. The looks he used to give me when we arrived back at Chessington were heart-breaking – pure disappointment and mistrust – and I wish to hell that I hadn't done it. I think the only thing that saved our friendship was the fact that Juan somehow believed I was a relative. Technically this was quite correct of course, as believe it or not we humans share 96.4 per cent of our genetic makeup with orangutans. Did you know that? Well of course you didn't! I only just looked it up myself.

That was our connection then, if you like, and as hard as it was for Juan being locked up in a cage twenty-four hours a day at least he hadn't suffered the same fate as his parents had. He was alive, thank heaven, and what he needed from me was not short spells of conditional liberty, however much I wanted to give them to him. What he needed was company, companionship and stimulation and so that's precisely what I resolved to provide him with. Whenever I wasn't filming and could escape from my other animal responsibilities at Clarence House, I'd be straight down to Chessington to see Juan.

'Where is he?' I'd bellow, as I made my way towards the ape house. 'Where is that awe-inspiring ape friend of mine?'

Watching Juan grow over the next few years was fascinating, but at the same time it eventually cut our relationship in half. As a baby, Juan had been as a human baby, with everything roughly in proportion. Then, when he got to about four or five years of age his legs and his arms began to grow apace, as did his shoulders. His hair too was now far more plentiful and you could tell that he was becoming a great deal stronger. From the age of about eight the power at Juan's disposal was immense, but because he was never able to use his strength naturally he could neither gauge nor control it. This meant that any physical contact between Juan and me could no longer be allowed and that was a wrench for both of us. Gorillas can expend their energy and test their strength by doing all kinds of things: running, climbing at low level or even fighting. Orangutans, on the other hand, need simply to climb and in the wild spend their entire lives swinging about in trees. These are Kapok trees, by the way, that are often hundreds of feet high. Juan, on the other hand – and it truly pains me to relay this to you, dear reader – lived in a concrete cage which had bars at one end and a pond and then a Perspex window at the other which separated

Juan from the public. Orangutans cannot swim so the pond was useless to him and the cage itself measured only about five metres square.

As soon as I arrived I would bang on the plastic and wave to Juan. He would then crawl to the edge of the pond and then hold up his arms, as if to say 'hello'. He only had two bars to swing on which were but a few feet from the ground and so the environment was diametrically opposed to what he would have had in the wild and hopelessly inadequate. Instinct was always denied the poor boy and so he was never able to *be* an orangutan. Isn't that tragic? These days I would have done something about it but back then I was as naïve as Juan was constrained and despite my efforts assisting the Ministry of Agriculture and Fisheries I was still just an animal lover and nothing more. In those days we didn't always consider the animal's welfare and although that seems shocking now – to some people, at least – it was indicative of how humans thought and behaved at the time.

As painful as it was being denied any physical contact with Juan it was certainly the right decision and this was proved to me one afternoon in what would have been the mid-1970s. I arrived at Chessington to see Juan as usual but as I approached the ape house I saw an ambulance parked up outside and a lot of people running around. To cut a long story short Juan had attacked a keeper out of sheer frustration and had done the man all kinds of damage. He wasn't killed, but he'd been very badly injured.

The assault was quite obviously a result of Juan's pro-
gression from adolescence into adulthood, as over the past
year or so both his demeanour and his behaviour had
changed quite dramatically. The Juan I'd first got to know
back in the 1960s had vanished forever and in his place
was a determined alpha male. An alpha male who desperately wanted to assert his power, lead his people and be
challenged. He was a king, for heaven's sake! The attack
was indeed unfortunate but surely it was to be expected.

I do an awful lot of voice-overs and as much as I adore
doing them I don't especially enjoy being cooped up in a
little sound studio for hours on end. Who would? Come
the end of the session I'm like a coiled spring and after
giving everyone a big hug and a kiss I make my way out
onto Wardour Street or wherever, throw my arms in the air
and thank the Lord that I am free again. But imagine being
stuck in one of those places ad infinitum and on your own?
It's enough to drive anyone mad. Instinctively I felt that
Juan was suffering from a deep depression, exacerbated by
boredom.

Alas, becoming King Louie from *The Jungle Book* would
never be possible to the extent Juan would have wished,
but after several nights lying awake thinking about it I
came up with a plan as to how I might be able to help him.
It wouldn't solve the problem of Juan's captivity, of course,
but it might challenge him and get him interested in life
again as he expended some of that energy and testosterone.
I had quite a bit of that too so I thought it might do us both
a bit of good.

The following morning, I got in my car and went down to Chessington. The zoo didn't open until about midday so I asked the keepers to let me in early.

'I want to try something out with Juan,' I said to them. 'But you have to let me go in with him. I've got to relieve his boredom.'

'We can't do that, Brian,' said the head keeper. 'I think he's beginning to lose his marbles. You saw what he did to Terry.'

'Yes, I know, but if you're all in there with me nothing can really happen. Please, I beg of you. Just give me half an hour.'

Although Juan was immensely powerful I was a black belt in Judo and if he attacked me I knew I could keep him away long enough to make my escape, or at least for the keepers to come to my aid.

They were quite naturally hesitant at first but after explaining exactly what I had in mind and how I intended to go about doing it they finally agreed. I can be extremely persuasive when I want to be, you know. How do you think I got to marry such a beautiful woman? It wasn't good looks, I can tell you that!

My plan, in a nutshell, was firstly to copy Juan's actions as best I could and try and cement, or at least enhance the notion that he and I were one of a kind. After that I'd wrestle with him for a bit. Nothing too rough, of course, but just enough for him to feel a bit more like a male orang-utan and not just a big ball of ginger wool. It was important that I entered the cage with an air of confidence and love so as the door opened I crawled in as bold as brass and then sat cross legged about ten feet away from him. Orang-utans do an awful lot of sitting and so apart from pulling a few faces and making a few noises, that was the extent of my impersonation. It seemed to work though and after five minutes or so Juan crawled over to me and sat about a metre away. Far more eye contact was now in play and after continuing to copy Juan for a while and then telling him what I had in store for him we eventually began to make contact. It started off with a little bit of shoulder slapping at first and then once I'd gained sufficient confidence I administered one or two playful pushes. This motivated Juan just enough for him to want to get involved with a little bit of wrestling. Nothing rough. Just a little bit of toing and froing. It was fun and the closest I got to being hurt was when he pushed his jaw into my chest and bit off two of my buttons. Because they eat only fruit, orangutan's teeth are terribly soft, unlike a gorilla's, and so I was never in any danger. I just lifted up his chin and said Ah-Ah-Ah, as I had with the gorillas.

After about thirty minutes the bout came to a natural and amicable end, which was exactly what I'd been hoping for. He was bored now and so I exited his cage. It was time for part three of my plan. This would have to take place on the other side of the pond as I had no idea what his reaction would be.

Once I was in position I began doing all kinds of physical movements while at the same time looking straight at Juan. I beat my chest, jumped up and down, slapped the top of my legs and even did a few push-ups. I also made lots of ape noises. The keepers sat watching in stunned silence.

Juan's reaction, as with the wrestling, was precisely what I'd been hoping for. As I began to beat my chest he stood up and walked to the edge of the water. Instead of beating his chest he waved his arms at me as if to say, *I'm the king of this castle you soft bugger!*

Anything I did he answered ten-fold and with tremendous enthusiasm. This was the first time he'd ever been challenged and responding was as natural to him as going to the loo. He was in his element, and so was I. Have you ever challenged a fully grown orangutan before? Well, if you ever get the chance, do it! From a safe distance, of course. There was more testosterone in that cage than in a stadium full of seventeen-year-old boys.

When I started doing press-ups, Juan walked over to his log. Apart from straw that's all there was in his enclosure. First, he picked up the log, which must have weighed about 400 pounds, and lifted it above his head. This alone was hugely impressive. I stopped doing press-ups at this point, then, after getting to my feet, I beat my chest and roared at him as loud as I possibly could. I did this in the hope that it would drive him on to do more and it worked a treat. There were two steel bars that ran the entire width of Juan's cage – kind of like elongated parallel bars – and as well as being about seven feet off the ground they curved sharply groundward at either end so that Juan could climb onto them. They were supposed to be his trees but were about as much use as a chocolate teapot.

After putting the log down from over his head Juan put it under his left arm and then carried it over to where the bars met the ground. I thought, *there's no way he's going to climb with that under his arm. It's impossible!* It wasn't. Juan climbed onto the bar one handed and after making his way to the middle he hung there holding the log tightly. The look he shot me was hysterical. His chin was raised and his lips pursed, as if to say, *Follow that, you great bearded tit!*

At first both the keepers and I simply stood there in awed silence. Emotionally I think we were all experiencing a mixture of extreme admiration and shock, yet when we finally came to our senses and appreciated the magnitude of what we had all witnessed, which was not merely some feat of strength but a rite of passage, we started to applaud. We did not laugh. We simply applauded. It had not been a pleasant experience by any stretch of the imagination as the encounter had been founded on hostility and confrontation. Yet it was something I knew had to be done and I had absolutely no regrets. Unbelievably, Juan held that log for at least three or four minutes and, as opposed to simply letting go of it, he climbed down just as he'd climbed up and then placed the log carefully back in its place. Astonishing! The whole operation did the trick and pulled him out of his depression.

I think we must have done this about seven or eight times in total and on each occasion Juan was as responsive as he was impressive. His *pièce de résistance* was always carrying the log onto the bars and each time we would applaud and I would then beat my chest and roar my approval. If I ever went to see Juan during opening hours, which was very often the case, I would go around to the back of the cage and, instead of going in with him, which I could only ever do when the zoo was closed, and even then when the manager wasn't in attendance, I would arm wrestle Juan through the bars. This was obviously a very crude form of arm wrestling but it enabled him to let off a bit of steam and assert himself. I used to find it enormous fun and as strong as I undoubtedly was at the time I was certainly no match for a fully grown orangutan. His hands were like hams and to compensate for the variance in strength I would have to use my speed. This used to frustrate Juan greatly but instead of getting angry as you'd expect, he simply emulated my actions and tried to beat me at my own game. He was a clever bugger and no mistake. I positively loved the guy.

I'm by no means trying to paint myself as being some kind of animal counsellor but these kinds of shenanigans undoubtedly helped keep Juan alive and gave him a purpose in life. They gave him an identity. He used to go crazy when I arrived. Not crazy as one of my dogs might if I've been away filming for a while, but as a boxer might when he sees his opponent approaching the ring. The moment Juan saw me his arms would go up in the air and he'd start screaming and clapping his hands. As much as I looked forward to seeing him I would have to psych myself up beforehand. After all, I wasn't there to throw bananas at him and take photographs. I was there to help him realize his identity and most important of all to help him feel like an orangutan. As the 1970s drew to a close I was busier than ever and as well as *Flash Gordon* being on the horizon I was being booked for all kinds of new television series. I constantly offered to buy Juan and return him to Borneo but all to no avail; the zoo remained adamant he had to stay. By now, family life too was completely bonkers as in addition to a young child at home we had a menagerie that would have filled two arks. But despite leading a very full and active life I always managed to find time to go and see Juan, and even though I was no longer allowed to have contact with him (we were eventually caught out by the powers that be) he still looked forward to seeing me, and I him.

One day while I was filming *Flash Gordon* at Brooklands, which is only a few miles away from Chessington, I went to see Juan but the sight that greeted me was heart-breaking. Alas, Juan didn't even flinch when I made my way noisily into the ape enclosure. He was sitting in the corner of his cage staring out through the bars and when I managed to attract his attention after banging on the Perspex window he simply stared straight through me. He was like a zombie. Nothing registered. As my heart began to sink I beat my chest and went through the movements I used when challenging him: press-ups, leg slapping, the lot. Nothing! His eyes were far, far away. Now in a panic I went to keepers and pleaded with them to let me get close to him.

'I don't want to touch him. I just want to be able to look at him in the eye.'

'It's no use, Brian,' said Juan's keeper. 'He's been like this for a couple of weeks now. It's like he's given up.'

Despite his rather grim diagnosis the keeper allowed me into the back of the enclosure so I could look Juan in the eyes and talk to him. The keeper was right though. His eyes were dead. Totally dead. Juan had given up on life.

I spent at least two or three hours trying to bring him round, but if you compared that to the amount of time he'd spent cooped up in that awful little cell it was little surprise that depression had eventually prevailed. I'm afraid I was naive enough to believe that me popping in and beating my chest every couple of weeks would make Juan feel like an orangutan and help give his life some purpose, but what about the thirteen days and twenty-two hours when I wasn't with him? What became of poor Juan then, and what did he do with his time? Well, I'm afraid the answer is that he was simply left to rot, ladies and gentlemen, and in the most basic and unhomely surroundings. He was fed and watered well enough but that was it. That's where the responsibility and indeed the interest ultimately ended.

To say I was distressed when I left the ape house would be a gross understatement and when I got back home I immediately started making enquiries again about trying to buy Juan. Looking back, it was a terrible state of affairs and the fact that I had to try and buy him in order to help him was a travesty. Although initiatives for releasing animals into the wild were only in their infancy then, I still wanted to give it a try. It may have sounded fanciful to some people but I managed to raise a lot of money for Juan's cause and we had some big hitters on our side. SO many people wanted to help him.

Unfortunately, after many meetings and more than a few sleepless nights our efforts came to naught and so the money was returned and Juan had to stay where he was. There was just too much red tape. The frustration I felt was crippling but of course that was nothing to what Juan must have been experiencing. I have never suffered from depression but know many people who have and as far as I can make out it is a relentless condition that eats away at you. Having to suffer something like this alone, however, and in a concrete cage is too awful to even think about. In the fifties, sixties and even in the seventies we were in the dark ages when it came to animal conservation.

To this day, we as humans seem to be obsessed with the concept of putting animals into cages and there's something vile about it. Juan was a broken animal, and for what reason? Because nobody had considered for one second what effect keeping a Bornean orangutan in complete isolation and in a concrete cage might have on his mental health. Physical cruelty to animals is the same as physical cruelty to children – unforgivable. But what about mental cruelty? Just because an animal can't express itself doesn't mean it cannot become depressed and experience fear or despondency, and our continued failure to recognize this fact is beyond embarrassing.

In the early 1980s, not long after I had tried to buy

Juan and take him back to Borneo, he was moved, without notice – traded for another animal, most probably – to a zoo in the United Arab Emirates. I never saw him again. I've tried to get word of him dozens of times but all to no avail. He was a commodity, you see, and only as valuable as the animals he could be traded for. I wanted to know what his new environment was like and if he'd made any progress mentally. I doubted it very much but one must always live in hope.

Juan would be in his early fifties now if he's still alive, and it's perfectly possible that he is. My heart says there's hope but my head says, how could there be? The last time I saw him he had given up on life altogether. Perhaps death would have been a happy release.

I once began to make a list of everything I had either done or achieved since getting to know Juan, as a way of comparing our lives, and from the point of view of me, the human, it made for quite impressive reading. I'd made films and television programmes by the dozen, appearing with some tremendously talented people, and was recognized wherever I went. I had climbed mountains all over the world and had explored every continent. I had a beautiful wife, a gorgeous daughter and friends I could rely on. I had enjoyed quite literally millions of experiences whilst knowing Juan all those years and in that time he had been sitting alone in a concrete cage while depression slowly got the better of him. I didn't start the list to beat myself up about it. What would be the point in that? All I wanted to do was to demonstrate to myself, and now perhaps to you, just how wrong it is to deny any animal its freedom and not to consider the true consequences of keeping them in captivity.

The first time I ever spoke to Virginia McKenna at the Born Free Foundation about this problem I quickly realized how wily and resilient you need to be when campaigning against it. It's all very well raising a few hundred quid and offering to build a new enclosure, but there are people out there like Virginia and her team who do this every day of the week and sometimes on an industrial scale.

I remember her telling me about a hotel she once stayed in somewhere in the Far East. She discovered, quite by accident, I think, that the owners of the hotel were keeping lions on one of the floors and in the most horrific conditions. As far as Virginia could make out they were being kept simply to impress the posh guests and were in cages only slightly larger than their bodies. Naturally Virginia was horrified by what she saw but because she was in a foreign country and not familiar with the laws there, or indeed the culture, she had to be very careful how she handled the situation.

'I had to lie, Brian,' she told me. 'I had to go to the manager, smile, and then tell him how nice it was to see lions in the hotel. I congratulated him. Then I had to think of a way of getting them out of there. It aged me, Brian. I felt deeply physically sick!'

Somehow Virginia managed to persuade the hotel owners to allow her to remove the lions from the building and then take them to one of the Born Free Foundation's enclosures. She was insane with anger, so she told me, yet she still managed to hold it all together. That's where I would fail, I'm afraid. Virginia has had her heart broken hundreds of times by what she has seen over the years, yet for the sake of the animals, she has always managed to remain calm and composed. I couldn't do that. I'd just kill the bastards. Put me in charge of a charity auction in a room full of millionaires and I guarantee that I'll make you a fortune. Put me in a room with somebody who is abusing animals, however, and you may as well just order an ambulance and a Black Maria. I wish them nothing but pain.

About eleven years ago, I had the enormous pleasure of visiting the beautiful country of Sri Lanka where I made a film for ITV and the World Society for the Protection of Animals about the Millennium Elephant Foundation; a marvellous organization that looks after elephants that have been kept and worked in captivity. Whilst there I met an elephant called Baby who had spent over sixty years – SIXTY YEARS – carrying timber and being made to take part in festivals. She was eighty-three years young when we met and as well as being blind in one eye she had developed crippling arthritis from being worked longer than some people live. But despite all of Baby's ills, and despite her being treated quite appallingly by some human beings, she was still capable of expressing love and for the two days I was there we were inseparable. This wasn't just for the cameras, by the way. After over six decades living in hell Baby the elephant was ready for some of the good stuff and I've never known another living creature exude so much positivity. She made everybody smile, all the time. How many animals – including humans – can boast a talent of such terrific magnitude? The fact that she wanted to shower some of this on me was a colossal privilege and is something I shall remember always.

There's a rather sad little irony here, my intrepid reader, but it at least allows me to finish the chapter on a positive note. It was because of Juan that I first became interested in helping animals held in captivity and my endeavours, as you can see from my experiences with animals like Baby, have afforded me many life-affirming encounters. The fact that I have Juan to thank is sad, in a way, but let's try and look on the bright side. He has inspired me to fight for animals who are held in captivity and if anybody reading this feels inspired to do the same then that's just marvellous. You see, good things *do* happen, and it's up to us to both create them and enjoy them. We are the guardians of this planet and we shall win!

7

TWICE AROUND THE
ARBORETUM

It turned out that Hildegard had been coveting the large Victorian cottage we had decided to move in to for quite some time. Just outside Bagshot, it had a similar amount of land to the old place but otherwise it was the absolute opposite, both in terms of size and location, and there wasn't a vicar, a church or even a main road in sight.

I'm happy to report that this is where we live to this very day, and over the past twenty-six years or so it has been home to literally thousands of animals.

I think I only saw the place once before we moved in and because I was going to be away filming it all had to take place without me. Hildegard didn't mind one bit. She'd found our Shangri-La and was looking forward to showing it to the animals and settling them all in.

By the time I arrived back from the shoot I'd almost forgotten what it looked like and because the move had only taken place a day or two earlier I was expecting chaos. Not a bit of it! The cottage itself was still full of boxes but that wasn't important. It was the garden and the paddocks I was interested in. The best way to describe what greeted me as I opened the kitchen door would be pastoral perfection. The four ponies were grazing happily in the paddock and two of the dogs, Willie and Benji, were frolicking on the expansive lawn. These two scallywags had been keeping us on our toes ever since they arrived. God, I love dogs! If I were the only human left on earth I'd be as right as nine pence so long as I had a couple of canines for company.

The scene was completed by three ducks we'd taken in just a few weeks before. I'd had a brand new pond dug shortly before we took up residence and as two of the ducks wrestled merrily upon the water the last of the trio quacked out a commentary from dry land. They were noisy little ducks but tremendous fun.

As I stood there drinking in the view I experienced the same feelings of optimism and excitement I'd had when we first moved in to Primrose Cottage, all those lovely, lovely years ago. We still had Bonzo, Jessie and Comedy and some of the other cats. Poor old Jessie was quite decrepit now and had been forced to forgo activities like grave bombing in favour of more sedentary pursuits. Eating, sleeping and digging now made up the majority of her days.

Much like at Cedars Lodge, the people who owned our new home before us also left behind all manner of outstanding organisms; the number of which almost doubled our clan's population. So, as well as ponies, ducks, cats and dogs we now had geese, hens and even peahens. They also left a flock of sheep behind but we had to have them rehomed. Hildegard was worried I'd want to take up shepherding and so she found somebody who knew what they were doing.

The pond that the ducks were enjoying, incidentally, had been dug specially to house my collection of Koi carp. I had about a thousand at the time and many of them were two or three feet long. They're beautiful creatures, don't get me wrong, but they're also an absolute bugger to keep and the task of transporting them from Cedars Lodge to Beeches cost more time and money than everything else put together.

I'd first become interested in Koi while living at Cedars Lodge, and I got a little bit carried away. I tend to do that sometimes, although I make absolutely no apology for it. What's the point of building a small pond and having four or five carp when you can dig a lake and have a thousand? It was exactly the same when I took up mountaineering. One minute I'm climbing Mount Snowdon and having a lovely time and the next I'm halfway up Mount Everest. You've got to think big, ladies and gentlemen, and remember – nothing's impossible! Adventure is the key to this millennium. If we stop taking risks, we start to lose. By the way, if you don't think keeping a thousand Koi carp is an adventure, just you damn well try it!

The pond I'd had dug held about 16,000 gallons of water and was five feet deep at one end and four feet at the other. The filtration system alone cost thousands, and there were lovely lights at the bottom as well as separate compartments for breeding and even somewhere to keep the eggs. I was a bit of a Koi carp expert for a while and people used to come from miles around to ask for my advice. In fact, I was once asked by a Japanese gentleman to give his new pond the once-over before he took owner-ship of a new Koi. A Koi, incidentally, that had set him back a cool £25,000! Twenty-five grand for one fish. Can you imagine? I also agreed to accompany this chap to Heathrow Airport when this fish eventually arrived and by the time it had made it through customs he was shaking like jelly. So was I, come to think of it. Koi carp must be kept in water that is between 65 and 70 degrees Fahrenheit and must have an oxygen level no lower than 5 mg per litre. It's difficult enough maintaining that on the ground, let alone at 38,000 feet!

For the first hour of us being there we had no idea whether this fish had survived the journey and the tension was almost palpable. Once it eventually appeared the little fellow was cock-a-hoop and as far as I know they lived happily ever after. By the way, this rare black Koi looked as if its scales were covered in glittering jewels . . . aston-ishing! You learn something new every day though, don't you? Brian Blessed, king of Surrey, the world's most dan-gerously virile man, used to be a Koi carp keeper!

Unfortunately, my adventures in keeping Koi carp came to a rather abrupt end, as within about three weeks of us moving in to Beeches Cottage our lovely new pond was overrun by an armada of bloody ducks. It happened almost overnight. I remember getting up one morning to let the ponies out and when I opened the kitchen door I was hit by a cacophony of quacks.

'Hildegard,' I cried. 'We've been invaded. Come and have a look.'

We couldn't believe it. Every inch of that pond was covered in feathers. It was like a duck convention! But while I was standing there going off my trolley Hildegard was quickly warming to the idea.

'I think it's marvellous that they've decided to live with us,' she said, smiling. 'And look. The three ducks who came with us from Cedars are still here.'

'But what about my Koi?' I complained. 'Ducks do crap you know, and it'll fowl up my filtration system.'

'I couldn't give two hoots about your filtration system,' said the emboldened Hildegard Neil. 'If those ducks want to stay here they're very welcome.'

Game, set and match to the feisty actress. I didn't put up much of a fight because at the end of the day, she was absolutely right. Those ducks had, for whatever reason, decided to come and live with us and evicting them would have been a travesty. I knew hundreds of people who'd quite happily buy the carp and so with a momentarily heavy heart but a much heavier wallet I found them all new homes. From that day on we nicknamed the cottage Duckville!

At the end of our paddocks there's an arboretum and then just beyond that there's a slip road that runs off the M3 motorway. Because it leads to a roundabout people don't drive terribly fast there and as well as being quite secluded there are also plenty of places to stop. Unbeknownst to us at the time, people tended to use this stretch of road to dump unwanted animals and even to this day we have all manner of poor creatures simply abandoned on our land. Even writing this makes me want to bloody explode and when I first became aware of the practice I went apoplectic with rage.

The most common victims of this shocking behaviour are greyhounds – the irony being that they simply adore humans and make the most marvellous companions. These dogs have obviously been bred for racing and have either lost a bit of speed or been injured. Either way, their so-called owners repay them for their labours by killing them or leaving them for dead. The problem is that greyhound racing remains a self-regulating gambling business and because breeding dogs is uncontrolled thousands dis-appear each year. Ireland in particular has a real problem with this. Even worse, they allow exports of greyhounds to China, a country with a very poor animal welfare record. In 2016 it emerged that a greyhound believed to be Irish had ended up in China, where it was boiled alive at a dog meat festival. Boiled alive, for heaven's sake! God it makes my blood boil!

Anyway, let's not turn this into a big rant-fest. There's a time and a place and this isn't it.

One day, as I was walking the dogs in the paddock, I saw what appeared to be a very large bird hobbling about near the fence. It must have been at least three feet high, and on closer yet cautious inspection I discovered that it was in fact a cockerel.

'What the hell are you doing here?' I asked him.

The poor thing looked half dead and by the time I reached him he'd collapsed in a feathery heap. 'You look like you've been in a fight,' I said picking him up. 'Let's get you back home and see what the vet says.'

At this point, if the cockerel had spoken English, he'd probably have said, 'Well of course I look like I've been in a fight you fat bearded fool. I'm a fighting cock!'

I had absolutely no idea how my new friend had obtained his catalogue of injuries and when the good vet enlightened me I was horrified.

'It'll probably be the same people who dump the greyhounds,' he said. 'Greyhound racing and cock fighting are like football and rugby to these people.'

I couldn't believe it. Not content with depositing dead greyhounds in my bloody field, now they were throwing punch-drunk cockerels over the fence. Apparently, Surrey's a hotbed for things like cockfighting and dogfighting. That's right, posh Surrey! (Sorry Surrey, you are also full of loving people.)

'They probably know you have ducks and hens so perhaps they think you'll look after him?' continued the vet.

I don't know if he was just being diplomatic by suggesting that certain people had wished to retire the giant bird but his theory did placate me slightly and so as opposed to concentrating all my efforts on combating the leery bastards I decided to focus on caring for the cockerel and nursing him back to health.

We ended up naming him Vessel – the cockerel, not the vet – after one of Hildegard's cousins. As well as being a deathly black colour his talons were about three inches long. He was like a harpy from hell! Not surprisingly, Vessel could be a truculent bugger sometimes and so in the end we decided to segregate him from the other animals. I shudder to think what he might have done to the hens but even the dogs seemed to be wary of him, and for good reason.

The only animals Vessel seemed to tolerate were humans, although there was one unfortunate exception who – regardless of the fact he'd rescued the bird and had spent about £700 saving his life – he simply could not abide. That exception was me. Hildegard, Rosalind and anyone else who happened to be around – and I mean, *anyone* – could pet Vessel until the bloody cows came home and he absolutely loved it. Not so his bearded sponsor. The moment he caught sight of me he'd start strutting around and ruffling his feathers. Then, once he thought I was in charging distance, the talons would come out and he'd go for me. Right in the bloody backside he used to hit me. There was no way in the world I was going to start running away from a male chicken and so, as opposed to fleeing for my life while screaming 'Hildegard, I'm being got at by a massive cock!', I used to stand there with a broomstick in my hands warding him off shouting, 'I saved your life, you ungrateful feather duster.' He had tremendous manoeuvrability and the closer he stayed to my person the harder it was for me to defend myself. It was like a boxing match!

One day this dark feathered demon actually ambushed me. He did! I'd just finished feeding the hens and I was walking back towards the house when Vessel ran out from behind a bush and went for me. The Lord only knows what I was thinking about at the time but because I was away with the fairies I didn't even have time to protect myself. BANG! Right in the tender region. As the assault was so unexpected I ended up falling backwards and before you could say 'cock-a-doodle-do' Vessel was standing on my chest trying to kick me in the bloody face, his talons missing me by millimetres.

Once I'd got over the initial shock of being floored by this feisty fowl I forced him off my chest, scrambled to my feet and began pursuing him around the paddock. I think he knew that this time he may have overstepped the mark and he put on an impressive turn of speed. As I stood there breathless and beaten he did a lap of honour around the perimeter of the field. For whatever reason I was anathema to that blasted bird and it seemed like he wouldn't rest until he'd finished me off. Nevertheless I still loved him and it was great to see him so healthy.

Unfortunately, Vessel wasn't the only one who wanted a piece of Uncle Brian at the time. I'd also become a target for some of the local teenage delinquents. It's different now, thank heavens, but back then there were air rifles everywhere and instead of finding something vaguely constructive to do with their time these little rascals had decided to take some pot shots at me.

I'd had another cabin built in one of the top paddocks, this time filled with gym equipment and not Shetland ponies. I lifted weights and used to do abdominal crunches, pull-ups and all kinds of things in there. Anyway, one day while I was halfway through a workout I suddenly heard a very loud bang. It was as if somebody had hit the outside of the cabin with a hammer. A few seconds later one of the windows smashed and it was then that I realized what must have been going on. I was under attack! I hadn't encountered a gun with live ammunition since my RAF days and so, after peeking through the broken window and spotting exactly where they were hiding, I opened the door, picked up a large stick and then ran at them as fast as I could.

'IT'LL TAKE MORE THAN A BLOODY AIR RIFLE TO SCARE ME YOU COWARDLY SODS!' I roared.

I have no fear, ladies and gentleman, and I wasn't going to be bullied on my own property for anybody. The moment the perpetrators saw me coming they ran off. They couldn't have been more than about fifteen or sixteen years of age. Perhaps they'd been hired by Vessel? It wouldn't at all surprise me.

Speaking of him, just you try guessing what became of the wily old devil. I bet you can't. Honestly dear reader you really couldn't make this up. One night, at about two o'clock in the morning, the hens started going absolutely crazy and so I immediately got up to investigate. At first I thought it must have been a fox. Every evening, once we'd fed the dogs and had shepherded the ducks and hens into their large sheds, we'd feed the foxes in the paddocks. At about 6 p.m., four or five of them would creep out of the bushes, usually with several cubs in tow. We would supply them with leftovers and rough meat from the butcher's and it would all disappear in seconds. In this way, we became friends with the foxes and it prevented them from attacking the ducks and hens. Despite this, you still got the odd chancer and after turning on the outdoor lights I ran towards the coop. When I got there, it was evident that although the hens had been disturbed by something they definitely weren't under attack. *Thank God for that*, I thought. It must have been a false alarm.

While I was there I thought I'd quickly go and check on the rest of the animals before returning to bed. It was then that I realized that Vessel was nowhere to be seen. I quickly shone my torch around the paddock and there, right at the top just before the arboretum, I saw what looked like two men running like hell. One of them was carrying a large sack and inside that must have been Vessel. I knew immediately what had happened. They had stolen him back!

The following morning I called the police and they confirmed my suspicions.

'It happens all the time, Mr Blessed,' they said. 'Word gets around about people who are willing to rehabilitate animals and so they dump them there hoping that you'll oblige. Once the bird is fit, they pounce and take it back.'

'Well I did oblige, didn't I? Seven hundred quid I spent getting that bird fit and all they're going to do is make him fight again.'

I was furious, but more than that I was sorry for Vessel. He was an impressive beast and as well as being a worthy adversary to me he had become an important part of our family. The thought of him being made to fight again filled me with anger and sadness.

Later that day a policeman came to the cottage to collect a few details and we got talking about cockfighting. Apparently, they'd been having a crackdown on the crime and after chatting for a good hour or so the policeman asked me if we'd consider homing a fighting cock they'd found just the day before. According to the policeman they'd actually found this poor bird wrapped around the spare wheel of a car.

'How the hell do you wrap a cockerel around a wheel?' I asked him.

'Quite easily, Mr Blessed,' he replied. 'It's easy to elongate a cockerel and so after drugging them they wrap them around the spare wheel, put them in the boot and then transport them.'

What a peculiar and rather screwed up species we are at times.

Like Vessel, this bird had been sporting all kinds of injuries when they'd found him and so when the policeman delivered him to us, the first thing I did was get the vet out.

'He's in better shape than the last one,' he said. 'But it's still going to be a few weeks before he's right again.'

Fortunately for me this bird was far less belligerent than Vessel and had no interest at all in head-butting me in the privates. Even so, within just a few days of us nursing him back to health he too was stolen by the gypsies. They must have been spying on us with binoculars or something and, despite all the extra security I'd put in, they had him away without even scaring the hens. Ah well – I did my best.

'That's it,' I said to Hildegard the following day. 'You can bring as many dogs, ducks, cats and ponies as you like to this place, but if I ever see another fighting cock on this land again I'm damn well moving house!'

Because we felt settled and still had a lot of land we started taking in more and more animals and after a while it became almost a full-time job. It felt as if the RSPCA were visiting us almost daily and as word got around that we were running a kind of sanctuary we began receiving hundreds of requests for help. Things are not quite as hectic these days as both Hildegard and I are approaching middle-age, but back in the early 1990s Beeches Cottage was like a holding pen for Noah's Ark. I honestly can't tell you how many dogs we used to have but it was well into double figures. I used to exercise them all by running up the paddock and then around the arboretum a few times – all part of my Everest training. You remember Peanut? Well, she was completely and utterly knackered. I used to put her in a rucksack and then take her with me. She couldn't bear to be left out of anything. Every dog in residence used to run with me and Peanut and it was one of the highlights of the day. I was always the first to drop out though. I'd be sitting there with Peanut sweating like a deviant and all the dogs would be barking, 'Come on Brian more please. Get up!' After a few minutes, I'd start feeling better and so we'd be good to go again. Never mind swimming with sexy dolphins. If you get the chance to run with a load of dishevelled hounds around an arboretum, just do it!

One thing I haven't mentioned yet is that I was forever disappearing off to places like Mount Everest. Both mountaineering and exploring had been obsessions of mine ever since I was a child and once I realized that it was within my power to attempt to scale these amazing mountains and go off exploring there was no stopping me. Over the years, I've written several books about my adventures and in 1991 I even made a film about an Everest attempt I made entitled *Galahad of Everest*.

The trouble is that while I was busy fulfilling these childhood ambitions of mine, Hildegard was left holding not just the baby – who was actually a young teenager now – but about fifteen dogs, ten cats, four ponies, three horses, fifty hens, a thousand ducks and even an abandoned ferret that the RSPCA said would be right up my street! Yes, ladies and gentlemen, we had a ferret. The poor thing had been abandoned by the gypsies because he was too old to kill rabbits and so he ended up with us. He was a sweet little thing but he had teeth like miniature razors so you had to be bloody careful.

Living with me at this time was not a bed of roses for my wife and in fact created great hardship. My first Everest expedition took me away for twenty-one weeks. The second, in 1993, took me away for sixteen weeks. We were climbing in the post monsoon season and the weather was frightful. I was nearly wiped out by a series of tremendous avalanches. Thank God Hildegard had no knowledge of it. The *Daily Mail* sponsored me and did a brilliant job, at one point saving the expedition and supplying it with helicopters and oxygen. Incidentally, this is the expedition where I reached 28,600 feet without oxygen at fifty-seven years of age – a world record. Aren't I marvellous?

I'm ashamed to say that I completely failed to appreciate the effect this was having on Hildegard and it wasn't until I received some letters from her that I began to realize how low she was feeling and what she had been made to sacrifice. I'm not going to bore you with the details of the expedition of course, but what I would like to do is include a passage or two from the letters Hildegard wrote to me as I think they demonstrate perfectly just how self-absorbed you can become when attempting to undertake these kinds of complicated excursions. More importantly though, they reveal how hard it was for Hildegard keeping her head above water mentally, physically and financially, and every time I even think about that period of our lives I am both humbled by her astonishing selflessness and haunted by my own self-interest. Despite all her woes

Hildegard did nothing but encourage me in my endeavours and as you'll see from the passages below she was battling all kinds of personal demons at the time. The term 'long-suffering' could have been invented for this astonishing woman.

10 September 1993

Darling,

I had a wonderful chat with Julian Champkin [the Daily Mail *reporter covering my attempt] yesterday, the first real news I've had of you for ages . . . Obviously the two letters from you were brilliant but they were written weeks ago and it was a relief for Julian to tell me you were fine and had climbed Island Peak, done a base camp stint, put your higher camps in situ and were coming right down off the mountain now to recover more fully than would be possible at base camp.*

I suppose I have not been terribly well (just a background cold) and that may be dragging me down as I am finding it all a bit of a grind and do have difficulty keeping my chin up sometimes. It still seems such an age before you get home and I do so miss the sharing. Duke does his level best to give me lots of love and attention – he is a real dear. Suzy is holding her own, Willie is OK but limping badly. Bodger and Duke fight a lot. As for Boo Boo, well she's still here, as dippy as ever. Poppet is at Rectory Farm in an effort to put some meat on his bones before the winter comes. All the other animals are fine and the ducks are splendid and safe and sound. Rosalind is off to Exeter on 4 October I believe. I thought she would get a full grant but I feel we are going to have to maintain her for at least the next three years. The council will pay her fees but I don't think they will give her a full grant. Times have changed greatly since our day as it seems parents are now expected to contribute financially so I'm afraid life is going to be even more expensive! . . . Sorry, I'm sure it all reads a bit strangely to you up on your mountain but I'm trying to paint a home picture for you of what's going on. The rains have come at long last; the ducks are thrilled and the grass is turning green so the ponies have something to eat again . . .

I need you to come home soon! I have always had a tendency to get depressed, which somehow or other does not happen when you are around. You keep me flying, I suppose, and I keep your feet on the floor so we achieve our excellent marriage and the peaceful joy we feel in each other's company. Let's be strong together when you get home. I miss you, I love you and I wish you the very best on the mountain. We are always together, as I see it, so as you climb I climb with you so you always have to take care of us both! And indeed all the other hearts and lungs that pulse at our cottage. GO UP, COME DOWN, COME HOME. Kisses, love, guts, calm, joy, acceptance all be with you and any other qualities you need.

Love,

Me xxx

21 September 1993

Darling,

It makes me happy to know that when you read this you will be safe with friends. I went to the mail box on Sunday to get the newspapers and found a letter from you in it. What a lovely letter and what a joy for us to read. I'm sorry the expedition is grim but I suppose that is the reality of expeditions on the whole.

Suzy was back in hospital a week ago with a fever of 103 after getting very agitated by rats in the barn. We have to scare off the bloody things somehow. Don't worry, she is sleeping peacefully at the foot of our bed; it was not as serious as last time but more blood tests are being done while they try to determine the problem . . .

This is a most peculiar letter to write as it is 21st of September and getting very close to the time you will be in the greatest danger and we are all worrying about you and yet here am I trying to write you a letter that will be fun for you to read when you are safely back at base camp, God willing and all things being equal, but as yet you have not made your summit bid and the time is drawing very near so I try so hard not to think about it but what with that and the pretty desperate finances (all will be well by March so don't fret) the things I don't think about with the front of my brain and deliberately suppress keep popping out in cold sores and a cold and now an itchy rash on my throat. It's very hard, darling, very hard indeed and of course now you are facing the worst of it. It is also the worst for me . . .

I think people feel I have an antenna connected to you. 'How's Brian getting on?' they all cry. I feel like screaming, 'How the f**k do I know? He was OK three weeks ago but he is in constant danger and could be in trouble as we speak. Please stop asking me "How's Brian", you're driving me nuts.'

Instead of course I patiently explain that I know almost as little as everyone else and say 'Read the Daily Mail, as I do.'

Come home safe and soundish and rejoin the fray; we love you, we miss you and we need you desperately. I love you so very much. Come home, you mad lunatic, where you belong. I can't wait to see you soooooooooooooon, be safe.

Love and kisses,

Me, Dukey, et al.

I dare say the majority of explorers have long-suffering partners at home, but how many have managed to bring up a child *and* maintain a makeshift animal sanctuary while their other half was off scaling Mount Everest? Not many I'll wager.

I arrived back home on 20 October 1993, three days after being near the summit of Everest. My blood, of course, was as thick as glue and I had lost over four stone in weight. I looked in a right pickle. God, it was good to be home with Hildegard, Rosalind and the animals! As I sat in the garden I sang a song I had heard as a child,

'You'll find your happiness lies, right under your eyes, back in your own backyard'.

The autumn sun shone gloriously and the numerous acres I had planted filled the landscape with yellow, green, purple and vibrant red . . . absolute heaven.

When Rosalind was about twelve or thirteen years of age she became interested in ponies and after taking up riding she started entering a few gymkhanas. Like Hildegard and me, she'd already turned into a committed animal lover and always has at least four or five dogs in tow. She's a real chip off the old block!

Because we'd quite enjoyed hosting some of the fetes at Cedars Lodge, Hildegard suggested we might stage one or two gymkhanas in the paddocks. And so, after erecting some jumps and dusting down the tea urn and the cucumber sandwiches, we threw open the gates! I must say we used to enjoy these events immensely as people would bring their entire families with them. This meant that in addition to having dozens of ponies trotting around the place we also had parents, grandparents, children and dogs by the lorry load. The animals used to absolutely adore gymkhana days and while the dogs who weren't deaf and blind would frolic in and around the arboretum, Peanut would march around the paddock and the lawn berating people who had the audacity to sit around on picnic rugs enjoying themselves. This situation was manna from Heaven to our four-legged despot. To keep myself occupied on these occasions I would often follow Peanut about and translate what she was saying to these rebuked individuals.

'Woof, woof, woof, wooooof!'

'Ah, yes. She's suggesting that you all take a running jump and get off home! Only joking, loves. Don't take any notice of her, she's only pretending.'

Or: 'Peanut says you should run twice around the arboretum. On your marks, get set, GO!' And indeed they did. What a sight that was – people, horses and dogs running in all directions.

Halcyon days indeed!

Never one to miss an opportunity, I used to put people to work while they were visiting us. I wasn't going to let all that talent and strength go to waste. Good heavens no! Some of them would always volunteer to help with things like tea, etc. but what I was interested in was getting my dreadful lawnmower fixed. It was one of those big sit-down jobs that the previous owner had left behind. You know the kind of thing. Anyway, I'd been itching to have a go on this ever since we moved in, but for the life of me I couldn't get the blasted thing to work. My brother had tried when he came down and so had my father, but none of us had had any luck. It drove me absolutely bonkers.

In the end I started making appeals before the gymkhanas started. 'Anybody here any good at fixing lawnmowers? If you are, please make your way over to the shed now.'

Pretty much every man from the local villages had a go at fixing it, including a professor and an expert mechanic.

It defeated them all. In the end I bought another one. I was sick to death of trying to mow my three and a half acres with hand mowers. What an absolute waste of time and effort – don't do it, ladies and gentleman.

Now the only downside to having so many horses and ponies about the place was that colic was never far away and for a time we had no end of problems. I've no idea why but horses and ponies seem to be prone to gastrointestinal conditions and as well as enduring unspeakable pain they can also die quite easily. Poor Misty the Shetland was a martyr to it and Hildegard and I would spend hours and hours with her trying to put it right. I remember once we really thought we were going to lose her. We couldn't get hold of the vet for some reason and because Misty was in so much pain Hildegard and I marched up to her stable with a two gallon drum of castor oil and set to work.

After pouring as much castor oil down Misty's throat as we could, Hildegard held her still while I attempted to turn her guts around. I have a bit of a talent for this and although I wasn't mad keen on sticking my hand up an animal's backside it usually did the trick. Sometimes we'd have two or three cases at a time and I'd spend hours covered in bloody shit. You've seen the episodes of *All Creatures Great and Small* when Christopher Timothy's standing there with his top off and his hand up a heifer's rear?

'There, there Buttercup,' he'd say in a soothing tone. 'We'll have you right in no time at all.'

Well, now imagine me on my knees doing exactly the

same thing to a Shetland pony, pouring with sweat and speaking words of comfort with Hildegard beside me weeping gallons in distress.

It was the strangest situation to be in though. One day I'd be in Tuscany filming *Much Ado About Nothing* for Ken Branagh and the next I'd be in a stable in Surrey greasing up Misty's rectum. Talk about a bloody contrast!

That reminds me. While I was making that particular film I taught Keanu Reeves how to meditate. Have we got time for a short actor interlude? Yes, I think we have.

Well, although Keanu was a very big film star at the time he wasn't much of a talker and so instead of just ignoring him I attempted to communicate with him by making silly noises. Imagine walking into a room and there's me holding out my arms going 'EEK, EEK, EEK.' It's enough to make anyone call for help. Strangely enough though, Keanu thought this was hilarious. After a while he even started responding to my greetings. I'd walk up to Keanu, hold out my arms and say 'FLEBBLE-EBLE-EBLE-EBLE-EBLE-EBLE-EBLE' and while I was doing this he'd lie on the floor and start making shapes. I wish to God somebody had filmed it. Anyway, if you're ever lucky enough to meet my mate Keanu, you know what to do.

We are both eccentrics and got on famously. While we were filming *Much Ado* Keanu was preparing to star in the Bernardo Bertolucci film, *Little Buddha*, and one day, completely out of the blue, he asked me about the dharma (truth). The thing is, I hadn't even told Keanu that I meditated and so was curious as to why he'd asked me.

'There's something about you, Brian,' he said. 'Something that makes me believe that you can teach me how to meditate.'

I spoke to Keanu at length about the subject of dharma and meditation and once I was satisfied that his enquiry was completely earnest I taught him a very simple meditation. The first he'd ever learned.

He also asked me one day what it was that made Buddha so impressive.

'It's almost impossible to answer your question, Keanu,' I said, 'but I'll do my best. Bertolucci is not doing you any great favour by offering you the part; it's a monumental task.'

For the next hour or so I pinned Keanu's ears back with the basic history of Buddha – particularly pointing out how the young man was born a prince in Lumbini, Nepal and gave up everything to head alone into the wild, intimidating jungle. He had a particular fear of tigers and at that time the forest was full of them. But in spite of his fear he survived for years, exploring many spiritual paths, until he reached enlightenment the week before he turned thirty-five.

'Look over there, Keanu,' I said, pointing to the dense wood. 'See that village about four miles away? I want you to reach that point by scrambling through the woods in the afternoon light. If you succeed, then make the same journey back in the dark.'

The wood was full of wild boar, not to mention several types of poisonous snakes, but Keanu set off without hesitation. Hours later he appeared on the veranda where I was sitting drinking coffee and looked for my reaction.

'Now you have a small taste of what Buddha had to face in those frightening forests,' I said quietly.

By the way, 2,600 years ago people reported that they had seen a large king cobra with its hood spread, like an umbrella, shielding the Buddha from the rain.

I think Keanu mentioned our conversation in an interview a few years ago and for a while afterwards he used to call me up to thank me. Hildegard would usually answer the phone and she had absolutely no idea who he was.

'It's somebody called Reeves, dear, although I can't make out his first name. Kaaaanoooo, is it?'

When he'd got off the phone I used to say to her, 'He's one of the world's biggest sex symbols dear. You've missed a trick there!'

Perhaps if I do another book I'll tell you about the time I took Sophia Loren up the Abruzzi Mountains.

I think the worst experience we ever had with the dreaded colic happened, unfortunately, while I was away filming one day. Rosalind had a pony at the time called Bessie and while I'd been out Bessie had been struck by it. I remember arriving back at the house as clear as day. It was late afternoon and as opposed to the usual fiesta of barks, meows and requests from Hildegard for everyone to quieten down a bit, silence reigned. Now, in our house that can only mean one of two things: either it's the middle of the night or something bad has happened. Eventually I found Hildegard in the living room curled up in one of the chairs and my poor dear wife was absolutely inconsolable. At first I thought Rosalind must have had an accident and when I asked Hildegard what had happened I was gripped by fear.

'It's not Rosalind,' she said. 'It's Bessie. She's dead.'

'What?' I said, taking her in my arms. 'But how?'

Slowly, Hildegard began recalling the whole sorry tale and to this day it's one of the most upsetting things that has ever happened to our family.

Bessie, who was a beautiful dark cherry colour, had been with Rosalind since she first became interested in riding and although they were never champions they were as close as any animal and its carer could be. Funnily enough, Bessie and Rosalind had recently won some sort of speed trial at a gymkhana over in Chobham and I remember admiring the rosette she came home with. She and Bessie were never expected to win anything and so we were all very, very proud.

Not long after I'd left the house that day, Bessie, who was out in the paddock, had started falling down and then standing up again. When Rosalind went to investigate she discovered that she was also screaming in pain and so with Hildegard out at the shops she called the vets immediately.

'For God's sake, don't let her lie down. She has colic,' they said. 'We'll be there in an hour.'

Poor Rosalind then spent the next twenty minutes screaming for help and desperately trying to keep Bessie on her feet, but by the time Hildegard arrived back home she'd died.

'Where's Rosalind now?' I asked Hildegard.

'She's in the bathroom. She's completely heartbroken, Brian.'

As I made my way down the corridor to the bathroom I could hear Rosalind weeping uncontrollably. The poor dear girl had struggled valiantly to keep Bessie upright and as I took her in my arms and hugged her I could see that she was covered in cuts and bruises. Bessie must have weighed at least half a ton and it was a miracle Rosalind wasn't seriously injured. There is no more upsetting sight to a parent than seeing a child of theirs in distress and watching Rosalind recall the horrors of what she had witnessed broke my heart in two, just as Bessie's death had broken hers.

Exactly one week later, at about six o'clock in the morning, Hildegard came running into our bedroom and told me that Misty had died during the night, again from colic. Why we hadn't heard her cries I don't know but we were absolutely devastated. That's the problem with animals, they will keep on dying! And it's no use saying, 'Well don't get too attached to them.' That's like asking somebody not to breathe.

Now, although I don't want to dwell too much on death, I would like to tell you what happened to our Exmoor, Poppet, because it's actually rather beautiful. He was forty when we had to have him put down and I'd been delaying the inevitable for months. I tend to do this I'm afraid and if one vet says an animal should be put to sleep I'll often ask another vet for a second opinion. It doesn't always work out but if the second vet says they can keep them going for a bit I'll usually ask them to do it. As long as the animals aren't in any pain I want to keep them alive for as long as is possible, even if it's only for an extra few days. I'm often mocked about the amount of money I spend on these extensions but the fact of the matter is you simply cannot put a price on life. I'm right, aren't I?

As I said, poor old Poppet had been on his way out for months and every time a vet got his black cap out and suggested putting him down I'd quickly call up another vet and order a stay of execution. It was a bit of a merry-go-round I suppose but Poppet had such a lust for life that I couldn't bear to see him go. Things had certainly changed though and instead of me calling from the gate and then watching him gallop through the paddocks like he had in days gone by, I now strolled out to where he grazed, stroked him for a while and then led him in. He couldn't even stand me scratching him anymore, the poor old thing. The excitement would have finished him off!

In the end Hildegard, my agent Stephen and one of our vets sat me down in the kitchen and told me that Poppet was now in pain and so keeping him alive would be for my benefit only. I didn't need to hear any more.

'Just give me a bit of time with him, would you,' I asked.

'Yes, of course,' said the vet. 'Stephen and I will come out to the paddock in about half an hour.'

I haven't mentioned Stephen Gittins yet as he's a bit shy but he's been looking after me now for about three hundred years. He's more like family really and as well as living with us for a while he too is animal crackers. Being a horse man, Stephen appreciated what Poppet and I meant to each other and so as opposed to putting Hildegard through the mill he offered to accompany the vet and hold my hand. Stephen was always there and never let us down.

With that I walked up to the paddock and found Poppet. He was always in the same place, just under one of the trees, and as he saw me approaching he swished his tail and gave me a quick nod of approval. He never, ever nodded at anyone else, by the way. Only me. He was the only horse I had ever been close to.

I didn't say anything when I reached him. I simply held him tight and then kissed him on his forehead. I don't know how many times I did this. Four or five hundred, maybe? The only thing I could do for him now was to fill his last moments with as much love as possible and when Stephen and the vet eventually arrived I was satisfied that wherever my friend was going he'd have more than enough love for the journey.

The scene, although sad, was perfect in a way as not only had Poppet enjoyed a long and happy life but he was going to leave that life on a beautiful day and in his favourite place.

As the vet gave Poppet an injection Stephen and I stroked him and held him tight but he would not die. Seeing that the injection had had no effect the vet eventually gave him a second shot into his neck.

'I think you'd better step back a bit,' said the vet. 'Just in case he falls on you.'

We did as we were told, and after just a few seconds Poppet sank to his knees and then slowly fell on his side. As this happened I ran to where he lay and once he was down I lifted up his head and held him in my arms. His large dark eyes were still wide open and seemed to me to be full of life, but as I went to place one final kiss on the forehead of my dear old friend they at last began to close. A few minutes later the vet confirmed what I'd hoped would never happen.

'He's gone,' he said.

That's not a bad death, is it? Do you know how I want to go? Peacefully, that's how! Then, once I've gone, I want to be thrown into a huge volcano. There's going to be none of that sombre black-suited rubbish for me, thank you very much, and you can stick your bloody eulogies right where the sun don't shine. Just chuck me in the volcano and then forget about me.

Do you know what I'm going to do before I bring the proceedings to a close? I'm going to tell you about Misty. Not Misty the Shetland pony, but Misty the dog. The reason I have decided to finish with this particular story is because I've yet to meet a more remarkable animal, and in addition to her dominating my life for fifteen years she epitomizes the bond that Hildegard and I have with our animals. Misty brings it all together, if you see what I mean.

But before I do, I'd like to do a quick straw poll if you

don't mind. OK, here's the question: what breed of dog do you think I'm most keen on?

Just cogitate for a moment . . .

OK then. You're thinking big, aren't you? Something powerful and hairy, right? A bit like me.

Well, up until about seventeen years ago, you'd have been absolutely on the button. In fact, ever since I became interested in dogs I'd dreamed of having an Anatolian Shepherd or a Mackenzie River Dog. Great big powerful creatures with teeth like talons. Remember Sabre from Clarence House? I'd always been the same when it came to animals and I would enthuse about them for hours.

The only person who used to repudiate my obsession with outsized canines was Hildegard who met my ramblings with a wry smile and a dismissive wave of the hand.

'Oh Brian, dear Brian,' she once said while I was planting some petunias in the borders at Primrose Cottage. 'One day you will experience a deep relationship with a tiny little dog.'

'What rubbish,' I refuted. 'I don't mind small dogs at all, but I much prefer large ones. I like powerful dogs!'

With another wave of her hand she continued. 'Little dogs can be very special Brian, and the love they generate verges on the mystical. It can be a life-changing experience. You mark my words.'

Well, my intrepid reader. To cut a long story short, fifteen years ago, I experienced such a relationship. It was in the year 2002 and at that particular time I'd just had a brush with death having recently completed an expedition to the fabled Lost World in Venezuela. Don't worry, I made sure Hildegard was happy and had plenty of help this time. I promise!

Anyway, on the return journey home from Canaima to Caracas our plane crashed into the dense rainforest. It was touch and go, but all eleven of us miraculously survived. Suffice to say that after many hours of hell and high water, not to mention the dreaded Penis Fish, which swims up your you-know-what and then opens its spikes, we came upon a brown and white scruffy-looking bow-legged Jack Russell that led us to a Pemon village and to safety.

At the time, back in England, among our many animals was a Jack Russell called Duke. My dear wife was completely devoted to him, and he her, yet the little swine gave me hell. He couldn't stand the sight of me. If I didn't do whatever he wanted straight away he would bully me from dawn till dusk. I can't even begin to remember the amount of times he gave me a nip. You can understand my amazement then – not to mention my shock – at being confronted by something similar in deepest Venezuela.

The shaman of the Pemon village informed us that he'd been bought from a shop in Caracas, and because he was so unique in the area he'd become the village mascot.

Fortunately for me the Venezuelan Jack Russell population seemed to hold me in slightly higher regard than the ones back in Surrey and during the few days we were there I spent many happy hours scratching him and tickling his tummy whilst relaxing in the village square. Watching that little dog's reaction to me tickling him was hysterical and, as he lay there with his tongue hanging out, obviously in the throes of ecstasy, the Pemon children all hooted with laughter while I made grunting Yeti noises at them. They'd certainly never seen anything like me before!

A week later I was back home. It was spring time and when I went out to say hello to Poppet, Champion (a black and white shire horse the RSPCA asked us to take in) and all the other boys and girls I realized how lucky I'd been to survive the crash. In celebration, I got all the dogs together in the paddock and we ran around the arboretum a few times. Then, after that, I took Champ out to crap on one or two private roads in Sunningdale. It was good to be alive!

Galvanized by the sights and sounds of spring I sprang into action and began planting hundreds of petunias and busy lizzies. The dogs, including Peanut, Duke, Benji, Willie and Suzy, who was a Manchester Terrier, joined me in the borders and as well as attempting to dig up everything I'd bloody well planted they made holes and then peed everywhere. It was a frolic on a grand scale! Little Suzy had belonged to a colonel who had long since retired and the poor old fellow simply couldn't cope. I saw him in Chobham with her one day and he was in a terrible state. Not only was he unable to walk Suzy sufficiently but his legs were obviously killing him. In the end I offered to rehome her and he agreed. I think it was a wrench for the poor old boy, as she was all he had.

As the horses and ponies neighed their approval from

the fields, the ducks in their hundreds floated down towards me in eager anticipation of any worms I might unearth. Whenever I do any gardening I like to sing and the ducks absolutely adore this. The dogs aren't so keen, but then that's their hard luck. The waterfowl's tune of choice is 'La Donna È Mobile' from *Rigoletto* and as I sink to my knees, take up the trowel and then start belting out this iconic classic they flap their wings like mad things. Ladies and gentlemen, I will never, ever grow up!

While the dogs and I were busy Hildegard came out to see what was going on.

'I'm going to the RSPCA in a minute,' she said, 'to see a couple of Jack Russells. Would you like to come with me?'

That's all we need, I thought. *More Jack Russells.* And people think I'm mad!

'Yes, of course I would,' I said gamely. 'Just let me get cleaned up.'

The RSPCA in Chobham is only about three miles away and is a delightful place. As well as being set in fields, it is run by the most likeable and brilliant staff. Thank God for them, and for anybody who works for an animal charity. You're all amazing people!

Along the cages we strolled, taking in the multitude of expectant canine faces before finally resting our eyes on two very small Jack Russells called Rosie and Misty. Rosie was brown and white and very shy and kept herself tucked away in the background. By contrast, Misty, who was black and white, thrust her nose and paws through the holes in the cage and enthusiastically licked my hand while she feasted her eyes on my beaming face. The manager of the RSPCA smiled. 'She's adorable, but I'll warn you now, she can be a bit of a madam.'

Once back at the car Hildegard admitted that her heart was over-ruling her common sense. After all, our menagerie was almost at breaking point and just two days earlier we had taken in a lovely female greyhound that had been abandoned on the M3. Her injuries had been appalling and after spending hours at the vets she was now resting in one of the stables. We named her Tilly, by the way, and she proved to be an absolute sweetheart.

Anyway, back to Hildegard.

She was still in two minds and after much deliberation she decided that we could only take one of the dogs. I left the choice to her and in the meantime, I went into London to voice the role of Sir Gregory for a new TV movie called *Mist – The Tale of a Sheepdog Puppy*. When I returned home that evening I was greeted by the usual onslaught and after much kissing and a bout of rampant stroking I strode into the kitchen.

Once the melee had died down a little I managed to gain access to the living room and sat myself down on the sofa. It was at that precise moment that I noticed a little stranger in the room, sitting upright and perfectly still in one of the small dog beds. It was a black and white Jack Russell. Hildegard smiled and said, 'It's Misty. She's settled in very well and the other dogs seem to adore her.'

'Misty eh?' I said. 'And aren't you lovely. Hello my little sugar plum.'

As I moved to an armchair closer to Misty's bed she jumped up onto my lap, snuggled under my armpit and stayed there all evening. Just before bedtime we all went out into the paddocks and ran ourselves into the ground. Young Misty was in absolute bliss. She was home, at last.

Later, as I sat on the bed, I placed Misty's little dog bed alongside and after giving her a goodnight kiss she curled up inside the bed and made herself comfortable. As I lay back on the pillow her tiny eyes never left mine and, in all probability, we fell asleep at the same time.

Day in and day out, month after month, we bonded together. Not that I remotely neglected the other animals, by the way. My love for all of them knew no bounds. But Misty simply lit up my soul.

'It's ridiculous,' I used to say to people. 'She's just a little tiny dog. How can something so small shake my heart and create such joy?'

It completely mystified me, and on top of that it was starting to cost me quite a bit professionally as I was turning down all kinds of jobs.

'No,' I'd say resolutely. 'I'm afraid I can't go away filming for ten weeks. Misty would be heartbroken.'

Some years prior to that, while I was filming Kenneth Branagh's *Henry V* at Shepperton Studios, the great actor Paul Scofield confided in me that he'd just turned down a film role worth two million pounds.

'I need the money Brian,' he said. 'My conservatory

has rotted and is in danger of falling down, but I can't possibly leave my dog Buster. I've only completed half his training.'

Now I was in the same boat with Misty. I've always been much in demand for my voice and I love narrating and voicing characters in films. It's great fun and very satisfying. There's a huge market out there and the emoluments on offer are often significant. Nevertheless, much of the time I don't have a penny to scratch my backside with, what with vet bills and everything else. Every time the doorbell goes my heart thuds, dreading the words: 'Brian. It's the straw man. Have you got three hundred quid on you?' We're all in the same boat to some degree, don't you think? Would I change any of it, given the chance? Would I hell! I'm as happy as a clam at high tide.

In the end, to stop my agent from having a fit, I started taking Misty to work with me. The old caravanette had gone by now as there was always somebody at home and as Misty was the only one who really pined for me it made sense to bring her along. I always took her little bed with us and as I worked she would sit there watching me intently. The thing is, she actually seemed interested in what I was doing and the directors, floor managers and wardrobe mistresses etc., all adored her.

Because she was always sitting down and paying attention she reminded me of Nipper, the dog from His Master's Voice, or HMV to anyone under eighty. You remember? The one peering into the old recording machine? I doubt if any dog in history has experienced so many different sound, film and TV studios.

On the few occasions when I had to leave Misty behind she would sit by the door waiting for me to return. This would often have Hildegard in tears as she wouldn't budge for anything or anybody. On arriving home, Misty would leap up into my arms yelping with joy.

'Here I am,' I'd say, hugging her. 'I'm home now. I'm home.'

Sometimes she'd become so excited that I'd have to take her up to the paddock and run with her, just to calm her down. It would take a while but eventually we'd stop and then retire to the sofa.

I must emphasize that Misty and I didn't have a lovey-dovey relationship. On the contrary. It was still, peaceful and mature. By day and by night she would watch me like a hawk with her warm dark eyes and she would appear to sense my every thought. On the odd occasion when I flailed with anger at the injustices in the world she would wait for me to calm down and then rest a gentle paw on my knee and make me smile. Everybody else would run to the bloody hills! Apart from Hildegard. She'd just shake her head and tut.

During this time, I purchased a new huge two-roomed log cabin like the one I had at Cedars, which is where I'm sitting at this very moment. When it was built, I filled it with rugs, Tibetan tankards and every conceivable object from my various adventures. To top it off I placed two large models of Sri Lankan elephants on top of the bookshelves and then sat back in my old armchair and looked out onto the garden I had created. By now it included an English wood, an African wild area with a twelve-foot model of a giraffe, a South American garden and a replica of the scene where Buddha attained Nirvana and freedom.

As all this was going on Misty was by my side constantly, and although she seemed happy with what I had fashioned she did express surprise at the tigress and her cubs snuggling under the six-foot golden Buddha. Each day she would ritualistically give the tigress a single bark before peeing nonchalantly on its belly.

On the sad occasions when I had to leave her for a time I would say, 'Sweetheart, I have to go out now, but I'll be back in a minute.' The word 'minute', seemed to convey to Misty that I wasn't deserting her and that I would be back. I'm sure many of you reading this will have experienced similar moments.

Year in, year out, this has been the pattern of my life, with springs, summers, autumns and winters passing away at a rate of knots. Misty was just two years of age when we gave her a home and by the time she'd reached her sixteenth birthday she'd become a thin old lady.

During that year of 2015 Misty became very weak. Nevertheless, she still loved her short walks. It was to be our last summer together. I turned down work and categorically refused to go on holiday to South Africa. It was all out of the question. I couldn't conceivably leave her. She needed me desperately.

I would put her in the car each day and take her to her

favourite haunts: the nature trail in the small wood in Chobham, the graveyards in Windlesham and the stream in the arboretum.

Once again, I started playing musical vets in order to keep Misty alive but eventually she just started to fall apart. She was in a dream-like state most of the time and had lost a tremendous amount of weight.

Sitting on the sofa in my cabin one day she looked at me. 'Come on,' she was saying, 'let me go, would you? I'm exhausted.' Two hours later, Gill and Pete arrived from Windlesham Vets. They were very sensitive, and devoted to Misty. After giving them a single bark each she nestled into my arms and they gently applied the needle. Misty's bright eyes stared into mine and gradually lost their light.

'She's at peace now,' said Gillian.

I'd shed a tear or two when I lost dear Poppet, who I loved dearly, but I was in absolute bits when I lost Misty. I still couldn't believe how such a tiny little thing could have had such a profound effect on my life. Here was a man who'd wept just a handful of times his entire life, yet now I was impersonating Niagara Falls.

I buried Misty in her favourite flower bed and I re-mained with her for several hours afterwards. When I eventually went back into my cabin one of our other dogs, Rocky, a Jack Russell who came to us from the RSPCA, joined me and sat on Misty's chair. 'Hello Brian,' he seemed to be saying. 'Come on, life goes on. I'm here!'

As much as I was going to miss my little pal I still had a tremendous amount to be grateful for, not least the memories of our companionship which will never leave me. Little Rocky was right though. Life does indeed go on and as somebody who thrives on being alive I owed it to myself, to Misty and, more importantly, to Hildegard, Rosalind and the animals to pick myself up, dust myself down and savour every moment. *Come on Brian*, I said to myself. There are creatures of all shapes and sizes relying on you. Not just for food and a roof over their heads, but for love.

I promised myself there and then that I would never mourn a life again. I would only celebrate. We in the West show death far too much respect and, as there's bugger all you can do about it, I propose we give it two fingers, ladies and gentlemen. Say, up yours, you boring sod! Then, once you've done that, I suggest you pick out a lovely big smile, sing a little tune ('La Donna È Mobile' always goes down well) and then go about choosing your adventure and making your life special! Life is the last word ladies and gentleman, Death is not! Death, thou shalt die!

Well, my sweet valiant reader, I'm afraid it is time for us to part once again. But before I go, shall I just bring you up to speed with what's occurring at our cottage? I think I should.

Hildegard and I are the only humans currently in residence, although there are always lots of people popping in and out during the day. There's Steve Knight, a good friend who drives me to jobs, and the girls Claire and Gillian who look after the horses and ponies. They're a smashing bunch of people and they help to keep this place alive. On the doggy front, we have Gloria, the aforementioned Rocky, and of course Rupert, who is so thick I call him Metal Mickey. There are no pedigrees in our house. Apart from me, of course!

Rupert and Gloria, who is an absolute darling, came to us via the same Welsh dog charity but they really are chalk and cheese. Gloria, who is somewhat cleverer than Rupert, was actually called Glory before she came to us and was described by the charity as an eleven-year-old golden male Labrador. Shortly after we agreed to take Glory, we were contacted by the charity, who informed us that 'he' was in season. Needless to say this discrepancy planted a certain amount of doubt in our minds and when 'he' eventually arrived we discovered that the male golden Labrador was actually a black female mutt! God only knows how old she is. She could be a hundred for all we know.

Unlike the vast majority of dogs who come to us via a charity, we were told all about Rupert and Gloria's backgrounds and once again they were polar opposites. Rupert had belonged to a frail old woman and had been doted upon all his life. Gloria, on the other hand, had been ill-treated beyond belief, to the point where her owner was actually put in prison for two and a half years, although I'd have given him life. Unfortunately, custodial sentences are still a rarity when it comes to animal cruelty, so you can image how bad things were. This man had kept dogs, ponies, geese and cats locked up in a cellar for years and years and poor Gloria was one of them. By the time the

RSPCA found these wretched creatures the majority had perished and the conditions in which they'd lived were some of the worst the inspectors had ever seen. When the vet got a look at Gloria he almost bloody fainted and immediately had to remove about six cancerous tumours from her body. Her mouth, too, was in a shocking state and he had to take out the majority of her teeth. Despite all this Gloria is the sweetest animal you could ever hope to meet and I love her desperately. We all do. She adores her walks and she adores where she lives, so from the hell that revolting excuse for a man created we have managed to help establish just a little bit of heaven. For all of us, really.

Three dogs doesn't seem like many compared with what we used to have but then once Rosalind turns up with her four hounds and then Steve Knight and the girls arrive with theirs, we usually have at least ten running about the place. It's as chaotic as it ever was! Steve's German Shepherd Sky, by the way, is an absolute behemoth and I often feel tempted to saddle her up, ride her around the paddocks and shout tallyho!

I'll tell you what has changed though. Rupert – who is about a foot high and all white with black ears – has become Hildegard's dog and I never saw that coming. In fact, when he first arrived my wife was most disparaging.

'He doesn't seem to have a brain,' she said. 'He just stands there like a lemon and barks occasionally. Are you sure he's a real dog?'

Well, over time Hildegard has become aware of Rupert's idiosyncrasies and slowly but surely, they've fallen madly in love with one another. Rupert only sleeps for about an hour at a time and in four or five places all over the house. Sometimes he goes trotting off to the paddock and gets lost. Oh yes, and he's got everything in the world wrong with him. Heart, lungs. You name it, they're all completely knackered. He even has an inhaler, for Christ sake! But, you see, all of a sudden, Rupert has a personality. He loves watching me do weights in the barn whilst eating a Bonio. All of a sudden, he's interesting.

Now, at seven o'clock every morning Rupert puts his face next to Hildegard's and then barks, 'Come on woman. Time to let me out for a pee.' They even have their own language. They speak 'rubbish' to each other fluently! Rupert's bark is a quite skew-whiff, but whenever he tries one out Hildegard will say, 'Who's a woopy poopy then, eh? Who's a woopy poopy? You are! Yes, you are, Mr Woopy Poopy. Off you go round the garden poop the poop.'

She's become as thick as he is!

I'll tell you what though, if Hildegard and I hadn't followed this path we'd have been two of the most financially secure paupers on God's earth. Does that make sense? But what is the point of having millions of pounds? You can only drive one car at a time and you can only live in one house. Do material possessions *really* make people truly happy? Do they? I don't think so. Some people might believe they do but their happiness barometers have obviously been tampered with and the mercury's been swapped for horse pee!

If you want to experience true happiness go out and get yourself a dog, a cat, rabbit or even a ferret! I'm not saying they can cure cancer or pay off your debts or anything, but what they can do is bring light into even the darkest hours, and when times are good they push them to perfection.

EPILOGUE

Michael Parkinson once said to me on his radio show, 'Brian, are you completely mad?'

'I hope so,' I replied. 'It's the only thing that makes sense.'

My friends, when people say you're mad, you know you're on the right track. Our Jack Russell, Rocky, is sitting in the armchair next to me with an amused look in his happy brown eyes. What did the wonderful Spanish writer Miguel De Cervantes say? 'Who knows where madness lies?' Rocky certainly does. He's thinking, *You're off your bloody box Brian!*

There are two things I want to address before I leave you. Firstly, I must apologise to my friends the gorillas for comparing their appendages to lipsticks. It's what you do with it that counts, and while we humans might be quite gifted in that department (well, some of us are), we are, of course, hopelessly lacking in others.

Before the late, great Dian Fossey began her work in Rwanda and the Congo, gorillas had an appalling reputation as violent brutes that would kill humans on sight.

Fossey demolished this myth by living alongside a group of mountain gorillas and showing that they are gentle giants with individual personalities and rich social lives. Very much like us, in fact.

Nevertheless, they continue to receive bad press and the film world is the biggest culprit. I must not be too harsh, however. There are one or two films that convey the truer side of our hairy friends and one of those films is Disney's *Tarzan*, in which I voice the role of the dreadful animal hunter, Clayton. What a ruthless swine he was. Normally I don't really like playing baddies but because the gorillas came out smelling of roses, I acquiesced.

Several years ago I narrated a film called *Gorillas in the Midst of Man* for the wonderful BBC Natural History Unit in Bristol. It's an absolutely amazing film where you see gorillas going about their everyday life in Rwanda. The film actually ends on a chorus of farting. It's true, I tell you! After gorging themselves all day on roots and bamboo, their bellies swell to a considerable size and as the gas builds up they simply have to relieve themselves. It's guffing on the grandest possible scale, as one by one they each grab a tree trunk, hold a leg in the air, and off they go! Each fart is as long as the millennium, and dozens of varying pitches of flatulence echo around the forest. If only we could get them on at the Proms. Imagine that! The Gorilla Symphony in G Trump major.

Bear with me a little longer, my handsome and patient reader. There have been a few darker moments in this book, as I touched on examples of cruelty to animals, when I admit I despaired of my fellow man. But then I remembered the Drake equation: $N = R^{\cdot} \cdot f_p \cdot n_e \cdot f_l \cdot f_i \cdot f_c \cdot L$

It was developed by the radio astronomer Frank Drake in 1961 and is used to estimate the number of communicating civilizations in our cosmos. The Milky Way galaxy – of which Earth is part – is believed to have 100 billion planets. The point being, my sultry little stargazer, that out in the cosmos somewhere, is life. And, let me tell you now, I am mad for it! MAD FOR IT!

Galaxies as far as our telescopes can see reveal possibilities of life way beyond our Milky Way. It's so exciting! So astonishing! The only question is, will we be around long enough to make contact? As I write this, Russia, North Korea and the USA are posturing like immature Neanderthals. Grow up, for God's sake! We, as a species, are on the cusp of discovering something amazing and all they want to do is fight.

Idiotic buffoons notwithstanding, I believe that we will make it. I think we will. We are very young and there are so many adventures still to be had. To see our planet on film or from space fills me with happiness and boundless optimism. The good guys win in the end and we are the good guys. You and me. Don't forget, when Pandora opened the box a second time a tiny blue creature flew out with iridescent blue wings. 'I am hope,' it said. 'I am hope.' Part of my hope is that one day I shall see all the animals I have known and loved in animal heaven. I'm quite sure Misty will be waiting for me to lead the way. My love and best wishes to you all.

284

Acknowledgements

Writing this book has proved to be a delightful experience, rekindling wonderful memories of animals, people, places and events from my adventures. It has been all the more enjoyable for giving me the opportunity to work with people I admire and love. This book has been a tremendous team effort. Once more I must pay homage to that truly remarkable fellow Yorkshireman James Hogg. Over the past six months it's been a colossal pleasure to pour out my stories to him in my cabin and see him respond with passion and delight, his moods ranging from infectious laughter to quiet sigh and tears of joy and sadness. He is a man for all seasons, ladies and gentlemen; if you are fed up with how gloomy the world seems to be getting, seek out James Hogg and he will restore your faith.

I must remind you, my lusty readers, that I still live in the nineteenth century and I am all at sea when it comes to computers, laptops, iPhones and email. I was brought up on 'Press Button A to speak' and 'Press Button B to get your money back'! In answer to a yeti's prayer, a guardian angel has entered my life by the name of Steve Knight; he takes it

Acknowledgements

all in his stride and spares me the complexities of modern life! On top of his many duties, he also drives me everywhere. His kindness, dedication and professional expertise brings order and stillness to my colourful existence.

My manager and great friend Steve Gittings has broken his back running hither and yon on my behalf, using diplomacy, encouragement and love in dealing with this project. He has never let me down. In those dreadful moments when we have had to put an animal down (particularly Poppet!) he has held me together with great strength and love! An astonishing man, a true Sir Galahad.

The backbone of my life whenever I become bogged down and uncertain is my wife Hildegard. She always lends a sympathetic ear and guides me in a new direction. Without her inspiration this book would never have been written.

Now it is time for the roll of honour. Sound drums and trumpet! Big, big love to my multi-talented publishers Pan Macmillan, led by the miraculous lady with the cheeky eye, Ingrid Connell. What a team they are. In vibrant drum beats I beat out their respective names: Tania Wilde (Editorial Services), Charlotte Wright (Picture Research), Stuart Wilson (Jacket Design), Sarah Patel (Publicity) and Alex Young (Marketing Campaign). Thank you for your vivid imagination and professionalism.

This book is a celebration, its object is happiness. Don't forget, ladies and gentlemen, to follow your dreams and don't let the bastards grind you down.

BRIAN BLESSED 2017